The
Thomas R. Brendle

Collection
of
Pennsylvania
German Folklore

Volume I

Edited by C. Richard Beam

Published by Historic Schaefferstown, Inc.

Copyright 1995
Historic Schaefferstown, Inc.

ISBN # 1-880976-11-0

Printed in the United States of America by Brookshire Printing, Inc., Lancaster, PA

TABLE OF CONTENTS

The Thomas Royce Brendle Collection of Pennsylvania
German Folklore: An Appreciation I

In Memoriam XI

Flotsam and Jetsam XIV

The Thomas Royce Brendle Collection of Pennsylvania
German Folklore 1

Geographic Origins of the Lore 113

Maps of the Geographic Origins 116

Index of Key Pennsylvania German Words 123

Index of Key English Concepts 139

Index of Informants 146

Bibliography 156

THE THOMAS ROYCE BRENDLE COLLECTION OF PENNSYLVANIA GERMAN FOLKLORE: AN APPRECIATION

by

C. Richard Beam
Center for Pennsylvania German Studies
Millersville University

Thomas Royce Brendle was born one hundred and six years ago in Schaefferstown on September 15, 1889 and departed this life on September 1, 1966 in Allentown, Pennsylvania.

Essential to an appreciation of the life and ministry of Rev. Brendle is the recollection that he was born at a time and in a place where the Pennsylvania German [PG] dialect was very much alive and German had not yet been replaced by English in the worship services of the Reformed Churches in rural Pennsylvania. Thomas Royce Brendle also had the good fortune of being born into the right family. His grandfather, Daniel D. Brendle, had served as the superintendent of the Reformed Church Sunday School in Schaefferstown for 44 years (*The History of St. Paul's Church*, 141). It was Grandfather Brendle who awakened the interest of his grandson in the flora and fauna of Heidelberg Township, Lebanon County, PA. T.R. Brendle's notes inform us that he frequently accompanied his paternal grandfather on excursions to the neighboring hills. This early exposure to the plant names and plant lore of the PG later developed into a lifelong preoccupation with the PG dialect and folklore (Brendle, T., *Perkiomen Region* 1.4:61; Milbury, 53-54). When young Brendle--he was only 19 years old when he enrolled--came to the Theological Seminary of the Reformed Church in Lancaster, he encountered professors who were sophisticated enough to appreciate the importance of the folk culture of the PGs, and they encouraged their young students to study the traditions of those to whom they would be ministering. Young "Roy" Brendle was but 21 years of age when he was graduated from the theological seminary in the spring of 1911 and he had responded to this encouragement.

During **Parre** Brendle's 50 years as a minister in the Reformed Church--after the first merger known as the Evangelical and Reformed Church, after the second merger to be known as the United Church of Christ--his workshop was the study in his village parsonage, the homes of his parishioners and the social centers of the communities which he served.

The work of the late **Parre** Brendle is unique in the annals of PG Studies. He took his God-given talent and planted it in the most fertile soil. Side by side with his published studies, which are an outgrowth thereof, his collection of PG folklore looms as a singular monument in the field of PG folklore research. Only the later field work and publications of Dr. Alfred L. Shoemaker are of comparative stature. But Brendle remains the pioneer, for at the time **Parre** Brendle was beginning his investigations, Alfred Lewis Shoemaker was yet in his infancy.

The singularity of the Brendle Collection calls to mind the dominance of the Washington monument in Washington, D.C. There are other great reminders of the accomplishment of great national leaders, but the Washington monument towers above them all. And thus it is with the Brendle Collection in spite of the fact that most of it awaits publication.

A moment's reflection will remind each of us that Brendle's feat cannot be repeated, should another with Rev. Brendle's gifts appear in Schaefferstown. Brendle was able to draw from deep wells full of water. His numbered folklore notes were recorded in the second quarter of this rapidly fleeting century, that is, roughly between 1925 and 1950. Among the non-sectarian Pennsylvania Dutch only the oldest generation speaks the dialect fluently and not all of those are bearers of traditional sayings and beliefs. It is virtually impossible to find a non-plain Dutch person under the age of 50 who is fluent in the dialect and at the same time who will sing **Schlof, Bobbeli, schlof** for you, let alone know that the Dutch word for candle is **es Inschlichlicht**.

In order to fully appreciate the magnitude of **Parre** Brendle's contributions to the field of PG Studies, it is necessary that we recall that the precocious "Tom" Brendle, who arrived at the seminary at the age of 19, was not the only young fellow from the Dutch country who came to a Reformed or Lutheran theological seminary with a knowledge of Standard German as well as of the PG dialect, thus with the basic equipment needed to function in "High" and dialect German. There must have been dozens of others who entered their respective seminaries bearing the same "talents." But young "Tom" Brendle was virtually the only one who had the vision to begin to study the folklore and folklife of his people and take the time--for years on end--to record every evening in his looseleaf notebooks that which he had overheard or elicited during visits to his parishioners, on fishing trips, at the local Grange Hall, or wherever his footsteps led him. And all this "academic" activity on the part of the late Rev. Brendle before there was such a thing as a department of folklore, let alone of "folklife," at any American university. Thomas Royce Brendle was indeed the "dean of PG folklorists," for his learning and personality not only enabled him to elicit from his informants literally thousand of bits of folklore, but it also placed him in contact with Professor John Meyer in Germany, a major figure in the study of German folklore. **Parre** Brendle drew on German publications on folklore at a time when such publications were rare in this country.

Before we turn to the collection itself, it is important that we bear in mind that the roots of the collection are in Schaefferstown, on the lower and upper Brendle farms to be exact, and in **die Reformiert Karich** in **Schaefferschteddel**. In his notes Brendle frequently recalls and records the Schaefferstown form of a word. When the young Rev. Brendle and his young family returned in 1913 from a two-year stint as the pastor of a missionary church in Abilene, Kansas and took up his duties as the pastor of the Sumneytown Charge of the Reformed Church in Montgomery County, Pennsylvania, he encountered the dialect in a somewhat different garb. Brendle's final 35 years in the ministry were spent in Lehigh (**Lechaa**) County as pastor of the Egypt Charge of the Reformed Church. There Brendle not only became familiar with Lehigh County Dutch, but he also met "Pumpernickle Bill," the late William S. Troxell, who wrote an almost daily dialect column for the Allentown *Morning Call* for over 30 years. Brendle and Troxell and others were among the founding fathers of the very first Dutch **Grundsau Lodsch** in the mid-thirties. This encounter with the dialect and our folkways in three distinct geographic regions alerted Brendle, the folklorist, to the variations within our culture.

After his father's death, who had been known as "Tom" Brendle all his life, Thomas Royce Brendle referred to himself as "Tom" and began to write his name as "Thomas R. Brendle" and no longer as "T. Royce Brendle." In the years following 1936 "Tom" Brendle filled approximately ninety looseleaf note books with his numbered observations and recollections, and subsequently other related data. Eventually Brendle typed many of his previously handwritten notes, so that today part of the collection is in Brendle's hand, part is in typescript.

Tom Brendle would collect his information on his daily rounds. For example, at Bible class meetings; on personal visits in the homes of his parishioners; on fishing trips; at a performance of a dialect play in the local high school; from members of his church consistories; from the caretaker of the Egypt Cemetery, which was located behind the parsonage in Egypt; frequently from a neighbor, Mary Koch; from recollections of things said by his father and grandfather Brendle; at a funeral; at the Laurys Sunday School picnic (for instance, on July 11, 1942); from his old friend and collaborator "Pumpernickle Bill" (William S. Troxell), who wrote a regular dialect column from 1925 to 1957 in the Allentown *Morning Call*, a daily newspaper; and from notes made from the manuscripts of radio broadcasts in the dialect by "Pumpernickle Bill" on radio station WSAN in Allentown (for example, "Funeral Rites"; Korson, 357).

An Overview Of the Contents of the Brendle Collection

The Brendle Collection proper consists of 93 loose-leaf notebooks. The numbered items in an individual notebook may be as low as 236 or as high as 2,792. For instance, volume one contains 1,804 numbered items recorded on 249 pages. (Brendle did not number his pages.) The entire collection contains approximately 55,000 numbered entries, even though Brendle's last numbered entry bears the number "57,124." Brendle's hand-written and typed notes are spread over approximately 24,000 pages.

All these figures will have to be approximations, for Brendle's numbering system was never exact. In some sections of the collection he renumbered items. As a result there were duplications and omissions of numbers. During the years of his retirement when the collection was with him in Hamburg, New York, he continued to work with his collection by making additions and corrections. Some of these additions were added to the numbered items or placed in the margins. These additions often spilled over onto blank pages and were not necessarily related to the neighboring entries. We must assume, therefore, that those additions and "corrections"--which are somewhat erratic and occasionally barely legible--must have been made between 1961, the year of his retirement from the active ministry, and 1966, the year he entered a nursing home in Allentown, where he died on September 1, 1966.

Since Pastor Brendle usually numbered each item as he recorded it, there was no need for him to number his pages. Sometimes he wrote on both sides of a sheet. When he typed his notes, he used only one side of the sheet. Brendle was fairly faithful to his original numbering system in the first 61 volumes. These volumes contain material recorded between May of 1936, the month volume one was formally opened, and February of 1961. (We have reason to believe that Brendle began making scattered notes at least 10 years earlier, that is, about the time he took up the pastorate in Egypt in Lehigh County.)

The final 30 volumes of the collection contains few numbered entries. It is clear that in his retirement in Hamburg, New York, that **Parre** Brendle was no longer rooted in the fertile Dutch soil of southeastern Pennsylvania. Hence, it is the first two-thirds of the collection which interests us the most, for in those 60 volumes Brendle accomplished what he set out to do. We quote in its entirety the foreword Brendle wrote for the first volume of his collected notes:

> In my associations with my people, I had heard many traditions, proverbs, expressions, etc. As the years passed I found that I was forgetting much that I had heard and was having only a faint memory of many things that at one time I knew well. Also such notes as I had made were not assembled.
>
> So in the year 1936 I began to make notes on all the lore that I heard. Day after day, I would make notes, as I heard matter which I felt would be worthwhile in making a study of the PGs.
>
> I wrote down daily what I heard and as I heard it. Often I noted the name of the informant; also my recollections which came back to my remembrance. There are frequent duplications. This is due to the circumstance that I did not trust to a memory of what I had written. I feel now that I should have noted more duplications for a study of frequency of occurrence and for variations and current interpretations of the original.
>
> I have loosely followed Lambert (Marcus Bachman Lambert, *A Dictionary of the Non-English Words in the Pennsylvania-German Dialect*, published by the PG Society in 1924) in spelling the dialectal words.
>
> When this collection was approaching 10,000 items, I felt that I should type the notes, for many of them had been written with pencil, and the numbering especially in the first volume, was not consecutive. In recopying the notes I was careful to make a faithful copy, adding little that was not in the original. Sometimes, where my notes were not clear to me, I have added a question mark.
>
> If I should not be able to use this collected material, I feel that the work has not been in vain, for I know that sometime someone will find it an ample source for study of the PGs.
>
> Everything unless otherwise noted was heard by me. I have used no printed matter, unless so indicated. All the material is what I personally heard. That should be remembered. Others may have heard things differently. That is what I heard and saw.
>
> Recopied 1941. I am keeping the originals.

The final third of the collection appears to have been assembled during Brendle's retirement in Hamburg, New York. He was no longer in daily contact with other dialect speakers other than Mrs. Brendle herself. He was experiencing the infirmities of advancing age. Thus there is a marked difference in the contents of the later volumes. Here we will find Brendle's annotated copy of Marcus Bachman Lambert's 1924 PG dictionary. In this copy are many additional dialect words which Lambert has not recorded. Since Brendle had assisted Lambert in the compilation of his dictionary, it is not surprising that Brendle made copious notes on lexical items as he heard them or as they occurred to him. In the compilation of a comprehensive PG to English dictionary we have made full use of Brendle's notes. The later volumes of the Brendle Collection are especially valuable for the inserted material. Here one finds letters, some to Brendle, some to "Pumpernickle Bill," who died almost ten years before Brendle ("Funeral Rites"). After Troxell's death in 1957 Mrs. Troxell turned over to Brendle lists of important information in the dialect which had been sent to Troxell by those who listened to his radio broadcasts.

One of the later Brendle notebooks contains what appears to be an English translation of the famous powwowing book, Hohman's *Long Lost Friend* (Yoder, 1976). In these volumes we find genealogical information on the Brendle family as well as on related families. Volume 71 contains a copy of Brendle's dialect play, *Die Mutter*, as performed on October 19, 1934, in Hershey, PA (Buffington, 194-222). A wheelwright's account book of the years 1768-97, which was copied in 1941, has been preserved here. A number of these later volumes contain the notes Brendle had made for a book on powwowing he was compiling prior to his final illness. Of especial interest are the folktales submitted in 1942 by listeners to the regular radio broadcasts by "Pumpernickle Bill" (Brendle and Troxell, 1944).

One of the most valuable documents which was copied verbatim by Brendle--in September and October of 1953--and preserved only in his collection is Edna Hurst's diary of the year 1900. The seventeen-year-old Edna Hurst was the youngest daughter of the only physician in Talmage, Lancaster County, PA. After she had taught in Arizona, Edna returned to Lancaster County and completed the teacher-training program at Millersville State Normal School in 1911. Edna's son was unaware of the existence of the diary until a copy was presented to him a few years ago. The 1900 diary of Edna Hurst Wenger will be printed in forthcoming issues of the *Journal of the Center for Pennsylvania German Studies*.

Illustrations of Some of the Categories Represented in the
Brendle Collection

The very first entry in volume one reads as follows:

1.

A child, visiting in a friend's or a neighbor's house, should not accept the first invitation to eat at the table with the family; it should wait for a second or third invitation.

Leb, Mont

Lest the child give the impression that it does not get enough to eat at home; to show no greediness. This also was the way of many grown-ups. Aunt Jane, my wife's aunt, 83 years old, almost always waited for a second request at the table for a second helping.

Ich hab en eemol gheese esse; sell waar genunk. Er is ken Kind, as mir en meh wie eemol heese muss. (I invited him once; that was enough. He is no child that one has to invite him more than once.)

There is also the feeling that the first invitation is due to courtesy, the second comes from real desire. **Do waard mer net fer's zwettmol gheese sei.** (One doesn't wait to be invited the second time.)

Often heard by me

A.

One person came as the family was gathered around the table: **Hock dich hie un ess mit**, (Sit down and eat.) said the man of the house. **Nee, ich will net; bin net hungrich**, (No, I don't want to; I'm not hungry.) answered the person. **Ach, kumm**

aan; ess mit, (Oh, come on; eat with us.) said the householder.

Nee, nee! (No, no!) answered the man. **Ya, well, dann!** (Very well, then!) said the householder, and the family took to eating. The visitor, who really was hungry, watched them, and after a bit, said: **Esse is awwer aa gut.** (To eat is a pleasant thing.) (**Es Esse schmackt awwer gut.**) (My, but the food smell's good!)

B.

A little boy came to a home at dinner time when the family was gathered around the table. Conversation as above. The hunger of the boy increased as the dinner progressed. As the pie was being passed around, he could restrain himself no longer and he cried out: **Seller Pei muss awwer gut sei!** (That pie must really be good!) In both instances the visitor was given to eat.

As is frequently the case in Brendle's notes, one piece of information seems to have reminded either Brendle or the informant of a related bit of information. Item number one is followed by several table prayers and a favorite bedtime prayer. This of course provokes the parody:

> Now I lay me down to sleep
> Upon my little trundle bed;
> If I should die before I wake,
> How would I know I am dead?

Or:
> If I should die before I wake,
> Goodbye to mother's buckwheat cake.

One parody, of course, reminds one of another. This is one on "Nearer, my God, to Thee":

> Nero, my dog, has fleas,
> Nero, has fleas.
> No matter what soap I use,
> Nero has fleas.

Item number 15 recommends: "When leaving a team of horses alone in a field, turn them away from the buildings and they will remain at the spot and not run away." This bit of lore reminds Brendle of the dialect expression: **der Blug verreisse**, meaning "to wreck a plow" (by the plowshare catching under a stump, a post, etc. and the horses have run away or are pulling too fast.)

Much weather lore has found its way into the Brendle Collection. This item is the very first bit of weather lore in the collection: **Wann die Hund odder Katze Graas fresse, gebt's Regge.** (When the dogs or the cats eat grass, there will be rain.)

The Brendle Collection is a storehouse of proverbs and proverbial expressions. They begin to appear very early in the first volume. For instance, **Was sich zwett, dritt sich.** (That which occurs twice, will occur a third time.) "Two funerals in short successions in a congregation portend a third one."

Here is a tale recorded in the first volume which Brendle heard from the lips of his father as well as from his grandfather:

> In the "bottom field" of the old Scheetz farm on the edge of Schaefferstown, where the sensational Scheetz murder took place, a man by the name of Houser of **Kannadaa** (Canada), the southern part of Schaefferstown, **hot Schtecheise gfischt ee Nacht**.(was gig fishing one night) ("The Tragedy of Old Schaefferstown") Around midnight he heard what he took to be the horses of the murderers galloping around for home and going through the woods he heard a voice calling, **Wuh-hie? Wuh-hie?** In his fright he answered, **Wuh-hie?** and thereupon a weight as of a two-bushel bag of wheat fell upon his back. The weight lay upon him all the way home, until unable to walk upright, he staggered against the door and collapsed.

Another tale from Schaefferstown:

> Dawson Hetrick, a schoolmate of mine in Schaefferstown, told me that one night his father and others went to a crossroad to mold magic bullets. While engaged in their work, one happened to look up and there suspended over them hung a millstone. In fright they rushed from under the stone and ran pell-mell all the way home. "If they had not been so scared and had kept on with their work, they would have succeeded in molding the bullets," said Dawson Hetrick.

Der Ewich Yaeger (the eternal hunter) has been at least heard of by every Pennsylvania Dutchman in the past. One night Tom Brendle's grandfather and Toms's uncle were out hunting. They were on the ridge that led back to **Walniss Brunne** (Walnut Spring) near Schaefferstown. As they went along the ridge, they heard **der Ewich Yaeger** on the slope across the **Haschdaal** (Deer Valley). They immediately turned back and went home, for it was dangerous to be out at night when **der Ewich Yaeger** was abroad. This could mean death or disappearance.

******

Let us skip forward to volume twelve, which contains almost 3,000 numbered items. The information in this volume was gathered in or near the town of Egypt in Lehigh County from March 6 to August 13, 1942, a five-month period during World War II, when travel was restricted. The folklore assembled and recorded in this volume represents a good cross section of the various categories of folkloristic and linguistic information which Brendle recorded in the early volumes of the collection. These were notes made when Pastor Brendle was in his most productive years and at a time when the generation born during the last quarter of the nineteenth century--a period when the PG culture was the dominant one in many of the rural sections of southeastern Pennsylvania--was well represented amongst Brendle's informants. In this fact lies the uniqueness of the Brendle Collection. Brendle assembled his collection from a generation which knew the dialect and the older ways well. As was already pointed out, Brendle grew up in Schaefferstown, which was thoroughly Pennsylvania Dutch during the period of his childhood and youth (A.S. Brendle). Brendle lived for almost half a century in two areas, which were at the time he served them as pastor, 1913-1961, heavily Pennsylvania Dutch and in part, rural.

Here are a few more examples of some of the categories to be found in volume 12:

1. <u>Proverbs and proverbial expressions</u>: **Sie sin aa Mensche.** (They are also human.) **Ich hab aa mei Menscherecht.** (I too have my human rights.)

2. <u>Riddles</u>: **Was is des? Six Zoll lang mit me Kopp un die ganz Welt eschdimiert's. En Daaler.** (What is 6 inches long with a head and is revered by the entire world? A dollar.) (From Mrs. Moyer, Egypt)

3. <u>Weather Lore:</u> When snow falls, it is said, **Sie roppe die Gens in Deitschland un schicke die Feddre rei.** (They're plucking the geese in Germany and sending us the feathers.)

4. <u>Counting out rime</u>: **Eene beene dunke funke/Raabi schnabbi dibbi dabbe/Ulla bulla Ros/Ib ab aus/Du bischt aus.** (From Mrs. Moyer, Egypt)

5. <u>Folk Cure</u>: For whooping cough: **Aus me blohe Glaas drinke. Mei Mammi hot immer en bloh Glass ghat fer die Kinner rausdrinke, wann die Blohhuuschde ghadde hen.** (My mom always had a blue glass for the children to drink out of whenever they had whooping cough.) (From Mrs. Charles Fries, Kreidersville)

6. <u>Seasonal Lore</u>: "At New Year one should eat pork and not chicken, **wann mer vorkumme will in die Welt.** (if one wishes to get ahead in the world) When a chicken scratches, it works backward, but when a hog roots, it roots forward. So if you would go forward in the world, eat pork, particularly at New Year; also at Christmas." (Mrs. Fries)

7. <u>Star Lore</u>: **Wann mer die Schtanne seht falle, schtarbt epper in die Freindschaft.** (When one sees the stars fall, someone will die in the family.) As a protective action, close your eyes or look away. (Mrs. Fries)

8. <u>Anecdote about a clergyman</u>: "A **Parre** was driving along when he came to a little boy playing with a **Kiehdreck. Was hoscht du? - Wees net! - Weescht net was sell is?' - Nee! - Sell is en Kiehdreck! - Guck, do kann mer sehne was die Lanning dutt. Ich hab net gewisst eb's en Bulledreck odder en Kiehdreck is!"** (What have you got there? - Don't know! - You don't know what it is? - No! - That's a cowflop! - Look there, one can see what an education can do. I didn't know whether it's a bullflop or a cowflop.) (Oscar Laub)

9. <u>Ascension Day</u>: "There was made for an old woman a nightcap, **en Schlofkapp.**" This happened to have been made on **Himmelfaahrdaag.** One day storms came **un sin yuscht iwwer em Haus gschtanne un sin net weckgezoge. Es hot arig gedunhnert un gegracht.** (and remained over the house and did not move on. There was a terrible thundering and cracking.) The persons in the house became frightened. Finally, they remembered the old belief and that the cap had been made on **Himmelfaahrdaag.** So they took the cap and hung it on the washline out in the yard. Then there was an awful clap of thunder. The cap was torn to shreds---and the storm moved on. (Brendle, 1951)

If space permitted it would be possible to retell a tall tale or one of the folktales about *Yenneveevaa, Die drei Brieder* or of *Der Buh und der Schwatzkinschdler* (Yoder, 1971b). Our last example of typical lore from the Brendle Collection is a tale involving Eulenspiegel and a preacher. This account was copied by Brendle from the manuscript for the February 18, 1942, radio broadcast of "Pumpernickle Bill." The story was submitted by James Stuber of Cherryville, PA. We quote "Pumpernickle Bill":

> Der James secht, der Ira Bickel hett sich mohl verdingt zu me Parre als Gnecht. Sunndaags maryets hett der Parre der Ira nausgschickt fer sei Weggel schmiere fer noch der Karich geh. Der Ira hett gsaat, er daed, un waer naus un hett der Wagge all eigschmiert mit Waggeschmier vun eem End bis ans anner. Wie der Parre nauskumme waer fer fattgeh, hett er der Ira gfrogt, was er geduh. Noh hett der Ira gsaat: "Ei, der Wagge gschmiert, wie du gsaat hoscht as ich sott."--"Ya," hett der Parre gsaat, "awwer du hoscht en dadde schmiere solle!" un gewisse noch der Ex vum Weggel. "Schur," hett der Ira gsaat, "ich hett aa, awwer ich hab net dadde draakumme kenne!" (Beam, 11-14)
>
> (James said that Eulenspiegel had hired himelf out to a preacher. Sunday morning the preacher sent Till out to grease his buggy before he went to church. Till said he would and went out and greased the buggy all over--from end to end. When the preacher was ready to leave, he asked Till what he had done. Till replied, "Why, greased the buggy as you said I should."--"Yes, said the preacher, "but you should have greased it there!" and pointed to the axles of the buggy.--"Sure," said Till, "I would have, too, but I couldn't reach there."

******

The Thomas Royce Brendle Collection of PG Folklore stands alone as a record of German-American folklife (Dorson, 1959; Klees, 450; Yoder, 1971a). In the last quarter of the 20th century the ranks of those who know the dialect well and recall the old ways are thinning rapidly. It would no longer be possible at this late date to replicate Brendle's solitary achievement. His folklore collection is his monument. He truly was "the dean of PG folklorists."

We hope that the publication of this the first volume in the Thomas R. Brendle Collection of Pennsylvania German Folklore will make it possible to publish subsequent volumes.

July 15, 1995
St. Swithin's Day

C. Richard Beam,
Center for Pennsylvania German Studies
Millersville University

THOMAS ROYCE BRENDLE
September 15, 1889 -- September 1 1966

IN MEMORIAM*

THOMAS ROYCE BRENDLE

With the death of the Reverend Thomas Royce Brendle at the Phoebe Home, 1925 Turner Street, Allentown, PA, on September 1, 1966, an era ended. The pioneer and "dean of Pennsylvania Dutch folklorists" is gone.

Born with a deep abiding love for historical research and folklore, the late Reverend Brendle collected volumes and volumes of Pennsylvania German folklore. As a pastor, counselor, and friend, the Reverend Brendle always lived close to his people. Their joys were his joys; their sorrows were his sorrows. The late Dr. Harry Hess Reichard said: "He seemed to have a peculiar faculty for cooperative research, as an eager student of folkways and folklore." With these gifts, he authored and co-authored several books.

The first of these was entitled *Plant Names and Plant Lore Among the Pennsylvania Germans*, which he co-authored with the late David E. Lick and was published in Part III, Volume 33 of the Pennsylvania German Society, 1923.

The next was *Folk Medicine of the Pennsylvania Germans: The Non-Occult Cures* and was co-authored with the late Claude W. Unger. It was published as volume 45 of the Pennsylvania German Society, 1935.

In collaboration with the late William S. Troxell, he co-authored *Pennsylvania German Folk Tales, Legends, Once-Upon-A-Time-Stories, Maxims, and Sayings: Spoken in the dialect popularly known as Pennsylvania Dutch*. This was published as Volume 50 of the Pennsylvania German Society, 1944.

Again in collaboration with William S. Troxell, he wrote a chapter, "Pennsylvania German Songs," in the book *Pennsylvania Songs and Legends*, edited by George Korson. This volume was published by The Johns Hopkins Press, Baltimore, 1949.

Among other writings of the late Reverend Brendle are: "The Flora of the Perkiomen Region," "An Old Time School Master," *History of the Falkner Swamp Reformed Church*, *History of the Old Skippack Reformed Church* and about 25 contributions relative to the history of the Reformed congregation at Egypt, PA.

The last publication of Pastor Brendle was *Moses Dissinger, Evangelist and Patriot*. This study appeared in Volume 58 of the Pennsylvania German Society, 1959.

Thomas R. Brendle also made significant contributions to the literature of Pennsylvania Dutch plays. His first play was *Die Mutter*. His second play, *Die Hoffnung*, was a war play and was his answer to the question: "What was the typical Pennsylvania Dutchman's attitude toward the first World War? These plays were published in *The Reichard Collection of Early Pennsylvania German Dialogues and Plays*, edited and re-transcribed by Albert F. Buffington, Volume 61, Pennsylvania German Society, 1962.

Thomas Royce Brendle was born on September 15, 1889 on the old Steinmetz farm at Schaefferstown, Pa. He was the son of the late Thomas Steinmetz Brendle and his wife, the late Mary nee Bomberger Brendle. Here he spent his childhood and school years.

From the Schaefferstown public schools he went to Albright College, then situated in Meyerstown. After three years at Albright College he completed his senior year at Franklin and Marshall College in Lancaster, Pa. He was graduated from F. & M. College in the year 1908.

In the fall of 1908 he entered the Eastern Theological Seminary of the Reformed Church in Lancaster, PA and was graduated from that institution in the spring of 1911. Following graduation from the seminary, Mr. Brendle was licensed to preach by the Lebanon Classis of the Reformed Church in May of 1911.

On May 30, 1911, Thomas R. Brendle was married to Anna Sarah Schwartz, the only child of the late Frank and Mary nee Kilmer Schwartz of Myerstown, Pa.

Rev. Brendle was called to Abilene, Kansas, where he was ordained into the Christian ministry on June 4, 1911. At Abilene he preached for two years at a mission church under the aegis of the Home Mission Board of the Reformed Church.

On July 28, 1913, he was installed as the pastor of the Old Goshenhoppen Charge in Montgomery County, PA. He became the Editor of the Historical and Scientific Society of the Perkiomen Valley, publishers of the *Perkiomen Region*. Although it is not commonly known, Rev. Brendle served as a public school teacher during and after World War I, when there was an acute shortage of teachers. He served the Old Goshenhoppen Charge of the Reformed Church for a total of 13 years, from 1913 to 1926.

In the year 1926, Rev. Brendle accepted a call to the historic Egypt Reformed Church, Egypt, Lehigh County, PA. He was installed at Egypt on April 18, 1926. He served the Egypt Charge for 35 years, from 1926 to 1961. Rev. Brendle served as an active minister in the Reformed Church for a total of 50 years.

The Reverend and Mrs. Brendle moved to Hamburg, New York, in June of 1961 and lived there at 19 Oakland Place for five years, until March 25, 1966, when they returned to their beloved Lehigh Valley, and moved into an apartment at 1104 Hamilton Street in Allentown, PA.

In April of 1966, Reverend Brendle donated his collection of folklore notes and much of his personal library to HISTORIC SCHAEFFERSTOWN, INC., where it is permanently and securely housed. This and other valuable materials will be housed in the Thomas Royce Brendle Memorial Library and Museum. The heart of Rev. Brendle's collection is over 40,000 hand-written and typed items of Pennsylvania German folklore: proverbs, folk sayings, dialect terms, expressions and human interest stories. These notations have been recorded in 90 spring-bound volumes and will be known as the Thomas Royce Brendle Collection of Pennsylvania German Folklore.

Reflecting on his activities as a collector of Pennsylvania Dutch folklore, the late Rev. Brendle once said:

> "During the early years of my ministry, particularly in the land of the Pennsylvania Germans, I had an inner feeling that much of the folklore would be lost forever among the sands of time, unless they were recorded. With this in mind, early in 1936, I started to hand record in notebook form, every dialect proverb, every dialect folk saying, and every dialect human interest story I heard in my daily contact with people."

In recent years the Rev. Brendle wrote that it was his fervent hope and prayer that his efforts have not been in vain, and that they would be of real interest, not only to the Pennsylvania German people and their descendants, but also to scholars of history everywhere. To this end HISTORIC SCHAEFFERSTOWN was organized.

No sketch of the late Thomas Royce Brendle would be complete without mentioning that in 1934 he was one of the original **Raad** members who started the now famous **Grundsau Lodge Nummer Eens an die Lechaa**. For many years, too, Rev. Brendle served as the Secretary of the Pennsylvania German Society and until his death was Secretary-Emeritus.

The *Morning Call* (Allentown, PA.) editorial of Saturday, September 3, 1966, stated:

"He achieved such notable success in his career because he gave himself so whole-heartedly to both. This is another of the great influences of a noble life."

No finer tribute can be paid to the memory of the late Thomas Royce Brendle than that which we find recorded in II Timothy, Chapter 4, Verse 7:

"I have fought a good fight. I have finished my course. I have kept the faith."

Leonard E. Shupp

*pp. 1-5, Volume I, Number 1, (January 1967) Historic Schaefferstown Newsletter.

FLOTSAM AND JETSAM

Collected among the Pennsylvania Germans
by
Thomas R. Brendle

Aafang Moi 1936
The beginning of May 1936

Notebook No. 1.
Recopied 1941.

TO VOLUME ONE OF MY COLLECTION

In my associations with my people, I had heard many traditions, proverbs, expressions, etc. As the years passed I found that I was forgetting much that I had heard and was having only a faint memory of many things that at one time I knew well. Also such notes as I had made were not assembled.

So in the year 1936 I began to make notes on all the lore that I heard. Day after day, I would make notes, as I heard matter which I felt would be worthwhile in making a study of the Pennsylvania Germans.

I wrote down daily what I heard and as I heard it. Often I noted the name of the informant; also my recollections which came back to my remembrance. There are frequent duplications. This is due to the circumstance that I did not trust to a memory of what I had written. I feel now that I should have noted more duplications for a study of frequency of occurrence and for variations and current interpretations of the original.

I have loosely followed Lambert [Marcus Bachman Lambert, *A Dictionary of the Non-English Words in the Pennsylvania-German Dialect,* published by the Pennsylvania German Society in 1924] in spelling the dialectal words.

When this collection was approaching 10,000 items, I felt that I should type the notes, for many of them had been written with pencil, and the numbering, especially in the first volume, was not consecutive. In recopying the notes I was careful to make a faithful copy, adding little that was not in the original. Sometimes, where my notes were not clear to me, I have added a question mark.

If I should not be able to use this collected material, I feel that the work has not been in vain, for I know that sometime someone will find it an ample source for study of the Pennsylvania Germans.

Everything unless otherwise noted was heard by me. I have used no printed matter, unless so indicated. All the material is what I personally heard. That should be remembered. Others may have heard things differently. That is what *I* heard and saw.

Recopied 1941. I am keeping the originals.

1.

A child, visiting in a friend's or a neighbor's house, should not accept the first invitation to eat at the table with the family; it should wait for a second or third invitation.
Leb, Mont

Lest the child give the impression that it does not get enough to eat at home; to show no greediness. This also was the way of many grown-ups. Aunt Jane, my wife's aunt, 83 years old, almost always waits for a second request at the table for a second helping.

"Ich hab en eemol gheese esse; sell waar genunk. Er is ken Kind, as mir en meh wie eemol heese muss." [I invited him once; that was enough. He is no child that one has to invite him more than once.]

There is also the feeling that the first invitation is due to courtesy, the second comes from real desire. "Do waard mer net fer's zwettmol gheese sei." [One doesn't wait to be invited the second time.]
Often heard by me

Stories floated around of persons coming at mealtime.

A.

One person came as the family was gathered around the table: "Hock dich hie un ess mit." [Sit down and eat.] said the man of the house. "Nee, ich will net; bin net hungrich." [No, I don't want to; I'm not hungry.] answered the person. "Ach, kumm aan; ess mit." [Oh, come on; eat with us.] said the householder. "Nee, nee!" [No, no!] answered the man. "Ya, *well,* dann!" [Very well, then!] said the householder, and the family took to eating. The visitor, who really was hungry, watched them, and after a bit, said: "Esse is awwer aa gut." (To eat is a pleasant thing.) ("Es Esse schmackt awwer gut.") [My, but the food smells good!]

B.

A little boy came to a home at dinner time when the family was gathered around the table. Conversation as above. The hunger of the boy increased as the dinner progressed. As the pie was being passed around, he could restrain himself no longer and he cried out: "Seller *Pie* muss awwer gut sei!" [That pie must really be good!] In both instances the visitor was given to eat.

2.

"Wer net will, hot schun ghat!" [He who doesn't want to eat, has already eaten.] Often spoken when someone invited to eat along does not accept the invitation. Whereupon, the others, with one saying, "Wer net will, hot schun ghat!" turn to eating.
Often used as a proverb.

Again in accepting the invitation when first given, one, to excuse his ready acceptance, is likely to say, "Mer waard net fer's zwettmol gfrogt." [One does not wait for the second invitation.] Another version is: "Do waard mer net fer gfrogt zu sei." [One doesn't wait to be asked.]

3.

The table prayer was often said by a child (by the youngest child) of the family. Table prayers are:

A. "God bless this (our) food. Amen."
B. "God bless this food,
   Which now we take for Jesus sake. Amen."
C. "Come, Lord Jesus, be our guest
   And bless what thou provided hast. Amen."

German:
"Komm, Herr Jesu, sei unser Gast,
Un segne was du uns bescheren hast. Amen."

This is a German prayer which was commonly used by our people. C. above is a translation of this German prayer.

4.

The favorite bedtime prayer of children is:

"Now I lay me down to sleep,
I pray the Lord my soul to keep.
If I should die before I wake,
I pray the Lord my soul to take. Amen."

A fifth line is often added:

"All this I ask for Jesus sake. Amen."

5.

A parody of the prayer, that was occasionally heard:

"Now I lay me down to sleep,
Upon my little trundle bed,
If I should die before I wake,

Fourth line to another parody:
Good-bye to mother's buckwheat cake
How would I know I am dead."
Bernville

In praying at bedtime one knelt on the floor, at a chair, or at the bed. In praying for a person sick in bed, one knelt at the bedside.

Parody on "Nearer, my God, to Thee":

"Nero, my dog has flees,
Nero has flees.
No matter what soap I use,
Nero has flees."
Not infrequently heard around 1907

6.

Expressions often heard from older persons:
A.
"Es is nimmi wie's fer Alders waar," with the implication that times have changed for the worse. This was a favorite saying of Jesse Zepp, Sumneytown, who always bemoaned the changes in the ways of life and man.

B.
"Es is nimmi wie's fer Lenger waar." [It's no longer the way it used to be long ago.]
C.
Another form: "Es (Sis) net (nimmi) wie fer Alders."
D.
"Sis nimmi wie's lenger zerick waar."
E.
"Sis nimmi wie's Yaahre zerick waar."
F.
"Sis nimmi wie's fer Yaahre waar."

7.
A beheaded fowl should not be held in the hand until dead. (Why?) [Brendle added later: Nothing should die in the hand.] *Leb*

Thus when a fowl is beheaded, the carcass is immediately thrown to the ground; and only (in the past) when the carcass was lifeless was it plucked.
Chickens, geese and ducks were decapitated with use of an implement. Doves were decapitated sometimes by a slinging motion with the fingers.
The carcass of a turkey was plucked dry or scalded. This was also true of chickens. Ducks were scalded and wrapped in cloths or a gunny sack, so that the heat would penetrate through the feathers.

8.
A fowl should be decapitated with one stroke. The reason given is that "as es ken hadder Dod hot." [so that it does not have a hard death.]
In butchering, if you pet the animal you are about to kill, "hot's en hadder Dod." [it will have a hard death.] *Frequent*

9.
Do not look into a mirror over another's shoulder. "Es gebt Schtreit." [There will be quarreling.] *General*

10.
Do not wash your face and hands out of the water which another has just used for the same purpose. "Es gebt Schtreit, wann mer aus der seeme Weschschissel wescht, wu en annrer (annres) sich gwesche hot." [There will be quarreling when one washes out of the same basin where another has already washed himself.] *Leb*

But drinking out of the same glass brings friendship. *Occasionally heard*

10.a.
In eating the men ate "am erschde Disch" [at the first seating] (the wife served). The wife ate "am zwedde Disch" [at the second seating]. She often would use her husband's glass. (When all could not eat at the first table, the wife waited and served.)

11.
If you whistle to a rabbit that is playing out in the open on a summer evening, it will come to you. *Leb*

A rabbit "peift" [whistles]. "Hoscht schun en Haas heere peife?" [Have you heard a rabbit whistle?] *Mont*

12.
"Siessgraut" [sweet cabbage] is another name for the dish "Weissgraut" [white cabbage] *Jane Kilmer*

13.
"En vierbleddrich Gleeblaat" [a four-leaved clover leaf] is lucky if found without looking for it. *General*

In the pulpit Bible, formerly privately owned, at Miller's Church, Laurys, Pa., there are quite a number of four-leaved clovers.

14.
Upon seeing the first evening star, make a wish and say:
"The first star I see tonight,
I make a wish,
And I wish it will come true." *Leb*

15.
When leaving a team of horses alone in a field, turn them away from the buildings and they will remain at the spot and not run away. *Leb, Leh*

15.a.
"der Blug verrisse" (tearing the wooden frame from the iron parts) - to wreck a plow (by the ploughshare catching under a stump or under a large stone, and the horses walking rapidly).
"die Mehmaschien verrisse" - wrecking the mowing machine, when the cutting bar hits a stump, post, etc. and the horses have run away or are pulling too fast.

16.
"Wann die Hund odder Katze Graas fresse, gebt's Rege." [When the dogs or the cats eat grass, there will be rain.] *Common*

17.
It is sinful to whistle on Sunday. "Du kummscht ins Feier." You will be punished in hell-fire. *Leb*

"Feier" here seems to be a corruption of "Fegefeuer" [purgatory] (?). "Du kummscht ins Feier" [You'll come into the fire] was frequently used to strengthen admonitions when I was young.
"Du kummscht in die Hell." [You'll go to hell.]
"Du kummscht ins Hellfeier." [You'll inherit the fires of hell.]
"hell-fire" at one time was not infrequently heard in English.
"Ich hab's in die Hell nei verfehlt." (I missed out all to hell.)

18.

If you sing (whistle) in the morning, you will cry before night. You will cry for your laughter.
Quite common in the past

"Du heilscht noch fer dei Laches." [You will cry for your laughter.] — for inordinate merriment.

This belongs to that series of beliefs and proverbs which have their origin in the recognition of a sequence of opposites.

19.

"Die Alde (those of a former generation) hen als gsaat [used to say]: 'Cornstalks should be so high on the Fourth of July that one can hide a whiskey bottle in the cornfield.'"
William Landis, Egypt

Whiskey bottle - "Drammboddel"

20.

"Wann mer sich begreemt, schpodde die Leit em yuscht (aus)." [When one complains, people just make fun of you.]

"Wann mer sich begreemt, lache yuscht die Leit." [When one complains, people just laugh.]

"Wer am (zum) Letschde lacht, lacht am Beschde." [He who laughs last, has the best laugh.]

"Wann mer sich beglaagt, lache die Leit." [When one complains, people just laugh.] "Wann mer sich beglaagt, watt mer yuscht ausgelacht." [When one complains, they simply make fun of you.] *Leh*

"Es batt nix as mer glaagt, die Leit lache yuscht." [It doesn't do any good to complain, people just laugh at you.] *Frequently heard around Egypt*

21.

"Die Hinkel mause so im Noochsummer." [The chickens molt so in late summer.] [reported an informant]

"Wann is Noochsummer?" [When does the Noochsummer occur?] said I.

"So in Augscht un September."

[Brendle added later:] Noch der Hawwerern. [After the oats harvest]

Note the pronunciation of "Noochsummer."
Jane Kilmer, Myerstown

22.

"Der Papp (short English a) hot als gsaat, 'Wann die Hinkel mol mause, no waer die Zeit fer saehe glei do.'" [Dad used to say, "When the chickens begin to molt, the time for sowing will soon be here."]
Jane Kilmer

22.a.

Weather proverb: "Noch Aller Seel un Heil kann's alli Daag eiwindere." [After All Souls' and Saints' Days, Nov. 1 and 2, winter weather can set in any day.] "Aller Seel is der erscht Nowember un Aller Heil is der zwett Nowember."
Carson Semmel, Egypt
Nov. 11, 1951

23.

On old Spanish coins which circulated at one time to some extent and which were occasionally met with in my father's boyhood, the words "Carolus magnus dei" appeared among others. These words were remembered after the coins had disappeared as: "Laddeinisch" [Latin]. These words were said to mean: "Kummscht du net, so hol ich dich!" [If you won't come, I'll fetch you.]
My father

24.

Another Latin phrase spoken: "Cum suet illius trisstissima et imago." also circulating in the community, was said to mean: "Fress Vogel odder schtarb." [Eat, bird, or die.] (A proverb) *Do*

25.
Proverb

"Zu viel Hund sin's Haases Dod." [Too many dogs are death to a rabbit.] Meaning: If you demand too much from a person, that one will perish; too many dependents will bring ruin to a man.
Quite frequently heard; Do

26.
A.
"Wann mer uff em Grankesbett draamt as mer gsund waer, schtarbt mer." [If one dreams in the sickbed that one is well, you'll die.]
B.
For a sick person to dream of plowing means an open grave—means his death. *Leb*

27.

"Mer sett sich net bedanke fer ebbes as em gewwe is fer blanze, wie Blummeschteck odder Roseschteck, schunscht dutt's net waxe." [One should not thank the donor for a plant which one has been given to plant, like a flower or a rose, otherwise it will not grow.]
A belief very frequently heard to this day.

28.
Proverb
"Was sich zwett, dritt sich." [That which occurs twice, will occur a third time.] *Commonly heard*

Two funerals in a short succession in a congregation portend a third one.

29.
Proverb
"Wer am letschde lacht, lacht am beschde." [He who laughs last has the best laugh.]
Not infrequently heard

30.
Proverb
"Wer lacht am letschde, lacht am beschde." [Same meaning as 29.] *This version infrequent; Leh*

31.
Proverb
"Schweige is aa gsiecht." Hard to translate.

"Silence is also a victory." "Silence also brings victory." *My grandfather*

31.a.
A man in Green Lane was called "Johnny Chick" because he had a reputation of stealing chickens. He had a favorite saying: "Geb dich drein. [Adjust; submit.] Apparently the essential meaning of No. 31.

31.b.
"Langsam wehrt am lengschde." [Slowly lasts the longest.]

32.
Open sores licked by a dog will heal.
Sam Faust, Obelisk

33.
A fireman on a railroad train could not get up steam. To the insistent requests of the engineer, he finally cried out, "Der Deiwel kennt do nix mache." [The devil couldn't do anything here.] Thereupon a man appeared at his side who said, "Loss mich moll do draa." [Let me take a hand here.] Then to the amazement of the fireman, he opened the door of the firebox, backed against the opening, flipped out a long hairy tail from under his coat and put it into the fire pot. At once the fire burst into fury and the engine became so hot that it seemed in danger of bursting "Un der Feiermann hot gebitt, er sett uffheere." [and the fireman begged him to stop.] The devil turned to the fireman and said, "Nochdem geb acht, was du saagscht." [After this watch out what you say.] and vanished. *My father*

"Wann der Esel (Deiwel) nennscht, kummt er gerennt." [Speak of a jackass (devil) and he'll come running.] *Both frequently heard*

34.
A man came to a farmhouse on a visit just as the family was beginning to eat dinner [the noon meal]. He was asked to eat along. "Nee, er will net esse." [No, he doesn't want to eat.] Not being asked a second time and being very hungry, he said, "Esse is awwer aa gut." [See Nos. 1 and 2.]

35.
In the "bottom field" of the old Sheetz farm on the edge of Schaefferstown, where the Sheetz murder took place, a man by the name of Houser of "Kannadaa" (Canada), the southern part of Schaefferstown, "hot Schtecheise gfischt ee Nacht." [was gig fishing one night] Around midnight he heard what he took to be the horses of the murderers galloping around the field. The riders called out, "Whoa! Whoa!" Frightened he started for home and going through the woods he heard a voice calling, "Wuh-hie! Wuh-hie!" In his fright he answered, "Wuh-hie!" and thereupon a weight as of a two-bushel bag of wheat fell on his back. The weight lay on him all the way home, until unable to walk upright, he staggered against the door, where he collapsed.

I often heard this tale told by my father and my grandfather.

35.a.
Mose Dissinger was holding services. While the church was "on", there was a noise at the door and Mose's wife entered. Mose said to the congregation: "Guck net rum. Es is yuscht mei Fraa mit em Eckschank uff em Kopp." [Don't look around. It's just my wife with the corner cupboard on her head.]

His wife had sold the corner cupboard and had bought a new hat. *Middle Creek*

35.b.
Near Palmerton I searched for Mose Dissinger stories. An old gentleman spoke of Dissinger's wife "mit em hochi Hut" [with a tall hat]. Maybe that hat was triangular in shape and Mose said, "Do kummt mei Fraa mit en Eckschank uff em Kopp." [Here comes my wife with a corner cupboard on her head.]

36.
A young dog when small passed through the handle of a "Biggeleise" [sadiron] will not grow large. Reference is made to the old "Biggeleise" with an iron handle. *May, 1926; Mrs. Henry Brown, Laurys*

37.
"Aagewaxe" [liver-grown] children are to be passed under the table three times. Sympathetic relation between "Beh" [legs] of the table and "Beh" of the mother, a rebirth symbol. *Do*

37.a.
Passing a child through a "Kummet" [horse-collar] warm from a horse's chest is also a cure for "Aagewaxe". (Symbolical of a birth)

38.
"Haahnekamm" - name for Linaria vulgaris, on account of the spurred flowers. *Do*

39.
"Geilstee, Gehltee" - Collinsonia. The first on account of the robust stalk; the second on account of the color of the flowers. *Do*

40.
"Ribbegraas, Bandgraas" - Plantago lanceolata. "Bandgraas" because it was used by children in playing; making baskets, ladders, etc. *Do*

41.
"Aranchzwiwwel" - Arisaema triphyllum. *Do*

42.
Tea made of "Holzfaare" (sweet fern) is good for colds. *Do*

43.
If someone has warts, give that person a cent for them and the warts will disappear. In the dialect:

"abkaafe fer en Cent". The idea seems to rest in "ab" — to buy *away, off, from*. *Do*

44.
Eggs set on Good Friday, "Karrefreidaag" (frequently heard instead of "Karfreidaag") gebt nidderbeeniche Hinkel." [produces short-legged chickens] *Do*

45.
Wheels of wagons used to haul home the harvest from the fields should be greased with fat ("Faasnachtkuchefett") in which the "Faasnachtkuche" ("Faasnachtskuche, Faasnachtkichlicher" [pl.]) [Shrove Tuesday doughnuts] were fried, to keep insects from the grain. *Do*

46.
The grains of seed corn should be passed through a knothole before planting, so that after being planted the crows cannot pluck it out of the ground. *Do*

47.
Frederick Stump was a noted Indian fighter. My grandfather often spoke of him. One day, pursued by Indians, he squatted down on the ground as if he were a stump and remained unnoticed by the Indians as they in passing sat on the stump. *My grandfather*

47.a.
That is, he changed himself by magic art into a stump.

48.
Dawson Hetrick, a schoolmate of mine in Schaefferstown, told me that one night his father and others went to a crossroad to mould magic bullets. While engaged in their work, one happened to look up and there suspended over them hung a millstone. In fright they rushed from under the stone and ran pell-mell all the way home. "If they had not been scared and had kept on with their work, they would have succeeded in moulding the bullets," said Dawson Hetrick.

49.
A preacher summoned by a member of a robber band to visit a sick person at night had to pass through a dark woods, where the band lay in wait to rob him. They were powerless to attempt the robbery, when they saw riding on either side of him a figure in white. *My grandfather*

50.
When my Aunt Stella Brendle, my father's sister, lay dying, my great-grandmother, who lived in Schaefferstown, was called down in the night. As she came down through the field, a lamb, as it seemed—and so she said—walked alongside of her. *My father*

51.
The night my Aunt Stella died the horse which she rode neighed continuously. *My father*

52.
A smokehouse was near the house in which my great-grandmother lived. An apple tree overhung the smokehouse. At night during her last days, when apples fell on the roof of the smokehouse, she would cry out, "Der Drach! Sis der Drach!" [a mythical creature] *My father*

53.
"Schteefens" [stone fence] - a fence built more or less irregularly on one side of a field with stones that were gathered in clearing and cultivating the field. "Poschdefens" - a fence made of posts and with 3, 4, or 5 rails to a panel. A panel was called a "Fach" in Lebanon County. "Waremfens, Schtaakefens" - the zig-zag fence. "Bordfens" - a fence around the garden or around small lots, made with boards a foot or so wide and closely spaced and set close to the ground. (To prevent the entrance of small animals or the entrance or escape of little chickens?)

The "Bordfens" on our farm was made of sawed boards, a foot wide. The clapboard fence was made of split (!) clapboards about 5" wide. Later there were sawed clapboards.

"Glabbordfens" - a clapboard fence. "Drohtfens" - a wire fence. "Heckefens" - a fence made of the osage orange. "Leinfens" - the fence between two adjoining properties. "Fensecke" - corners at the end of a field of a "Poschdefens" or the corners of a zig-zag "Schtaakefens."

53.a.
A stone wall laid up around a garden (at one time not uncommon), a field or a cemetery was a "Schteemauer." Cf. the P.G. words "Gaardemauer" [garden wall], "Karichhofmauer" [churchyard wall]. At Blechersville, "Blecherschteddel," south of Myerstown, there was a beautifully laid wall on the side of the field lying along the road and the same kind of wall along the yard opposite the field. "Schteemauerfens" [stone wall fence] - a stone fence at a field was a "Schteefens."

54.
"Riggelfens" - a word sometimes applied to both the "post fence" and the "stake fence." The word "Riggelfens" was used, however, by some specifically for the "stake fence" to distinguish it from the "post fence." "Riggelhaufe" - the pile of reserve rails to be used in repairing fences or in building new ones. "eifense" - to enclose with a fence. "Ich hab der Mischthof eigfenst." [I fenced in the barnyard.] "Fenseschtreeme" - the land along the fence which cannot be turned by the plow and is not always cultivated—though often cultivated by hand for cabbage or other vegetables.

55.
"An die Fens hie bluge" - to plow closely along the fence. "An die Fens draa naus" - to go out along the fence.

"Fense-eck, Fenseck" - 1. In the case of a post fence

(this is the word in English) the corner of the field. 2. In the case of the stake fence (the word in English with this meaning) the recess formed by the fence.

The "Fenseschtreeme" noted in No. 54 is the strip of land that lies uncultivated. This strip is cleaned of weeds and brush. This is done after haymaking and after harvest. This is spoken of as "Fense butze (ausbutze)," "Fenseschtreeme butze (ausbutze)" or "Fense-ecker butze (ausbutze)." The last in the case of stake fences particularly.

55.a.
"Fenseschtreeme (hie)bluge" - to plow close to the fence.

56.
My grandfather, D.D. Brendle, with another man, was out hunting one night in the mountains. The dogs would not hunt. They kept close to my grandfather and his companion. The dogs hung close to their legs. Then by the light of their lanterns they noticed a little black animal, strange to them. This they took to be one of the pack of the "Ewich Yaeger" [eternal hunter] and came home immediately. *My grandfather*

57.
My grandfather and my uncle were out hunting another night. They were on the ridge that led back to "Walniss Brunne" [Walnut Spring]. As they went along the ridge, they heard "der Ewich Yaeger" [the eternal hunter] on the slope across the "Haschdaal" [Deer Valley]. They immediately turned and came home, for it was dangerous to be out at night when "der Ewich Yaeger" was abroad. This meant death or disappearance. *My father*

58.
My father repeatedly said that "der Ewich Yaeger" was nothing more than the cackling of wild geese migrating at night. He did not call the wild goose "der Ewich Yaeger," but he explained the legend through the noises. Evidently "der Ewich Yaeger" was connected with a nocturnal noise made in the sky.

59.
When the sexton was notified of a person's death, he rang the church bell for a brief time and then tolled the number of years the deceased had lived. This was called "die Leicht aabelle."
Church near Quakertown, Rev. Franklin Slifer, June 1936

60.
At Ben Salem Church, out from Lehighton, the men communed first, then the women. After the benediction at the communion table the men straightway returned to their seats, but the women bowed and then returned to their seats. "In my pastorate." *Do*

61.
Mrs. Charles Snyder of Ballietsville tells me that when she was young, the people as they approached the communion table made a curtsey. This was at the Egypt Church. I was told this repeatedly.

62.
A dead fetus was called "abschtennich" [repulsive], "en abschtennich Geburt" [a repulsive birth].
Mrs. K-, a midwife, Laurys

63.
A woman who has given birth to a child should not get up "vum Kinsbet" [from parturition] on a Sunday; or "soll net uffschteh" [should not get out of bed].
Do

64.
A male child, "en Buh" [a boy], is foretold if the mother becomes large in front; i.e. if her condition is most noticeable in the front. *Do*

65.
A female child is foretold if the mother's condition is most noticeable in the rear, "pushed out." *Do*

66.
The afterbirth should be buried in a brook ("Rann") or in a gutter. Also: in the ground or in the manure pile. *Do*

67.
A corpse should not lie unburied over Sunday. (Is this belief connected with Easter Sunday, the resurrection?) *Leb*

68.
Twins are due to a double, i.e. successive coitus.
Common belief

69.
To speak straight from the shoulder and to call a spade a spade is "die deitsch Waahret schwetze" [to spead the German truth] or "ihm die deitsch Waahret saage" [to tell him the German truth].
Particularly in Mont

69.a.
Also: "Fer die deitsch Waahret saage: Er liegt!" [To tell the whole, blunt truth: He's lying!]

70.
Proverb
"Wann du ebbes recht geduh hawwe witt, muscht's selwer duh (duh's selwert). [If you want something done well, properly, you must do it yourself.]
Note the form "selwer". The Mont. Co. form is "selwert". *Leb*

71.
"Es kiehl Wedder im Schpotyaahr macht die Haase fett." [Cool weather in fall makes the rabbits fat.] "Die Haase warre net fett bis mir en hadder Reife ghat hen." [The rabbits don't get fat until we've had a hard frost.] *Common beliefs*

72.
The worms which are occasionally found in the skins of rabbits are killed by the frosts. If there is warm weather up to the hunting season, the rabbits are sure to have worms. *Common belief, Mont*

72.a.
"Die Haase sin wermich." [The rabbits are wormy.] A hunter at Sumneytown would press out the worms or skin the rabbits and not tell his wife of the worms (skin worms), who would then cook the rabbits. "Die Werm schadde nix!" [The worms do no harm.] Generally hunters threw the carcass away. The worms were found around the neck.

73.
Proverb
"En alder Haas losst sich net leicht fange." [An old rabbit is not easily caught.] ("fange" refers to a snare?) *Quite frequently heard*

74.
"En alder Haas hockt net gern im freie Feld." [An old rabbit doesn't like to sit in an open field.] *Mont*

"Du findscht net glei en Haas im Midde vum Feld." [You won't often find a rabbit in the middle of a field.] *Leb*

74.a.
A rabbit nests up not far from a fence, so as to escape if flushed.

75.
"En Haas geht hinnerschich ins Nescht." "En Haas backt (English a) in sei Nescht." [A rabbit backs into his nest.]

76.
"Wann en Haas mol uffgyaagt is (aus seim Nescht geyaagt), geht er nimmi in sell Nescht (datt nei)." [When a rabbit has been chased up (chased from his nest), he'll never go back to that nest (back into it).] *Leb*

77.
There are cats which roam the fields, which are spoken of as "Feldkatz" or even "wildi Katz." Such a tomcat is "en Heckekaader." These are said to mate with the rabbits. The progeny has the general appearance of a rabbit with a head like that of a cat and WITH HORNS. I often heard hunters of Sumneytown tell of killing such progeny. In Egypt two hunters told me of shooting rabbits with cats' heads and horns. (Why the horns? I cannot understand.)

78.
My father tells me that he can distinguish between the calls of the male and that of the female partridge. (Isn't the female silent?)

79.
"Hiesicht" [regard; view] (Mont, Leh); "Hinsicht" (Leb). "In eenre Hiesicht is es recht un in der annre letz." Looked at in one way, it is right, in another way, it's wrong. The word is in common usage; see Lambert's "hiesig."

80.
An old undertaker of Mahoning Valley told me on Labor Day in 1935 that when he started practicing, an old man came to him at a funeral and said, "Es is ken Leicht [It's no funeral], if the corpse doesn't stink." (Does "Leicht" refer to corpse?) Evidently the corpses were in a state of decomposition.

81.
When the sky is filled with small cumulus clouds, they say in Upper Lehigh County, "Die Schof gehne fer Wasser. Marye geb's Rege." [The sheep are going for water. Tomorrow it will rain.]

82.
Small cumulus clouds are called "scheffiche Wolke" (sheep-like clouds) in Green Lane. They are a sign of rain on the morrow. ("scheffich" comes from the dialect word "Schof" [sheep].
Isaac Smith, Green Lane,

83.
In walking through the cemetery, one should not step across a grave. (You will disturb the rest of the dead. Since cemeteries are now mowed, this belief has disappeared.) *Leb*

83.a.
"Du nemmscht die Ruh." [You rob the dead of their rest.] You cause the dead to become a ghost.

84.
When my Aunt Stella was buried, Peter Mock, a friend of the family, cut a swath with a scythe 13 feet wide through the meadow for the funeral cortege on the way to the church. Isolated this incident might have no significance, but...

85.
When I was a student pastor at Bernville in Berks Co., I was asked to conduct the funeral of a woman who had been maid on a farm several miles north of Bernville, but who died in Leesport, Berks Co. On the way from the house to the church we left the public road and drove through a lane that led across the farm, where she had been the housekeeper. Was there a belief back of these two instances?

86.
In colonial times housing was small and the means of preservation limited. Bodies were interred soon after death. Later the pendulum swung to the end of keeping the bodies as long as possible. This was done to keep the bodies for the accomodation of distant relatives and maybe to be sure they were dead. Oft

times, no doubt, the bodies were in the first stages of decomposition.

"Sie hen en lang ghalde. Sei Gsicht waar am blo warre." [They kept him a long time. His face was turning blue.]

87.
"Batsche, Batsche, Kichliche,
Marye kummt's Marichliche.
Iwwermarye noch emoll,
No backt sie en ganzer Zuwwer voll."

[Patty cake, patty cake,
Tomorrow tiny Maria is coming.
The following day again,
Then she'll bake a whole tubful.]

Mrs. Ed Wagner, Northampton

88.
"Ich heier aa die Lisabeth,
Ich heier sie aa doch net,
Weil sie ken Geld hot,
So maa ich sie net."

[I'll also marry Elizabeth,
On the other hand I won't marry her,
Because she has no money,
I don't like her either.] *Do*

Note the form "maa" [maag].

89.
"Aa Beh Zeh
Deh Ee Eff Geh
Haa Ie Kaa Ell Emm
En Oh Peh Kuh
Ar Es Teh Uh
Ix Ipselon Zett
Un des is Aa Beh Zeh."

[A B C
D E F G
H I K L M
N O P Q
R S T U
X Y Z
And this is A B C.]

Mrs. Rudolph, Cementon

90.
"Hiwwelli [a little hill] up, Hiwwelli down,
That's the way to Schaefferstown."

Henry Bomberger, Lititz

91.
The bogeyman was called "Bautz" in Lebanon County in speaking to children. "Der Bautz grickt dich." [The bogeyman will get you.]

92.
Proverb
"Unni Druwwel hot mer nix." (Wie en Kopp voll Leis un en Haus voll Kinner.) [Like a head full of lice and a house full of children.] If you have no trouble, you have nothing else to be troubled about. *Mont*

93.
Proverb
"Der Druwwel as mer mit sich nemme kann, is ken Druwwel." [The trouble that you can take with you is no trouble.] Your own personal trouble is very little.
Mrs. Joe Fenstermaker

94.
Proverb
"Druwwel hot unser eens net; Mer hot yuscht Sarye." [Our kind doesn't have trouble; We only have burdens.] Here trouble is something like blindness, cancer, tuberculosis. *Astor Ritter*

95.
Proverb
"Seller Druwwel kann mer sich schpaare." [You can spare yourself that trouble.] The matter is settled. Don't worry about it.

96.
Proverb
"Der greescht Druwwel macht mer sich selwert." The greatest troubles are fancied ones. *Leh*

97.
Proverb
"Vanne hui, hinne fui."
[In the front nothing, in the back nothing.] *Leb*

98.
Proverb
"Zu viel Eise, gaar ken Schwees." [Too much iron but no fusion.] *Ed Bolig, Sumneytown*

"Zu viel Eisi im Feier, gaar ken Schwees." [Too many irons in the fire, no fusion at all.] *Mont*

98.a.
"Zu viel Eisi im Feier." — an expression indicating that too many things are being done at the same time.

99.
Proverb
"Wann's Fass voll is, laaft's iwwer." [When the barrel is full, it will overflow.] *Rather commonly heard*

100.
Proverb
"Wann's Moos voll is, laaft's iwwer." [When the measure is full, it will run over.] "Moos" — the measure. *Mont*

101.
Proverb
"Wann mer bei der Welf is, muss mer mit ne heile." [When you're with the wolves, you have to howl with them.] *My grandfather*

102.
Proverb
"Zu viel vum Gude." [Too much of the good thing.] "Genunk is genunk." [Enough is enough.]

103.
Proverb
"Des is zu viel vum gude Ding." [This is too much of the good thing.] Even the poor worm will turn. Enough has been borne.

104.
Proverb
"Wann du's recht (geduh, gemacht) hawwe witt, muscht's selwert duh." [If you want to have it done right, you have to do it yourself.] *Mont*

105.
Proverb
"Es nemmt zwee fer fechde." [It takes two to fight.] A very common expression by one who would be neutral.

106.
Proverb
"Es nemmt zwee fer fechde, awwer eens muss es aafange." [It takes two to fight, but one must begin it.] This as an answer to No. 105, by one who would be partisan. *Not commonly heard; Leh*

107.
Proverb
"Wann mer zu viel Eise im Feier hot, dutt's em gern verbrenne." [When one has too many irons in the fire, one is apt to get burned.]
Mrs. Harvey Barndt, Sumneytown

108.
Proverb
"Wie mer der Schtul macht, so hockt mer." *Leb*
[As the chair is made, so one sits.]

109.
Proverb
"Wie mer der Schtul macht, so sitzt [sits] mer." *Leb*

110.
Proverb
"Wie mer's Bett macht, so leit mer." *Mont*
[As the bed is made, so one lies.]

111.
Proverb
"Zu viel verreisst der Sack." [Too much tears the bag.] *Common*

112.
Proverb
A.
"Wann mer sich uff Mensche verlosst, is mer verlore." [When one depends on man, all is lost.] *Leb*
B.
"Wer sich uff Gott verlosst, is net verlore." [He who depends on God is not lost.] *Leb*

113.
Proverb
"Wer viel schwetzt, liegt gern." [He who talks freely, lies easily.] *Leh*

114.
Proverb
"Wer viel schwetzt, liegt viel." [He who talks much, lies much.] *Leh, Mont*

114.a.
"Er hot sich moll uffgeblose." [He exploded; he shot off his mouth.]
"En Laus im Graut is besser wie gaar ken Fleesch." [A louse in the cabbage is better than no meat at all.]

115.
Proverb
"Wer zu letscht (zum letschde, Mont) lacht, lacht am Beschde." [He who laughs last, has the best laugh.] *Leh*

116.
Proverb
"Verschpreche macht schuldich." [Promises make commitments.] *Mont*

117.
Proverb:
"Verschpreche macht Schulde." [Promises make debts.] *Leh*

118.
Proverb
"Ee Lieg bringt die anner mit sich." [The first lie produces the next.] *Leh, Leb, Mont*

120.
Proverb
A.
"Ee Lieg is die anner wert." To him who lies, a lie.
B.
"Wer bedriegt, watt bedroge." [He who cheats, gets cheated.] *Leb*

121.
Proverb
"Ee Ehr is die anner wert." One good turn deserves another. *Mrs. Ed Wagner, Northampton*

122.
Proverb
"Wann mer uff em Hund sei Schwanz drett, gauzt er." (If your words find their mark, there will be a reaction on the part of the person hit.) *Leb*

123.
Proverb
"Wann mer uff em Hund sei Schwanz dreet, greischt er." [If you step on a dog's tail, he'll yap.]
Mont

124.
Proverb
"Wann mer uff em Hund sei Schwanz dreet, gnabbt (English short a) er." [If you step on a dog's tail, he'll yap.]
Leh

125.
Proverb
"Es nemmt zwee fer hure, awwer die Fraa hot's immer geduh." [It takes two to fornicate, but the woman always did it.]
Leh

(I do not have the correct verbage of the last part. The meaning is that while two have part in the act, the blame is unequally borne.) Richard Peters says, "Ich glaab, as es daere Weg waar: 'En Weibsmensch dutt net leenich hure.'" [I think it was this way: A woman does not fornicate singly.] "Velleicht waar's: 'En Weibsmensch kann net lee hure.'" [Perhaps it was: A woman cannot commit fornication alone.]

126.
Proverb
"Ee Hurer wees glei, wu der anner hiegeht." Immoral men know all the immoral women.
Leh

127.
Proverb
"En banger Mensch is im Himmel net sicher." [A fearful person is not safe in heaven.]
Mrs. Raymond Remaley, Egypt

128.
Proverb
"Sie hebt ihre Kopp in der Heh as wann sie's frisch gebacke Brod in Schweezeland rieche deet." [She carries her head as if she were smelling freshly baked bread in Switzerland.]
Do

129.
When ants are in mass outside their burrows, there will be rain.
Thomas Hoffman, Egypt

130.
"Wann beese Weibsleit ins Feier gucke, brennt's." If a fire in a stove doesn't burn, have a cross woman look at it.
Mrs. Raymond Remaley, Egypt

(Many of the above proverbs came from Mrs. Remaley.)

130.a.
"Sie hot sich verschmiert." [She besmeared herself.]

131.
"Baschdert" — a scrub woodland; a wet pastureland with scrubby trees.
Green Lane

132.
"Schlack" — a second growth scrubby woodland. Both terms (131 and 132) for a second growth scrubby woodland are used in Green Lane. "Schlack" comes from "Ausschlack" [young shoot, sucker].

133.
If a cellar under the house or the ground cellar, "Grundkeller, Kiehlkeller", sweats, there will be rain.

134.
If the flagstones in a springhouse or cellar sweat ("schwitze") on hot days, there will be rain. "Kellerschtee" — flagstones in the cellar.
Mont

135.
If the native sycamore tree sheds its bark and displays a nude bole and branches, the winter will be mild. The native sycamore tree at Macoby Bridge, Green Lane, was the weather prophet for the community.

136.
"Wann die Schof nach der Lechaa gehn (gehne), geb's Rege." "Schof" — fleecy clouds. When the wind blows the fleecy clouds towards the Lehigh River (eastward), there will be rain.
North Whitehall, Leh

137.
"hallich" — jolly, lively, pleasant. "Heit waar er awwer hallich." [Today he was very lively.] "uffgelebt" in Mont. Co. has the meaning of "hallich", a Leb. Co. term.

138.
If you cut yourself, lay a spider web on the wound to stanch the flow of the blood.
Mrs. Lottie Strauss, Treichlers,

139.
For a bad cut, lay a rag soaked in vinegar on the wound to stop the blood.
Do

140.
For the "Brand" say:
"Do geht en Fraa iwwers Land,
Sie hot en schneeweissi Hand,
Un des is gut fer der Brand."

[Here goes a woman through the land, she has a snow-white hand, and this is good for gangrene.] Stroke 3 times with your right hand and blow away 3 times. The right hand and not the left hand is used in "brauching" [powwowing].
R. H. Scheirer, Undertaker, Orefield

141.
"Wu der Dod nausgeht am Karber, bleibt's blo." That part of the body where death left the body remains blue. This is a very interesting belief.
Do

The body is a house. Through the window or or door by which death escapes, that part, mouth, eyes, nose, ears, remains blue.

142.
Game: "Hide and Go Seek."
"It", the seeker, stands at a tree with an arm over the eyes. "It" counts 10 and then goes forth to seek the remaining players. The one first found and touched became the next one "it". The search was kept up until all had been found. *Do*

143.
Game: "Fox and Geese."
The players were divided into two groups. The first group would drop paper cut fine. The foxes would follow. *Do*

144.
Game: "Follow the Leader."
As the leader went, over and through fences, etc., so the ones that follow went. *Do*

145.
Counting out for the game "Follow the Leader"
"Rich man, poor man, beggar man, thief." Certain counting out rhymes were used for certain games. *Do*

146.
Counting out rhyme:
"Eens, zwee, drei,
 Hicke, hacke, hei.
 Der Schnee geht weck,
 Die Katz leit im Dreck."

[One, two, three,
 Hicke, hacke, hei.
 The snow goes away,
 The cat lies in the dirt.] *Do*

147.
Game: "Hopscotch."
Stand on one foot, jump up and kick with the foot upon which you are standing. *Do*

148.
Game: "The Farmer in the Dell."
Played by mixed groups. A ring was formed. The farmer was in the middle. The boys had been counted out to find out who was to be the farmer. The ring circles around, the players singing:

1.
"The farmer in the dell,
 The farmer in the dell,
 Hei hoh, the dairy ho,
 The farmer in the dell."

2.
"The farmer takes a wife,
 The farmer takes a wife.
 Hei ho, the dairy ho,
 The farmer takes a wife."

Here the farmer in the ring selects a girl and takes her to himself in the ring.

3.
"The wife takes a child, etc."
Here the girl selects one from the circle and takes her into the ring.

4.
"The child takes a dog, etc."
The child selects one and takes him into the ring.

5.
"The dog takes a cat, etc."
The dog selects one and takes her into the ring.

6.
"The cat takes a mouse, etc."
Here the cat selects one and takes him to the others into the ring.

7.
"The mouse takes a cheese, etc."

Here the mouse takes one out of the circle to the others within the ring. The game begins anew with the first one selected "it." *Do*

149.
Game: "Nipsi."
A small piece of wood was taken, pointed at both ends. It was hit on one end, and flying upwards, it was hit for a distance. The game was to see who could cover a certain distance with the fewest strokes. *Do*

150.
Game: "Kick the Wicket."
A piece of hose was laid across from one brick to another. The player kicked out this hose and tried to touch three bases (one of them home base) before the hose was returned. *Do*

151.
In burials, a wife is to lie to the left of her husband a husband to the right of his wife. A persistent custom. "Wann's net so geduh watt, is es ganz letz." [If it is not done so, it is considered to be completely wrong.] This is also the position in marriage. *Do*

152.
When a corpse is taken into the church, it should be feet first. The corpse should be with the head to the right and facing those approaching the casket for viewing. *Do*

153.
Upon a death the mirrors are to be covered. "Wann der Dod sich im Schpiegel sehnt, geht (gebt's) glei noch

eens." [When death sees itself in a mirror, another one will die soon.] *Do*

154.
In tolling at Unionville, Neffs, Pa., the full number of years is tolled—then a pause—and the number of days till the funeral. *Do*

(Scheirer, a native of Allentown, gave the games as played in Allentown, when he was a boy.)

155.
Babies were rocked to sleep with the lullaby:

"By-O-Baby,
By-O-Baby,
By-O-Baby,
Go to sleep."

The melody used was "Sieh, hier bin ich, Ehrenkoenig" or "Come, Thou Fount of Every Blessing." The melody was hummed (Leb, Leh). Words were improvised, but usually English words.
(Charles Millson)

156.
Expression
"Datt is wu der Schuh em drickt." [That is where the shoe pinches.] That is where he is in trouble.
Common usage

Of a young girl, unmarried and pregnant, "Sie is in Druwwel." [She's in trouble.] "Er hot sie in Druwwel grickt." [He got her in trouble.] A pregnant woman is "in Famillye Weg" or "in Famillye Umschtende" [in a family way, circumstances].

156.a.
The plant "Alder Mann" is not to be planted close to the plant "Aldi Fraa," because "der Alt Mann macht die Alt Fraa doot." [Southern wood kills common mugwort]

157.
Proverb
"Allemol wann en Schof blatt, verliert's en Maulvoll." [Every time a sheep bleats, it loses a mouthful.] *Not infrequently heard*

158.
For a toothache put an unburned match head in the cavity.
Mrs. Lottie Strauss

159.
For sore eyes put fried out rabbit's fat on the eyelid be careful not to get any in the eyes. That would cause blindness. *Do*

160.
To keep chicken pox, measles and other children's diseases away from a child, hang a small bag around its neck, in which are camphor and "Deiwelsdreck" [asafoetida] have been placed. *Do*

161.
For a felon or splinter mix lard and flour to a paste and lay on. This will draw out the core or splinter. Or tie on a piece of bacon with a cloth. *Do*

162.
"Er is unnich em Wedder." He is sick. He has been sick for some time. *A common expression, Do*

163.
Six weeks after the katydids begin to sing there will be the first frost. *Henry Summers, Green Lane*

164.
"Glee odder Graassume sett mer friehyaahrs saehe vor em letschde Froscht." [Clover or grass seeds one should sow in the spring before the last frost.]
Oscar Mickley, Egypt

165
"Riewesume muss gsaet sei vor en Gwidderrege, schunscht geht's net uff." [Turnip seeds must be planted prior to a thunderstrom, otherwise they will not come up.] *Frank Sterner, Egypt*

166.
"Riewe, roh gesse, sin gut fer ebbes as im Maage reibt." [Turnips eaten raw are good for something that's bothering your stomach.] *Leb*

A hair in the stomach: A man had "Maagedruwwel" [stomach trouble]. The physicians were of no help. A tramp came along: "Riewe gerode." [He advised turnips.] A ball of hair was passed. (Evidently the same story as No. 167.) *Leb*

167.
There was a man who had been sick for a long time. His stomach was out of order. He went to this doctor and to that doctor and spent a great deal of money. There was no cure. One day a man came along to whom he told of his illness. The old man told him that he had a hair in the stomach. To get rid of the hair he was to eat a raw turnip. He did so and was cured. A typical "folk medical experience." *My father*

168.
"En Yuddebiewel (the Jewish Bible) bringt Unglick ins Haus." [brings misfortune into the house] Emil Smith's wife asked me how she was to get rid of a "Yuddebiewel." Emil had told her that she was to burn it. But she said that she had been taught that it was sinful to burn a Bible or to sell one. What was she to do? I told her to keep the Bible. As long as the New Testament was in a Bible, it was not a "Yuddebiewel." She kept it. (See No. 14,410)

Later I saw this Bible. It was a Jewish Bible. I had not thought that there would be one in Egypt and had concluded that it was a German Bible with the Apocrypha.

169.

Professor Kegel of Lehigh University suggests that our game of "Barley open" comes from the German game "Baer lauf."

170.

"Er schpitzt sei Naas (Ohre), wann er des heert." His curiosity, interest, concern, will be aroused when he hears this. A horse, a dog, listening, "schpitzt die Ohre" [points the ears].

171.

"Wer net haricht, muss fiehle." "Wer net hariche will, muss fiehle." He who will not obey must learn by experience. He who will not follow counsel must learn by experience. *Quite commonly heard*

172.

"Wer net folgt, muss fiehle." He who does not obey must learn by experience. *Leb*

173.

Passing two persons who are standing or walking side by side, will take away their good fortune (will cause them to quarrel). *Common belief*

174.

"Wilder Meerreddich" — Lepidium virginianum. The leaves resemble the upper leaves of the "Meerreddich" [horseradish]. *Mrs. Tilghman Frantz's mother, October 14, 1927*

175.

"Seiohrebledder," Plantago major, were laid on to alleviate the pain of wasp stings. *Do*

176.

"Gensgraut" — the common daisy. Chrysthanthemum Leucanthemum pinnatifidum. *Do*

177.

"Kar(e)betlumbefarb Blumme" — Solidago, farm and barnyard species. She says that the flowers and the plants were used to color the carpet rags before taking them to the weaver. *Do*

178.

"Scheissmelde" — Chrenopodium ambrosioides. The name on account of odor and the flower clusters. *Do*

179.

— Gross of Snyder County says there is a tradition that barn decorations are due to the federal tax on windows; that decorations were put on the barn to take the place of real windows. Personally, I believe that there is the remembrance of a federal tax on windows still extant. I do not, however, believe that that is the historical basis for the barn decorations, or for the slatted windows, or for the closed windows, so characteristic of the barns of Snyder and Northumberland counties. Gross says that painting the gate blue when a marriageable daughter was in the home, was done by others besides the Dunkards. His father built a new fence around the house yard and painted the gate blue when his sister was 18 years of age. It proved useless, for she did not marry until she was some 20 years old, and the lover didn't come through the gate. *BB*

180.

"Smartweed," Hydropiper, boiled in vinegar, is good for sprains. On October 12, 1927, I, Marcus Diehl of Egypt, Abe Wenger of Egypt, a man from Fogelsville, were at Promised Land in Pike County, at the boarding house run by Charles Wilson. *Heard in that group, plus Wilson*

181.

The inner bark of the white oak is used for sprains, as a wash. *Do*

182.

"Schofribbetee" [yarrow tea] — a tea used for the stomach.

183.

The juice of "Schpitzeweddrich" [narrow-leafed plantain] is used as a wash for sumac poisoning.

185.

Indian turnip, [jack-in-the-pulpit], Arisaema triphyllum, dried and grated into sweet milk was taken for stomach cramps. *Do*

186.

The berries of the Staghorn sumac were taken in warm water for a sore throat. (In Green Lane the berries of Rhus glabra in vinegar were used as a gargle for a sore throat.) *Do*

187.

Catnip tea for colds. *Do*

188.

Peppermint, Mentha spicata, is good for stomach cramps. *Do*

189.

Boneset tea for fevers. *Do*

190.

A tea of sweet fern is a tonic. *Do*

191.

The bark of sassafras root is used for a tonic. (How? In liquor?) *Do*

192.

"Seiohrebledder" [pigs' ears] were used as "greens" when young. *Do, Abe Wenger*

193.
"Potly" (so called by Wilson), Portulaca oleracea, used for "greens". *Do*

194.
Marsh marigold, milkweed, pigweed (Chenopodium album) were all used as "greens". *Do*

195.
Young shoots of Pteris aquilina were used as "greens". They were canned for winter use. The taste is similar to that of sweet peas and mushrooms. *Do*

This was served at the table on October 13, 1927, by the Wilsons.

196.
"Reetzelche" [riddles]

"Was guckt me halwe Hinkel gleich?" [What looks like half a chicken?] — "Die anner Helft." [The other half] *Hatty Solt, Egypt, Spring, 1936*

197.
"Was verennert sei Naame?" [What changes its name?] — "En Weibsmensch, wann sie heiert." [A woman, when she marries.] *Do*

198.
"Was is elder as sei Mudder?" [What's older than its mother?] — "Essich." [Vinegar]

199.
"Wie kann mer der ganze Weg noch der Schtadt reide im Schadde?" [How can one ride the whole way to town in the shade?] — "Wann mer abschteigt un laaft wu's kenner hot." [If one dismounts and walks where there is none.] *Do*

200.
"Ferwas hot der Eileschpiegel als gheilt, wann er barignunner is un glacht, wann er barignuff is?" [Why did Eileschpiegel weep when he went downhill and laugh when he went uphill?] — "Wann er barignunner is, hot er gheilt, weil er widder nuff gemisst; un barignuff hot er glacht, weil's glei widder barignunner gange is." [When he went downhill, he wept, because he had to go up again; and uphill he laughed, because it would soon go downhill again.] *Do*

201.
"Was geht die Schteeg nuff un regt's net aa?" [What goes up the stairs and does not touch them?] — "Der Schmok." [Smoke] This may have come from the time of the open fireplace. *Do*

202.
"Was hot's Hatz im Kopp?" [What has its heart in its head?] — "En Grautkopp." [A cabbage head] The stem in a cabbage is called "Hatz". *Do*

203.
"Was hot's Hatz im ganze Leib?" [What has its heart in the entire body?] "En Baam." [A tree] "Es Hatzholz" — the heartwood. *Do*

204.
"Ferwas schpringt en Fux der Barig nuff?" [Why does the fox run up the hill?] — "Vor sei Schwanz." [In front of his tail] *Do*

["fer" is the unaccented form of "vor", hence "vor was?" (in front of what?) could be misunderstood as "ferwas?"]

205.
"Ferwas schteht die Uhr im Haus?" [Why is the clock standing in the house?] — "Wann sie greesser waer wie's Haus, deet's Haus in der Uhr schteh." [If it were bigger than the house, the house would be standing in the clock.] *Do*

206.
"Wann is en Fux en Fux?" [When is a fox *a* fox?] "Wann er lee is." [When he's alone.] [The second "en" really should be articulated as "ee" (one). *Do*

207.
"Wie kenne drei Leit drei Oier deele un es bleibt noch eens in der Schissel leie?" [How can three people divide three eggs and one remains in the bowl?] "Wann der letscht die Schissel mit em Oi nemmt." [If the last one takes the bowl with the egg.] *Do*

208.
"Was hot's greescht Schnuppduch in der Welt?" [What has the largest handkerchief in the world?] — "En Hinkel. Es butzt sei Naas iwweraal uff die Erd." [A chicken. It cleans its nose everywhere on the earth.] *Do*

209.
"Was waar gebore un is net gschtarwe?" [What was born and hasn't died?] "Du un aa viel annre." [You and also many others.] *Do*

210.
"Wie lang schloft die Katz uff em Hoi?" [How long does the cat sleep on the hay?] — "Bis der Aamet druff kummt." [Until the second cutting is placed there.]

211.
"Wer es macht, der saagt es net. Wer es nemmt, der kennt's net. Wer's kennt, der will's net." [He who makes it, does not say so. He who takes it, doesn't recognize it. He who recognizes it, doesn't want it.] — "Falsch Geld." [Counterfeit money] *Do*

211.a.
"Es elft Gebot: Loss dich net verwische." [The Eleventh Commandment. Don't get caught.]

211.b.
Proverb

"Was is es elft Gebot?" [What is the 11th Commandment?] — "Loss dich net verwische!"

"verschniert" [drawn up with strings, etc.] — used in reference to the oldfashioned corsets which were often drawn up too tightly.

212.
The mother of Preston Smith, cashier of the Egypt Bank, told him that an illegitimate child was going to be named "Essich" [Vinegar]. — "Ferwas?" [Why?] asked the son. "Weil's en Mudder hot un ken Vadder." [Because it has a mother and no father.] [A secondary meaning of the word "die Mudder" in Pennsylvania German is "mother of vinegar."]
Riddle
"Was hot en Mudder un ken Vadder?" [What has a mother and no father?] — "Essich." [Vinegar]
Common

213.
When a widower with children marries a widow with children, the children are called "zamme(r)gebrochde Kinner" [children which have been brought together].
This term is used in Leb, Mont, Leh. Heard by me.

214.
Proverb
"Ee Ehr is die anner wert." [One honor, favor, is worth another.] "Sie hen mer die Ehr net geduh fer mich eilaade." [They didn't do me the honor of inviting me.] *Quite frequently heard*

215.
A. "Gwidderrut" — lightning rod. *Mont*
B. "Gewidderrutschtange" — lightning rods *Leh*
C. "Gwidderschtang" — lightning rod

216.
"Aftergscharre," pl. — old style harnesses with broad leathern parts, put on the rear horses of a four-horse team. Made with a broad piece of leather coming around the hindquarters of the horse, which would enable the horse to hold back the wagon, going downhill. We used "Aftergscharre" on the farm when I was a boy. My grandfather called them "Aftergscharre", but my father and the workmen who assisted in the farm work called them "Hinnergscharre" and the harness of the lead horse "Veddergscharr".

The lead horse or horses had a different kind of harness, not as heavy, and without the rear "breeching" to hold or pull back. This was "es Veddergscharr."

Lambert [p. 160] has "Veddergscharr" but not the companion "Hinnergscharr." The term "Aftergscharr" was also used by Mrs. Ed Wagner, Northampton.

217.
The mournful howling of a dog denotes misfortune to the family to which it belongs. *General belief*

218.
"unheemlich" [unsettling]. The howling of a dog at night is "unheemlich." *Mrs. Ed Wagner*

219.
If, as you enter a house, you stumble, "bischt net willkumm." [you are not welcome.] *Do*

220.
If you stumble over a step, there will soon be a wedding. *Charles Hoffman, Neffs*

If you stumble going up a stairway or over steps going up, there will soon be a wedding.
Mrs. Joe Fenstermaker, Egypt

220.a.
I heard someone say to another man, who was about to be married, "Iwwerdem brauchscht die Drebbe nimmi geh." [Soon you will no longer have to go the stairs.] Could it mean that as a single person he had to sleep in the attic, as a married person on the first floor? [It still is the custom among the Old Order Amish and Old Order Mennonites for the parents to sleep downstairs in the first floor bedroom called "die Kammer" in the dialect.]

221.
One should not whistle, be boisterous or indulge in laughter on Sunday. *Earlier a common belief*

Rev. C. E. Held of Sumneytown lost the respect of Mrs. Harvey Barndt when, invited to her home for a Sunday dinner, he came around the house whistling.

222.
If you laugh or sing early in the morning, you will weep before night. *Earlier frequently heard*

223.
"Ich bin net vun geschder (heit)." [I wasn't born yesterday (today).] I am not a stupid person. "Er hot mer sell weis mache welle, awwer ich bin net vun geschder." He wanted to have me believe what he said, but I knew better. *Common expression*

224.
"So ehrlich wie die Naddschtann." [As honest as the North Star.] "Er is so ehrlich wie die Naddschtann; du kannscht en Haus uff en baue." [He's as honest as the North Star. You can build a house on him.] *Not infrequently heard*

225.
"Grischtliche Fraa; grischtlicher Mann" — Christian woman; Christian man. "Sie waar immer en grischtliche Fraa." She always lived a righteous life, according to her faith. "Er hot en grischtlich Lewe gfiehrt." He lived a life of Christian righteousness.

226.
Plant late cabbage "graad vorm lengschde Daag. No hald's lang." [right before the longest day. It will keep over the winter.] *Said by Dr. Henry Leh, according to Henry Musselman*

227.
Finding a needle, a pin, a horseshoe, means good

luck. The needle or pin should not be taken up at the pointed end. *Common belief*

228.
"En Breddich muss an der Mann gebrocht warre." [A sermon must strike the hearer.] It must evoke reactions within the hearer for repentence and better living. "It must hit home." *Common expression*

228.a.
"an der Mann bringe" [to get a point across; to impress someone with a fact or a situation.]

[The following 15 entries are identified as proverbs.]

229.
"Es is niemand so dumm as er net Leit finne kann graad so dumm wie er." [There's no one so stupid that he can't find someone just as stupid.]
Mrs. Raymond Remaley

230.
A.
"Es is niemand so schlecht as er net sei Aahenger hot." [There's no one so bad that he does not have his followers.] *Mrs. Caroline Jacoby, Sumneytown, Do*
B.
"Der bees Feind" — the devil. "Er is gschprunge as wann der bees Feind hinnich em waer." [He ran as if the devil were behind him.] *Often heard, Leb*

231.
"Er wees net genunk fer aus em Rege." [He doesn't know enough to come in out of the rain.]
Mrs. Raymond Remaley

232.
"Er wees net genunk fer heem geh, wann's regert." [He doesn't know enough to go home when it rains.] Said of the son of a prominent lawyer in Allentown.
Occasionally heard

233.
"Vun scheene Wadde kann mer net lewe." [You can't live from beautiful words alone.]
Mrs. Raymond Remaley

234.
"Besser aus der Welt wie aus der Fashion." [Better out of the world than out of fashion.] *Do*

235.
"Er is ken hohli Buhn wert." [He's not worth a hollow bean.] Utterly worthless. *T. S. Brendle, Leb*

236.
"Geld vergeht, awwer der Unflot bleibt." [Money vanishes, but the negative effects remain.] *Do*

237.
"Der Dod losst mer ruhe." The dead, one lets rest.
Common expression

238.
"Der Dod losst mer lieye." (Note "lieye".) [One lets the dead lie.] *Do*

239.
"Mer losst der Dod mit Fridde." "Mit Fridde" has the sense of "at peace". "Mit Fridde" is a common usage. *Do*

240.
"Mer veracht net die Dode." [One does not disrespect the dead.] *Do*

241.
"Mer losst der Dod, was er is." [One lets death be what it is.] *Do*

242.
"Mit der Dode fecht mer net." "Mer fecht net mit em Dode." [One does not fight with the dead.] *Do*

243.
"Wann mer nix Gudes saage kann vum Dod, saagt mer nix Schlechdes." [If one is unable to say something good about the deceased, one doesn't say anything bad.] *Mrs. Raymond Remaley*

244.
"Wohlwinscher" [well-wisher], sg. and pl. Only heard by me in th plural. "Ich kann net saage, as ich der N— N— net gleich; yuscht ich bin kens vun seine Wohlwinscher." I cannot say that I do not like the man, but I am not one of those who always wish him well. The word has practically the sense of "political supporter".

245.
"Was mer saeht, ernt mer." [What one sows, one harvests.] *Common expression*

246.
"Was mer verdient, grickt mer." [That which one earns, one gets.] *Do*

247.
"Sis ihm recht gschehne; er hot's verdient." [He got what he deserved; he earned it.] *Do*

248.
"Wer schtichelt, der schtecht." [He who needles you, sticks you.] Spoken when a person givea a sly hint for a favor. *Pierce Nothstein, Ormrod*

249.
"Er watt ee Daag zerick bezaahlt." Some day he'll be paid back. Some day he will be punished for what he has done in this life.

249.a.
Mrs. Miller's husband committed suicide leaving her and nine or ten children and a heap of debts. She took up her burden, saying, "Sis en schlechdi Gluck as net e paar Hinkliche uffziege kann." [It's a poor mother-

hen that cannot raise a few chicks.] She brought them up successfully. This saying is a local proverb in and around Egypt.

250.
"Fluche is schlimmer wie schtehle. Wann mer schtehlt, hot mer ebbes. Wann mer flucht, hot mer nix." [Profanity is worse than stealing. If one steals, one has something. If one curses, one has nothing.] This was taught, I am told, by the Rev. Samuel Leinbach in catechetical instruction some 60 years ago and still circulates among the people.
Egypt

251.
"Wer's erscht schmeckt
Hot's Heffel uffgedeckt."
[He who smelled it first
Uncovered the pot.]
Mrs. Raymond Remaley

252.
"Die siesse Schnitz vanne gesse; die saure kumme hinnenooch." [The sweet slices are eaten up front; the sour ones come on behind.] *Do*

253.
"Ich schmeiss dir aa moll en Schtee in der Gaarde." [I'll throw a stone into your garden some day.] Some day I will do you a good turn.
John Sowers, Sumneytown

254.
"En blindi Sau findt aa alsemol en Eechel."
Common
"En blindi Sau findt aa alsemol en Eechel, wann's voll (genunk) leit." [A blind hog will occasionally fnd an acorn, when they're lying all about.]
Mrs. Raymond Remaley

255.
"Die Lieb fallt graad so gern (leicht) uff en Kiehdreck wie uff en Ros." [Love falls just as easily upon cow manure as it does on a rose.] Each one makes and loves his own choice. (This one I gave to Dr. Fogel.)
Harvey Ziegler, Souderton

256.
"Not (German, Noth) lannt schreie." [Need, necessity learns to cry out.
My grandfather

257.
"Not brecht Eise." [Need, necessity breaks iron.]
Mont

258.
"Wu nix is, geht aa nix verlore." [Where there is nothing, nothing will be lost.] Harry Miller, a farmer with a large farm and much cattle, but with many debts, lost a number of cattle. I tried to console him, whereupon he gave me the proverb above. A doubtful comfort.

259.
"Er hot sei Naas verbrennt." [He burned his nose.] He meddled into that which was of no concern to him and got a rebuff. *Common expression*

260.
"Yuscht ee Muss in der Welt." [There's only one must in the world.]
Common expression, the usual form

261.
"Sis yuscht ee Muss un sell is: Du muscht schtarwe." [There is but one must and that is: You must die.] This is spoken when someone says, "Des muscht duh" and the person rebels at the statement or command. *Rather common expression*

262.
"Was hilft's [sic] (unusual use of 's) der Kuh Muschgaatnuss, sie frisst [sic] doch Hawwerschtroh." [Of what help will nutmeg be to the cow; she eats oat straw.] *My father*

263.
"Fress, Vogel, odder schtarb." [Eat, bird or die.]
Not infrequently heard at one time in Leb

264.
"Der letscht bezaahlt alles." [The last pays all.] "Der letscht muss es Licht ausblose." [The last one must blow out the light.] Two persons are rooming together. One goes to bed first. The other is to raise the window and put out the light. "Der letscht bezaahlt alles."

265.
"Mer kann immer lanne." [One can always learn.]
Common expression

266.
"Mer watt net zu alt fer lanne." [One never gets too old to learn.] *Do*

267.
"Sis noch ken Engel vum Himmel gfalle." [No angel has fallen from heaven yet.] Every person has faults. *Heard rather often, Leb*
This proverb was applied to Mrs. N— N— who had become obnoxious. It was said: "Sis noch ken Engel vum Himmel gfalle als wie die N— N— un die hot mer heere blatsche." [No angel has yet fallen from heaven except N— N— and one heard her crash when she landed.]

268.
"Alli ebber hot sei beesi Zeide (Seit)." [Everyone has his bad moments (side).] There is no person but becomes angry at one time or another.

268.a.
English: "The longest way round is the nearest way home."

17

269.
Proverb
"Sis noch ken gelannder vum Himmel gfalle." [No learned person has ever fallen from heaven.]
Common expression

270.
Up at Scheidys, near Egypt, there was a Sunday school. Among the teachers was a certain Betz. She had become with the years overbearingly knowing. All things were to be done according to her way. Then there came to her ears the knowledge that others were saying, "Sis noch ken gelannder vum Himmel gfalle except (English) die Betz." [See No. 269.] And that broke up the Sunday school.

No. 267 is spoken as a dig at a person who would be overly good. No. 269 would be applied to a person who would be overly clever.

A SERIES OF PROVERBS

271.
"Die gebrotne Dauwe fliege ihm ins Maul." [The roasted doves fly into his mouth.] When I became pastor at Sumneytown [in 1913], I was very much entertained by the people. One day a man said to me, "Parre, dir fliege die gebrotne Dauwe ins Maul." [Pastor, the roasted doves just fly into your mouth.]

272.
"Die Lanning kann em niemand nemme." [You can never be robbed of your education.] Heard in those families that are sending children away to school at personal sacrifices.

273.
"Guder Verschtand is iwwer alles." [Common sense is above all.]
Infrequently heard

274.
"Guder Verschtand is iwwer Gesundheit (Gesundheet)." [Common sense is above health.]
Heard, though infrequently

275.
"Die Yuchend (Yugend) muss dowe." [Youth must get rid of excess energy.]
Heard quite frequently

276.
"Die Yuchend (Yugend) muss gedobt hawwe." [Same as No. 275.]
Infrequent

277.
"Owwe hui, unne fui." [Above lovely, below lousy.]
Heard at Sumneytown, also at Egypt

278.
"For a very sore throat, take cornmeal and wet it with water to hang together, then melt lard and mix the cornmeal and the hot lard to form a paste and keep hot on a stove and put the cornmeal paste between two rags. Then have one paste rag on the stove always ready and hot and one always on the throat every half hour to prevent diptheria."

— Verbatim from a written communication to me by Mrs. Lottie Strauss, Treichlers, Pa. [Nos. 278 — 294 are quoted verbatim.]

279.
"For a little (mild) sore throat take one teaspoon of coal oil and tie a woolen stocking around your neck."
Do

280.
"Lettuce ("Gaarde Zelaat," leaf lettuce) is good for the nerves."
Do

281.
"Red beets and (beef) liver are good for the blood."
Do

282.
"Tomatoes and hot pepper are good for the liver."
Do

283.
"Celery is good for rheumatism."
Do

284.
"Spinach cleans out the stomach."
Do

285.
"Asparagus cleans the kidneys."
Do

286.
"Rhubarb is a mild laxative."
Do

287.
"If you see your child is going to get measles, scarlet fever or chicken pox, and it don't come out good, make them dried eleberrie flour (elderberry flour) tea and send them to bed." Verbatim.
Do

288.
"For sore eyes: If it snows on the first of March, gather all the snow you can in a clean dishpan and let that snow melt in the house. Then put that snow water in a clean bottle and store away and any time you have kind (?) or tired eyes, wash them with this snow water. This water you can keep 20 years and will never get stinky. My grandmother and mother and aunt have tried to see how long it could be kept. My grandmother, Julia Breyfogle (pronounced Breifogel), was 84 years old in 1909, mother of 4 children, all dead. My mother, Mrs. Agnes Foster, mother of 8 children living, 2 dead. My aunt, Mrs. Ellen Handwork, mother of 18 children all living yet."
Do

289.
"For a bad cold at night squeeze a lemon; add all the sugar the juice takes and take a spoonful every half hour until relieved."
Do

290.
" — or 1 cup of hot water with 1 heaping teaspoonful butter and sugar to taste and drink all at once. You won't cough, for it greases the throat." *Do*

291.
"To break up a cold take a teaspoon of baking soda in a glass of water and drink this." *Do*

292.
" — or go to bed and have someone bring to your bed 1 bowl of hot water, the juice of a lemon, 3 tablespoons whisky; sugar to taste; drink this as hot as you can and cover up good and sleep and sweat." *Do*

293.
" — or eat onion sandwiches before going to bed." *Do*

294.
"For diarrhea drink 1 glass sweet milk with cinnamon and sugar to taste." *Do*

295.
Proverb
"Wann alli Fehler en Hoischtock waer, waert die Welt voll." *Leb*
[If all mistakes were haystacks, the world would be full of them.] All the space in the world would be taken up. *Common in variations*

296.
People down at Norristown said of Sumneytown: "Summnitaun, wu die Fix un die Haase enanner 'Gude Nacht' gewwe." [Sumneytown, where the foxes and the rabbits bid one another "Good Night".]

296.a.
The father of Ralph Beaver Strassburger had courted a girl at Green Lane. Strassburger lived at Schwenksville. The girl, however, married Landis, the superintendent of schools of Montgomery County. "Jim" Jacoby was on the train going to Philadelphia. Strassburger got on at Schwenksville. Addressing "Jim" he said No. 296 "un die Maed nemme die Buhwe mit ne ins Bett" [and the girls take the boys with them to bed]. To which "Jim" replied, "Du settscht's wisse; du waarscht oft genunk datt drowwe." [You should know; you were up there often enough.]

297.
People of Sumneytown said of Dietz's Mill and of Finland, "Datt gewwe die Fix un die Haase enanner 'Gude Nacht'." [See No. 296.] This expression was used to describe a wild locality.

298.
"Er macht Geld wie Hoi." [He makes money like hay.] *Common expression*

299.
"Er macht Geld wie Hoi, yuscht net so lang." [He makes money like hay, just not as long.] This form is not heard as frequently as No. 298, though both are common.

300.
"Wu mer sei Geld verliert, muss mer es widder finne." [Where one loses one's money, one must find it again.] *Salfordville*

Jacob Gable, a hotel keeper, lost a good bit of money in the Green Lane brewery. To "raus kumme" [make good the loss] he and others bought the brewery and ran it. This proverb was used to describe their action.

301.
"Liewer sei Gebetbuch wie sei Gaul." [Rather his prayerbook than his horse.] (Rather your religion than your wealth.) *Mrs. Raymond Remaley*

I cannot get the sense of the saying. I suspect that it is used to minimize a disaster. Rather have it happen to your prayerbook than to your horse. There may be a story back of it.

302.
"En fauler Gaul iwwerlaadt sich gern." [A lazy horse likes to overload itself.] *Egypt*

303.
"En fauler Esel draagt (Leb Co) (drecht, Mont Co) sich gschwinder dod wie en fleissicher." [A lazy mule works himself to death quicker than an industrious one.] When a person to save steps takes a heavy load, instead of going twice. *Common*

304.
"Unne gfrogt findt mer nix aus." [No questions, so answers.] *Common*

305.
"Unne gfrogt lannt mer nix." [Without asking, nothing is learned.] Not as frequently heard as No. 304.

306.
"S macht nix aus wie gross es Grummbierschtick, sie gucke alsnoch noch em Himmel fer mehner." [It makes no difference how large the potato patch, they still look to heaven for more.]
Mrs. Raymond Remaley

307.
"Die Fraa draagt (drecht)[See No. 303] die Hosse." [The wife wears the pants.] *Common*

308.
"Die Fraa hot's Backebuch." [The wife has the pocketbook.] Nos. 307 and 308 mean that the woman is the head of the household. She has the final word.

309.
"En schlechdi Hausheldern kann mehner nauskehre as zwee Menner neischaufle kenne." [A poor housekeeper can sweep out more than two men can shovel in.] *Leb*

310.
"En schlechdi Hausheldern kann mehner nausschaufle wie zwee Menner neibringe kenne." [A poor housekeeper can shovel out more than two men can bring in.] *Leb*

310.a.
"Er verschteht net meh als wie die Sau vun Sunndaag." [He understands no more of the matter than a hog does of Sunday.] *Mrs. Raymond Remaley*

311.
"Er verschteht net meh vun der Sach wie en Kuh vun Sunndaag." [He understands no more of the matter than a cow does of Sunday.] *Leb*

312.
"En schlechdi Fraa kann mehner nauskehre wie en Mann neibringe kann mit re Warfschaufel."
Jane Kilmer, Leb

313.
"Ferda (Ferdas) is ken Antwatt."
Mrs. Raymond Remaley
"Ferda" was a common answer to the question, "Why did you....?" [Ferwas hoscht....?] — "Ferda" = Oh, because.

314.
"Was mer net im Kopp hot, muss mer in die Fiess hawwe." [That which one does not have in the head, one has to have in the feet.] A person who forgets why he came must come again. *Very common*

315.
"Besser iwwel gfaahre wie schtolz geloffe." [Better to drive poorly and to walk proudly.]
Mrs. Raymond Remaley

316.
"Rumgedreht iss aa gfaahre." [Turning around is also traveling.] *Ed Bolig, Sumneytown*

317.
"Gaar net gschosse is aa verfehlt." [Not firing at all is also a miss.] *Do*

318.
"Was em net brennt, brauch mer net blose." [What doesn't burn need not be blown.] Why bother about the affairs of others? *Leb*

319.
"Sis immer's bescht, wann mer sei Fauscht in der Sack macht." [It's always better when one makes his fist in his pocket.] Or: "Mach dei Fauscht in deim Sack." [Make your fist in your pocket.] Don't show your anger.
Mrs. Caroline Jacoby, Sumneytown

320.
"Ee Vadder kann besser 99 Kinner ernehre wie 99 Kinner ee Vadder." [One father can support 99 children better than 99 children one father.]
My father

321.
"Eis hot ken Balge." [Ice has no (supporting) beams.] *Sumneytown*
Do not venture on an undertaking that looks good only on the surface. A proverb?

322.
Proverb
"Zu viel Eise im Feier verschmelzt em Deel." [With too many irons in the fire some are bound to melt.] *Mrs. Raymond Remaley*

323.
"Wie geht's? Hinnich die Dier schteht's." [How are you? It's standing behind the door.] *Do*

323.a.
"Wie geht's?" — "Besser." [Better] *Often heard*

324.
"Katz un dick
Is aa en Schtick."

[Short and thick
Is also a piece.] *Do*

325.
Proverb
"Denk zweemol, schwetz eemol." [Think twice, speak once.] *Not infrequently heard*

326.
"Denk zweemol, schwetz eemol, awwer net wann Feier ausbrecht." [Think twice, speak once, but not when fire breaks out.] *Mrs. Raymond Remaley*

327.
"Wann sie nimmi wisse was die Fashions (English) sin, hockt er sich uff der Barig un geigt sie raus." [When they no longer know what the fashions are, he sits on the mountain and fiddles them out.] *Do*

328.
"Do will ich net iwwer der Damm un versaufe." [Well, I don't want to go over the dam and drown.] I don't want to go out on a limb. *Do*

329.
"Wann sie satt gsoffe hen, breiche sie ken Esse." [When they have drunk themselves full, they need no

food.] I do not see the reason for the proverb, though the meaning is evident. *Do*

330.
"Die Bense mache die Daaler." [Cents make dollar.] *Common proverb*

331.
"Wer net Acht gebt uff en Bens, gebt net Acht uff en Daaler." [He who cannot take care of a cent, cannot take care of a dollar.]
Rather commonly heard

332.
"Save the pennies; the pennies make the dollars."
Heard in English in Leh

333.
"Geb mer en Schtick Brod,
 Der Becker is dod.
 Der Fresser lebt noch."

[Give me a piece of bread,
 The baker is dead.
 The eater lives yet.]
Mrs. Raymond Remaley

334.
"Babier nemmt alles aa." [Paper accepts all.] *Do*

335.
"Sis en schlechder Bettler, as ken Ausrett hot." [It's a poor beggar who has no excuses.] For one who finds an excuse for his actions. *Leb*
Also: "Sis en schlechdi Hur, as ken Ausrett hot." [It's a poor adultress who has no excuse.]
Green Lane

336.
"Es gebt immer en Schtund, as der Bettler sei Hemm drickle kann." [There's always a time when the beggar can dry out his shirt.]
Mrs. Raymond Remaley

337.
"Wer immer schafft, hot nie ken Ruh." [The one who's always working never has any peace.] *Do*

338.
"Ganz aarmi Leit schaffe alli Daag." [Very poor people work every day.] *Do*

339.
"Leis misse aa lewe," [Lice must live also.] said Mary Gucker when she had head lice. *Sumneytown*

340.
Game
"Here we go round the Mulberry Bush."
A ring is formed by the children playing the game. The players go around in a circle singing:

1.
"Here we go round the Mulberry Bush,
 Mulberry Bush, Mulberry Bush.
 Here we go round the Mulberry Bush,
 So early in the morning."

2.
"This is how we wash our clothes,
 Wash our clothes, wash our clothes.
 This is how we wash our clothes,
 So early in the morning."
 (Imitating the washing of clothes.)

3.
"This is how we hang up our clothes, etc."
 (Imitating hanging up clothes.)

4.
"This is how we iron our clothes, etc."
 (Imitating ironing.)

5.
"This is how we sew our clothes, etc."
 (Imitating sewing.)

6.
"This is how we bake our bread, etc."
 (Imitating baking.)

7.
"This is how we go to church, etc."
 (Imitating going to church.)
Lottie Straus, Treichlers

341.
"Aller Anfang is schwer." [Every beginning is difficult.] *Common proverb*

342.
"Erfaahring macht kluuch." [Experience makes wise.] *Leb*

343.
"Er sett's noch eemol mache; no sett er schtobbe." [He should do it once more, then stop.] Spoken contemptuously of the work of another.
Not infrequently heard

344
"Wer *die* Hack gemacht hot, sett noch eeni mache un noh's Hackemache schtobbe (uffgewwe)." [Whoever made *this* hoe should make one more and then stop (give up) hoe-making.]
"Er sett noch *eemol* breddiche un noh schtobbe." [He should preach (only) one more time and then give it up.] These are espressions which I have heard. They imply derogation of workmanship.
Common

345.
"Haahnekamm, Hinkelbiebs,
 Frehlich Maedchen, du warscht hibsch."

[Cockscomb, hen peep,
Cheerful maiden,
You were lovely.]

(Could this be something like this: Haahne komm, Hinkel biebsch, Frehlich Maedchen, Du warscht hiebsch.?)

THREE P.G. EXPRESSIONS MEANING "TO GO TO BED"

346.

A. "Nau will ich ins Bett." [Now I want to go to bed.] *Common form*

B. "Nau will ich noch em Bett." [Now I want to go to bed.] *A common form*

C. "Nau will ich noch Bedde geh." [Now I want to go to bed.] *Occasionally heard*

347.

D. "Nau geh (gehn) ich ins Hoi." [Now I'm going into the hay.] *Berks*

E. "Nau will ich moll uff's Schtroh." [Now I'm going into the straw.] *Mont*

348.

F. "Nau geh (will, gehn) ich ins Nescht." [Now I'm going in the nest.] *Do*

G. "Nau geh (will, gehn) ich uff die Schtang [pole]." *Leh, Do*

Chickens would be given poles on which to roost.

348.a.

Ducks, during laying season, were driven into some pen for the night, for the sake of the eggs, which otherwise were dropped by the duck in the water. Guinea hens were regarded as good watch dogs, on account of their cackling when intruders came into the barnyard at night. Chickens had the run of the barnyard. Their nests were made at any convenient place. Boxes with straw were put here and there for their use. They were fed in the evening, usually with corn and rye. "Hinkelschtell" [pl.][chicken houses] were made by building a straw stack on a low scaffold made of boards or rails. The top of the pig stable was often a "Hinkelschtall" (chicken coop) or the top of a wagon shed. The chickens were not penned up.

349.

Game:

"One, two,
Button my shoe.
Three, four,
Close the door.
Five, six,
Pick up sticks.
Seven, eight,
Lay them straight.
Nine, ten,
A big fat hen.
[11 -12 missing]
Thirteen, fourteen,
Boys a courting.
Fifteen, sixteen,
Maid in a kitchen.
Seventeen, eighteen,
Maids a waiting.
Nineteen, twenty,
My stomach is empty.
Please, mother,
Give me something to eat."

Mrs. Lottie Straus

(How was this game played?)

A SERIES OF DIALECT WORDS

350.

"Eegner," owner. "Wer is der Eegner vun dere Bauerei?" [Who's the owner of this farm?] *Leb*

351.

"ehner," sooner (Leb Co); "ehnder," sooner (Mont Co).

"Ich hab net eener (ehnder) kumme kenne." [I was unable to come sooner.]

352.

"Grundkeller" (Leb Co), "Kiehlkeller" (Mont Co), "Grummbierekeller" (Leh Co) = deep outside cellar used for refrigeration. Used where there was no springhouse to store milk, butter and eatables in the summertime; potatoes, turnips, cabbage, apples, etc. in the wintertime.

"Der Grummbierekeller" today is not "der Kiehlkeller." The large potato farmers build special cellars for the storage of potatoes.

353.

"Unnerschrief," deputy sheriff (Leh Co). Sometimes referred to merely as "em Schrief sei Mann" [the sheriff's man].

354.

"Zuck, pl. Zick" (Leh Co), the rifling of a gun, of a rifle. "Die Bix hot en guder Zuck." [The gun has good rifling.]

"Die Zick sin ausgewaare." [The riflings are worn out.]

355.

"Wolkebruch uff Redder" = an expression to denote something extraordinary. "Des is en Wolkebruch uff Redder" was said of a very good draft horse. *Leb*

I do not see how it came into being.

356.

"hinnich en" [after him], "hinnich re" [after her]. "Der Parre waar hinnich en." The preacher had him on the carpet. The sense has been carried over into our English expression: "The preacher was after him." The preacher admonished him. Also: The preacher besought him for a good purpose, wanted him to serve as a deacon, etc.

357.
"winnisch" = inquisitive. *Egypt*
"Winnisch" usually means recalcitrant, stubborn.

358
"Er will un will net." He steadfastly refuses. Accent on the two "wills".

369.[sic]
"Er will un will net." He does and he doesn't. Accent on the "net". Heard also: "Er will un will aa net." Accent on "aa".

370.
"Weis der Friede," an expression of surprise or amazement. "Geschder hawwich en fatt gyaagt un weis der Friede is er heit schun widder do." [Yesterday I chased him away and wouldn't you know he's here again today.] *Leb*

371.
"gezoge" = rifled. "Die Flint is gut gezoge." This gun is well rifled. See No. 354. *Egypt*

372.
"unerwaard," unexpectedly, unexpected. "Des is so unerwaard uff uns kumme." [This came upon us so unexpectedly.]
"Mer hen unerwaarder Bsuch grickt." [We got unexpected company.] *Mont*

373.
[sich] "umbringe," to commit suicide. "Er hot sich um's Lewe gebrocht." [He took his own life.] *Leb*
"Sie meene er deet sich noch umbringe." [They are of the opinion he might commit suicide.] "Er hot sich umgebrocht." [He took his own life.]

374.
"sich's Lewe gnumme," committed suicide. *Mont*

375.
"sich aus em Weg gschafft" — committed suicide. Nos. 373. 374 and 375 are heard throughout. No. 373 seems to be the most common in Leb Co. No. 374 is most common in Mont Co.

376.
[die] "Schwett" — group. "Die ganz Schwett waar ken hohli Buhn wert." The whole crowd was not worth a hollow bean. *Leb*

377.
"schwiege" [sic] — to remain silent. "Schtill gschwiege is aa gsiegt." [Remaining silent is also a victory.] *Lanc*

378.
"Schtammglied" — a charter member. *Leh*

379.
"Schtammgascht" — one who boards with a family or at a hotel over a period of years. "Is der N— N— Freind (related) zu's Benners?" [Is N— N— related to the Benners?] — "Nee, er is yuscht en Schtammgascht." [No, he's just a permanent boarder.] *Leb*

380.
"Schpuckerei" — the whole matter of spooks. "Die Leit fer Alders hen viel an die Schpuckerei geglaabt." [Years ago many believed in spooks.]

381.
"Schpuck" — a spook.

382.
"schpucke" — to spook. "Datt, saage die Leit, deet's schpucke." [People say that it's haunted there.]

383.
"schpuckich" — ghostly. "Do seht's awwer schpuckich aus." [It look ghostly here.] Nos. 380-383 in common usage.

384.
"Schpaltgscharr" — splitting tools.

385.
"schmaert" — smart, clever, industrious, righteous. Adjective and adverb. "Du hoscht mich schmaert bsucht." [You visited me faithfully.]
Polly Schaeffer, Cementon

"Er is zu schmaert fer ihn." [He's too smart for him.] "Sell is en schmaerder Bu." [That's a clever boy.] "Er is schmaert geloffe." [He walked smartly.]

386.
"geboost" — [boose] "Er hot net viel geboost." He didn't accomplish much. *Willis Gibbel, Lititz*

387.
"Rolldier" — folding doors; doors that are rolled from the bottom.

388.
"Regebrunne" — cistern. *Common term*

389.
"Raudebusch" — a rowdy.
Henry Troxell, Ruchsville
"Busch" from German "Bursch."

390.
"Mausfall" — a mousetrap.

391.
"Raddefall" — a rattrap.

392.
"Raus mit der Farb!" [Show your colors!] = Show where you stand.

393.

"Blazier" — pleasure; "blazierlich" — pleasant; [sich] "blaziere" [to have a good time]. "An die Allentown Fair kann mer sich arig blaziere." [One can have a good time at the Allentown Fair.] Words quite commonly used.

394.

"parbes" [on purpose] "Er hot's parbes geduh." He did it on purpose (in our English). "Er hot's fer Parbes verbroche." He broke it purposely. *Do*

395.

"Oierschlingel" — omelet. Word used in Weissenberg, Lehigh Co. *Amandus Bittner(?)*

396.

"Mess" — a cooking measure. "Ich hab en Mess Brunnegraas gekaaft fer fimf Cent." [I bought a mess of watercress for five cents.] "Geschder hawwich Pissebett gsucht." [Yesterday I was looking for dandelion.] — "Hoscht grickt?" [Did you get any?] "Ya, en scheeni Mess." [Yes, a nice mess.]

397.

"Lieyebaschdel" — a dirty liar. "So en Lieyebaschdel." *Egypt*

398.

"bei Lewe un Gsundheit" — with life and health. Used as an expletive: "Bei Lewe un Gsundheit, duh sell yo net!" [Don't do that by any means!] "Wann mer lewe und sind gsund, wascht uns widder sehne in zwee Woche." [If we are alive and well, you'll see us again in two weeks.]

399.

"Duh sell bei Leiwe net!" A strong negative expletive. [Don't do that on your life!] "Bei Leiwe" [= on your life]

400.

"Lenz" [spring; Lent]. On warm spring days my neighbor[in Egypt], Mrs. Koch, is likely to call over to me: "Gewwacht, der Lenz grickt dich." "Der Lenz kummt der uff der Hals." [Watch out, spring fever will get you.] Seems to be an old name for spring.

401.

"Schtaabkiddel" — dust coat. Our English "duster".

402.

"Klubbe" - "Waard bis ich ihn mol in die Klubbe grick." Wait till I get him in my clutches.

403.

"Keefer" (singular and plural) — trader, merchant. (Mostly of one who purchases.) "Duwackkeefer" — tobacco dealer.

"Geilskeefer" — horse dealer; "Kiehkeefer" — cow dealer. All in general use in Lebanon County.

404.

"Liewer Yammer" — an expression used to express surprise at some misfortune or disaster. "Liewer Yammer, was hot's do gewwe?" [What happened here?] *Leb*

404.a.

"Gott im Himmel!" [God in heaven!] A common exclamation signifying surprise or dismay. "Is sell nau net Gott in Himmel(s) schee?" [Isn't that marvelously beautiful?] "Er is Gott in Himmel(s) reich." [He's almighty rich.] "Ich hab en Gott in Himmelser grosser Haas gsehne, awwer er is Gott in Himmels gschprunge." [I saw an almighty big rabbit, but he ran like mad.]
"Gott in Himmel, was duh ich yuscht, wann's so aahalt?" [My God, what will I do, if this continues?]

405.

"Yesuwidders" [Jesus....?]. "Des is Yesuwidders warm." [It's almighty warm!] At one time quite frequently heard around Egypt. *Frank Sterner, Egypt*

406.

"iwwerschlucke" — to get something in the wrong throat. *Dal. Kohler, Egypt*

407.

"niwwer un riwwer" [back and forth]. "Ich hab's em niwwer un riwwer gsaat, er sett uffheere." I told him right and left that he was to stop. I told him again and again that he was to stop doing what he was doing. (Our English) "Er is niwwer un riwwer gange." He went over and over. (Our English) Both the German and the English are commonly heard.

408.

"Hoisume" — seed that is found on the haymow or drops to the floor of the barn when the hay is unloaded.

409.

"hinlenglich, hielenglich" — sufficient for the purpose.
"Waar unser Geld hielenglich?" "Did our money reach?" (Our English) Enough to pay all bills. "Is der Sume hielenglich?" Is there enough seed for the sowing? *Common in Mont*

410.

"Lightning on the horizon on hot summer evenings without audible thunder is said to be due to the heat and is called 'heat lightning.'" I can only recall the English name.
"Guck, wie's wedderleecht." [Look how it's lightning.] — "Sell is vun der grosse Hitz." [That's from the great heat.] *Leb*

411.

"en Gschiss un Wese" — a big ado.
Young Jacob Spengler was a cattle dealer. He was

always more or less in financial straits and had gotten a good bit of money from his wealthy father, to whom he had given notes. His father lived with him. "Sei Daadi is hatt grank warre. Un der Yung hot gmeent, er deet schtarwe. So ruft er en Nochber, en guder alder Mennischt, nei, fer mit ihm uffhocke darich die Nacht. [His father became very ill. The son thought he would die. So he called in a neighbor, a kindly old Mennonite, to sit up with him through the night.]

"Geye Middernacht fangt der Alt schwer un langsam aa zu schnaufe. Es hot gscheint, as wann's am letschde waer. So hot es gedaueret bis geye Mariye." [Toward midnight the old man began to breathe slowly and heavily. It seemed as if it were going toward the end. Thus it continued until toward morning.]

"Noh, uff eemol waar der Alt ganz ruhich. Der Yung geht ans Bett, guckt en scharf aa, dreht sich rum zum Nochber un saagt: [Then all of a sudden the old man became quiet. The young man went to the bed, looked at him closely, turned around to the neighbor and said:]

'Nau is der Daadi doot. Nau will ich wennich darich die Schubblaade, eb's en Gschiss un Wese gebt unnich die Gschwischder.' [Now Dad is dead. Now I want to go through the drawers a bit before there is a big ado amongst the brothers and sisters.]

"Un er is aa graad an die Schubblaad un aafange suche. Wie er datt waar, saagt der Mennischt, 'Jake, kumm, guck, dei Daadi is net doot.'" [And he went to the drawer and began to search. As he was there the Mennonite said, 'Jake, come, look your father is not dead.']

"Der Jake kummt zerick ans Bett, seht wie sei Vadder widder am Schnaufe waar un saagt, 'Nee, er is net doot, awwer er waar bei Gott doot!'" [Jake comes back to the bed, sees how his father is again breathing and says, "No, he's not dead, but, by God, he was dead!"]

Told in Sower's Store, Green Lane, ca. 1920
Mason Light, Allentown

412.
"grundaarm" — very poor. *Leb*

413.
"Graabhof" — burial grounds. So called by Dunkards, Lanc. Co. *Abe Wenger*

414.
"Gott erbarmlich" [enough to evoke the mercy of God], an adverb with the sense of very. *Leb*

415.
"Glockezieher" — sexton. *Leb*

416.
"mit Goddes Hilf un Beischtand" [with God's help and support]. Used as a qualifying expression. "Mit Goddes Hilf un Beischtand will ich browiere es zu unnernemme." [With God's help and support I will attempt to undertake it.]

417.
"Gaardebauer" — trucker, truck gardener. *Egypt*

418.
"Es gebt Gwittre uff die Nacht." There will be a thunderstorm towards nightfall. There will be a thunderstorm tonight.

419.
"Heit griege mer noch Schtarm." [There'll be stormy weather today.] *Mont, Leb*
"Heit griege mer noch Gwittre." [Today we'll get a thunderstorm.] *Mont, Leb, Leh*
"Heit griege mer noch en Gwidderschtarm." [Today we'll get a thunderstorm.] *Leb*
"Heit griege mer noch en Wedder." [Today we'll get a thunderstorm.] *Mont*

420.
"Gehaer, Ghaer" — hearing. "Mei Gehaer is schlecht." I can't hear well. *Leh*

421.
"Gottsdunner!" [God's thunder], an expletive.
Mrs. Meisner, Lehighton

422.
"frosich" — gluttoneous. *Mont*

423.
"freilich" — certainly, surely.
Mrs. Caroline Jacoby, Sumneytown

424.
"Des is verschtanne." This is easily understood. To be sure! Quite so! *Common term*

425.
"farichderlich" [frightening], adverb with the sense of "very." "Er is farichderlich schtarick." [He is terribly strong.] *Leb*

426.
"farichderlicher Mann," a very powerful man.

427.
"furichbaar" [to be feared] — sense of "farichderlich." [No. 425.] *Mont*

428.
"furichbaarer Mann" — No. 426. *Mont*

429.
"(O) Elend, du hoscht mich!" [Oh, trouble, you've got me!] An expression of dismay, "wann ebber gebodde is." [when someone is defeated]
Frank Sterner, Egypt

430.
"Dodeschtreech," the tolls of the church bell announcing the death of a person. *Leb*

431.
"Drawatz, Drawutz," a misunderstanding between two persons. *Mont*

432.
"gedeckert," gossiped. "Sie hot gedeckert darich's ganz Schteddel." [She gossiped through the entire town.] *Egypt*

433.
"Daagshelling" [daylight]. "Alleweil kummt die Daagshelling frieh." [This time of the year it gets light early.] *Common*

434.
"Lewesdaag, Lebdaag" [day of my life; in my life]. "Ich hab mei Lewesdaag (Lebdaag) nix so gsehne." [Never in my life have I seen such a thing!] *Leh*

435.
"Blutschwamm," bloodwort. *Mrs. Koch, Egypt*

436.
"Schlack," a layer of sheaves of grain in the mow. The man on the mow who lays the layer, "dutt's schlagge." [makes the layers] The sheaf of wheat was always thrown with the butt end towards the one who was to "schlag" [make the layer]. The butt end of a sheaf is called "der Orsch" [the ass] and the top end "der Kopp" [the head]. *Leh*

437.
"Backmoldgratz," scraper for the doughtray. *Do*

438.
"altleinisch," old-fashioned. *Do*

439.
"altfrenkisch," old-fashioned. *Mont*

440.
"Erzschwindler," arch-swindler. *Leh*

441.
"Erzliegner," arch-liar. *Do*

442.
"Erzbschisser," arch-cheat. *Do*

443.
"Holzax," the common axe.

444.
"Schpaltax," a heavy axe used as a sledge and as an axe to split logs. *Do*

445.
"Absatz," heel of the shoe.

446.
"abgebleecht," faded. *Common word*

447.
"Schneidmesser, Schneideise," drawing knife. *Both in common usage*

448.
"Kett," chain"; "Hunskett," a light chain, dog chain; "Kiehkett, Halskett," a short, rather heavy chain. *Leb*

449.
"Raziermesser," razor. Not as common as "Balwiermesser."

450.
"beleschdiche," to deride or malign a person. *Mont*

451.
"beleidiche," to deride. *Leb*
"beleschdiche" seems to have a deeper meaning of malignity.

452.
"Dachwerk," roofing. *Egypt*

453.
"Gibbelwerk," gabling. *Do*

454.
"Summerflecke abschlagge" [to knock off freckles], to wash the face in dew on May 1st and to bring hands down on that part of the body to which they [the freckles] are to be transferred. "Uff der erscht Moi sett mer die Summerflecke abschlagge." [On the first of May one should wash away one's summer freckles.]

455.
"eens uff die Beh schtelle," to help somebody get on their feet; to set upright. Charles Hoffman of Egypt, aged, had a child with his maid. At the hotel sometime thereafter he boasted, "net alli ebber an mei Elt kann eens uff die Beh schtelle." [Not everyone my is age is able to father a child.] *Norman Remaley*

Often heard is the form, "eens uff die Fiess schtelle (setze)," meaning, to help someone; to support someone.

P.G. EXPRESSIONS

456.
"meiner Sex" [of my six; my gosh!] "Mer meent, meiner Sex, so ebbes kennt net sei!" [My gosh, one would think something like this couldn't be!] *Common*

457.
"Grund der Arde (Erde)" [Ground of the earth] *Berks, Leb*

458.
"liewer Grund" [dear ground, earth], *Leb;* "Du liewer Grund!", *Leb, Berks;* "meiner Grund", *Leh;* "Du Grund!" — most common and widespread of the four expressions.

459.
"meiner Seel" [my soul]. "Mer wees, meiner Seel, ball net was zu duh." [My soul, one soon won't know what to do.] *Leb*

460.
"meines Daag des meines Lewens!" [my day of my life] *Much used by Dr. Harvey Scholl, Green Lane*

"Mei Lebdaag hawwich nix so gsehne." [Never in my life have I seen the likes of this.]

461.
[What in the ... is going on here?]
"Was der Deiwel [devil] geht do aa?" — "Was der Beddel [dickens] geht do aa?" — "Was der Schinner geht do aa?" — "Was der Dausich geht do aa?" — "Was die Hell geht do aa?" — "Was in Goddesnaame (Gotts Naame) [in God's name] geht do aa?" — "Was in der Himmelswelt [the world of heaven] geht do aa?" — "Was in der Welt [world] geht do aa?" — "Was die Grenk [deuce] geht do aa?" All frequently heard, one as much as the other.

462.
"O Yammer, ich hab so grossi Schmatze!" [Oh suffering, I have such terrible pain!] "O Yee, ich hab so grossi Schmatze!" "O du Yee, ich hab so grossi Schmatze!" "O Gott, ich hab so grossi Schmatze!" "O mei Gott [oh my God], ich hab so grossi Schmatze!" "O du liewer Zuschtand [my goodness], ich hab so grossi Schmatze!" *All frequently heard*

463.
"Kannscht in die Hell geh, wege mir!" [You can go to hell on my account!] "Kannscht in die Hell neigeh!" [same meaning]

"Kannscht mich im Orsch lecke!" [You can lick my rear end!]

"Kannscht mich hinne lecke!" [same meaning] "Kannscht der Baam nuffgraddle!" [You can go climb a tree!] "Kannscht zum Deiwel geh!" [You can go to the devil!] "Kannscht mir der Buckel nuffgraddle!" [You can climb up my backside.] "Kannscht mer der Buckel gratze!" [You can scratch my back!] *All common in a divergence of motives*

[addendum] "Kannscht in die unnerscht (siwwet) Hell neigeh!" [You can go to the lowest (seventh) hell!]

464.
"Kannscht zum Dunnerwedder hiegeh, wu du witt!" [You can go, thunderation, wherever you want!] "Kannscht zum Dunnerwedder duh wie du witt!" [Thunderation, you can do whatever you want to do!]

"Kannscht zum Deiwel duh was du witt." [You can do the deuce whatever you want to do!] In a disagreement of purpose.

465.
[God, etc., what have you done now?]

"Gott, was hoscht nau geduh?" "O, Gott, ..." "Gott im Himmel [God in heaven] ..." "Liewer Gott [dear God], ..." "Liewer Droscht [dear consolation], ..." "Der Deiwel [the devil], ..." "Himmel [heaven], ..." "Harr Gott [Lord God], ..." "Harr Gott Sackerment [Lord God sacrament], ..." "Dunnerwedder [thunderation], ..." "O Hell, ..."
All heard, one as much as the other

466.
"Chimmni!", "Chimeni!", "Chimeni Peters!", "Chimeni Patz" (English a), "Chimeni Riwers!"
All heard, one as much as the other

467.
"bei Gott" [by God], "bei Tschudes" [by Judas], "bei Gripes", "Tschudes Pikes" [Judas Priest].

468.
"Harr meins Lebens" [Lord of my life], "Harr Gott" [Lord God], "Harr Yesus" [Lord Jesus].

469.
"Dunnerwedder" [thunderation], "Harr Gott, Dunnerwedder," "Heilich Dunnerwedder" [holy thunderstorm], "Greitz Dunnerwedder" [cross and thunderation], "Himmel Dunnerwedder" [heaven and thunderation], "Sackerment Dunnerwedder" [sacrament and thunderation], "Heilich Dunnerwedder" [holy thunderation], "Schtann Dunnerwedder" [star and thunderation].

[addendum] "ungebutzder Seikopp" [uncleaned pig's head]; "gaar ewich" [eternal].

470.
"bei Galli" *Very often heard*

471.a.
"noch emol" [one more time]. This was often added to expletives. "Dunnerwedder noch emol." "Harr Gott noch emol."

[addendum] "Verdamm sei!" [Be damned!] "Nau will ich verdamm sei!" [Now I'll be damned!] "Gott verdamm sei!"

471.b.
I have heard the word "Ferd, Fard," horse, used. It is not in common use. I always took it that it was used as a sign of respect to the pastor when he came calling. "Schpann em Parre sei Ferd aus un fieder en." [Unhitch the pastor's horse and feed him.]
This I heard when I was pastor at Old Goshenhoppen.

(Calvin St... uses "Fard" but only of the minister's horse. Jan. 1953.) *Mont*

472.
"Mund" [mouth]. "Es basst net zum Mund." [It doesn't suit to the mouth.] Of uncouth language. *Leb*

473.
"So siwwe Schtock uff em Bodde naus." [Seven stories lined up on the ground] Meaning obscure to me. *Leh*

474.
"Er hot sich ganz bucklich (schepp) gelacht." [He laughed himself crooked.] Meaning: He laughed very boisterously. *Common expression*

475.
"Er hot sich ganz schepp gelacht." Meaning = No. 474. "Er hot sich grank gelacht." [He laughed himself sick.] "Er hot's Lache nimmi halde kenne." [He was unable to contain his laughter.]

476.
"Er hot sich die Feischt voll gelacht." [He laughed his fists full.] He has great inner (hidden) delight at another's discomfiture.

477.
"Ich hab's Lache schier gaar net halde kenne." I could hardly keep a straight face. *Common expression*

478.
"Sis nix fer driwwe lache." "Sis nix fer lache driwwe." This is no laughing matter.

479.
My father said that the guns of Gettysburg were heard at Schaefferstown; that on the day of the Battle of Gettysburg, he was picking apples in one of the fields. (There used to be an early apple ("Ernabbel") tree that could have had ripe apples at that time of the year.)

480.
My uncle, A. S. Brendle, often told me of the posters which were at the crossroads during the Civil War: A flag on a broken staff with the caption "Shall it fall?"

481.
Tom Miller of Schaefferstown told us in school, when he taught the high school, how the Army of the Potomac cried out after McClellan had been relieved of his command, "Give us back our old commander!"

482.
There is a small house on the cemetery at Egypt, which is known as the "tool house." In it are stored tools, lawnmowers, etc. This house is called by the older persons, "Dodeheisel" [death house]. There were two rooms in the "Dodeheisel." It may be that the building was erected with the purpose of keeping the coffin there in emergencies.

483.
"Dodsdaag," the day of death. "Wann dei Dodsdaag mol kummt, wascht du ordlich deemiedich sei." "When the day of death comes, you will be quite humble." *Not infrequently heard*

484.
"Graabschrift," the inscription on the tombstone. *Not infrequently heard*

When reference is had to the inscription on the tombstone, it is commonly with the words: "Uff em Graabschtee heest's ...," "Uff em Graabschtee saagt's ...," "Uff em Graabschtee leest's ..."

485.
"Wann's Graab eifallt, hot der Dod ken gudi Ruh." [If the earth on the grave caves in, the deceased has no rest.] This is said of newly made graves. In filling the grave after burial, care is taken that the ground becomes tightly packed. If shortly thereafter the ground "settles" (P.G. "seddle", to settle, a dialect verb)—within a month or two months or so—then the corpse doesn't sleep well.

486.
"Wann's Graab neifallt, leit der Dod net gut." [If the grave falls in, the deceased is not lying well.] Such a happening, when I was a boy, was sure to give rise to "en Gschwetz" [gossip] among the people as to the reason why the dead did not sleep well.

487.
"Wu ich daheem waar uff die Bauerei." When my home was on the farm; when I lived on the farm as a boy. "Datt waar ich moll daheem." [I was at home there at one time.] "Bei ihm waar ich moll daheem." [I lived with him at one time.] *Common expressions*

488.
A woman giving birth to her first child will get rotten teeth and will lose hair. The strength which goes into the teeth and the hair goes into the child. (This is interesting. Is it an evidence of the recognition of secondary sexual characteristics?) *Leb*

489.
Babies that get teeth early will not walk early. *Do*

490.
"Wann Kinner mol Zeh griege, kenne sie aafange esse." [Once children get teeth they can begin to eat.] They can be fed more solid food. *Common*

491.
"Glei Zeh,
Glei meh."
If a child gets teeth "glei" [early], there will soon be another baby in the family.
Heard by my wife at Myerstown

492.
"Kinner as frieh laafe, fange net gern frieh aa zu babble." [Children that walk early do not begin to talk early.]
Common

493.
"Er is so grummbeenich as er ken Sau in en zwee Fuuss Alley schtoppe kennt." He is so bow-legged that he could not stop a pig in a two-foot alley. *Lanc*

494.
"Ich hab nix davor gekennt." I could do nothing to avoid or prevent what happened. I am blameless.
Common

495.
"Alles was recht is, hot Gott lieb,
Wer Schof schtehlt, is ken Bockdieb."
[God loves all that is right. He who steals the sheep is not the ram thief.] *Jim Jacoby, Sumneytown*

496.
"Alles was recht is." [All that is right, proper.] This is a commom expression with which the speaker strengthens an appeal to an impartial consideration of the merits of the matter.

"Nau, ihr Leit, alles was recht is, awwer meent ihr es waer Ursach do gewest fer duh wie er geduh hot?" [Now, you folks, all that is good and proper, but don't you agree there was reason enough for him to do what he did?]

497.
Verses on the Signs of the Zodiac "uff die Zeeche" [on the signs]:
"Der Leeb, der brillt,
Die Wog, die gilt,
Der Schitz, der schiesst,
Der Wassermann giesst,
Der Fisch, der schwimmt,
Der Schteebock schpringt,
Der Schtarweyan schticht,
Die Yungfraa schpricht,
Der Grebs, der glemmt,
Der Schtier, der rennt,
Der Widderbock schtosst,
Die Kinner sin blos."

[The lion (Leo), it roars,
The balance (Libra), it tells,
The archer (Sagittarius), he shoots,
The water bearer (Aquarius) pours,
The fish (Pisces), it swims,
The billy goat (Capricorn) jumps,
The scorpion (Scorpio) stabs,
The virgin (Virgo) speaks,
The crab (Cancer), it pinches,
The bull (Taurus), he runs,
The ram (Aries) bucks,
The twins (Gemini) are bare.]
A. A. Kleckner, Egypt

498.
A double meaning riddle:

"Ich geh hinnich's Haus,
Un henk mein dinner langer raus,
Un denk in meinem Sinn,
Ach, wie lummerich un wie dinn."

[I go behind the house
And hang out my thin long one
And say to myself:
Oh, how limp and thin!]

Answer: An old-fashioned money bag.
James B. Jacoby

499.
"Ich hab ihn mol der Jacket (English a) verhackt." A common expression meaning to circumvent someone; to get the better of someone, openly or secretly; to forestall someone. "Er hot sich aamache welle beim Parre, awwer ich hab ihn der Jacket gut verhackt." [He tried to make up to the pastor, but I fixed his wagon.] "Er hot arig gross gschwetzt, awwer ich hab ihn der Jacket verhackt." [He talked very big, but I cut off his water!]

500.
Proverb
"Mer muss schaffe, as mer seelich watt, reich watt mer hennicher net." [One has to work to be blessed (saved), rich one will never become.] Given as a reason for always working. I have heard it also as an excuse for not working hard. *Mrs. Mary Koch, Egypt*

501.
Game
"Pig in the Parlor" Players form a ring with "it" in the center. The ring circles around, the players singing:

"There is a pig in the parlor,
There is a pig in the parlor,
There is a pig in the parlor."

They stop circling around and letting go the hand of the partner on the left side, the boy passes over in the front of the partner on the right, holding her hand, taking the left hand of the next person and swinging between them to take the right hand of the third person. This is done while singing:

"Your right hand to your partner,
Your left hand to your neighbor,
Your right hand to the stranger,
And all promenade."

And then promenade with the new partners, singing:

"And we all promenande,
And we all promenade,
Your right hand to your partner,

Your left hand to your neighbor,
Your right hand to the stranger,
And all promenade."

In the passing which takes place during the singing of the second stanza, "it" cuts in. This leaves one alone, who becomes the pig. The circle forms anew, singing:
"There's a new pig in the parlor."
This game was played on August 30, 1936, at Willoughby Troxell's family reunion.

502.
Proverb
"Der Abbel fallt net weit vum Baam, mit aus er schteht am Barig." [The apple doesn't fall farm from the tree unless it's standing on a hill.]   *Green Lane*

503.
"Es waar als en alt Sprichwatt." [It used to be an old proverb.]   *Leb*

504.
"Wann die Grabbe nidder fliege, gebt's kalt schtarmich Wedder." [When the crows fly low, there'll be cold stormy weather.]   *John Shupp, Mechanicsville*

505.
"Waarmer Abrille un kiehler Moi,
  Fillt mer die Scheier mit Schtroh un Hoi."

[Warm April and cool May, one fills
 the barn with straw and hay.]

(Note "mer" and "Abrille".)
H. H. Bomberger, Lititz

506.
"Morgenschtund hat Gold im Mund,
Wer dies verseimt geht ganz zu Grund."   *Do*

507.
"Morgen, Morgen, nun nicht heite,
Schprechen immer traege Leit.
Was noch heite kann geschehen,
Lass bis Morgen nicht anschtehen."

[Tomorrow, tomorrow, but not today,
The shiftless ones always say.
What can happen today,
Don't put off until tomorrow.]   *Do*

508.
"Winsche nicht in der Welt,
Alles was dir gefellt,
Wenn es dir nitzlich waer,
Geb Gott dir's selber her."

[Don't wish for yourself,
All in the world that pleases you.
If it's useful to you,
God will see that you get it.]   *Do*

NOTE: May one conclude that where a higher German is retained, that there is a printed source, maybe a generation or two back? The above came from a Mennonite community, where of course traditions are well preserved. [Bomberger may have been a Mennonite, but Lititz is an old Moravian community.]

510. [sic]
"Was hawweswert is, is aa frogeswert." [That which is worth having, is worth asking for.]   *Mont*

511.
"Was net frogeswert is, is net nemmeswert." [That which is not worth asking for, is not worth taking.]   *Do*

512.
"Was net frogeswert is, is net schtehleswert." [That which is not worth asking for, is not worth stealing.]   *Egypt*

NOTE: In Nos. 510, 511, and 512 "hawweswert, frogeswert, nemmeswert, schtehleswert."

513.
"Hawwergees," katydid. "Du Hawwergees!" spoken in good natured raillery. "So en verdammder Hawwergees!" [Such a damned katydid!] = an epithet of contempt.

Julius Wilde, *Die Pflanzennamen im Sprachschatze der Pfaelzer, ihre Herkunft, Entwicklung und Anwendung*, 1923, page 40, traces "Haber" [P.G. Hawwer] back to Old German, coming from the same root as Latin "caper," meaning "goat."

514.
Proverb
"Des is Muunschei gfochde." [This is fighting by the light of the moon.]
My wife; a common expression in Leb

Fighting against the inevitable; useless work. For example, our housewives clean the house on Friday, so that everything is spick and span over Sunday. Now if someone would clean the house on Tuesday with the expectation that it would remain clean and that she would not have to go over it on Friday, "Sell waer no Muunschei gfochde."

515.
Children in playing would put the double-winged maple seedpods upon their noses with the pretense that they were spectacles.

516.
"Sauerambel" [sorrel], Rumex acetosella. It was used for pies during the Civil War by persons around Skippachville.

517.
It was customary in picking apples from the trees to leave a few apples hanging on the tree, "so as wann

mer der Weg kummt, as mer als noch eener hot." [so that, when one came by that way it was possible to eat one.] *Mont*

I heard it said, "Mer losst paar Ebbel uff der Baam henke fer die Aart." [One permits a few apples to hang in the tree to show the kind of apples.] Here there may be a very old belief.

518.
A young lady who can peel a whole apple without having the peeling break, will soon marry. *Leb*

519.
"En Maedel, as en Abbel zu dick scheelt, gebt ken gudi Hausheldern." [A girl that peels an apple too thick will not be a good housekeeper.] "scheele", to peel; "en gscheelder Abbel," a peeled apple.
All commonly used

Strange that such a commonly used word does not appear in Lambert. [Brendle had the same problems with Lambert's P.G. orthography that many others have had. The word "schaele, etc." appears on page 131.]

520.a.
In the spring the young boys would break off the ends of maple branchlets. Then they placed bottles over the ends to collect the sap. The sap, called "Saft" in the dialect, was known to them as "sugar water". There were those who bored holes with the gimlet into the bole of the tree and drank the sap with the straws. The real sugar maple was very rare in the lower end of Leb. Co. and the tree which was tapped for "sugar water" was Acer saccharinum. (There is also the cultivated "Silwer Meebel" of town and village.)
Memories of childhood in Leb

520.b.
The bark of the sweet birch was chewed, particularly in spring. It was taken from the smaller branchlets. Sometimes a sapling, two to three inches in diameter, would be bent over. This would cause the bark to spring loose at the bend and to crack. Thereupon it peeled off in fairly large pieces. Latin: Betula lenta. *Do*

521.
The leaves of the wintergreen, "Bruschttee," Gaultheria procumbus, were chewed. They were also eaten by some persons as a tidbit while roaming in the woodlands.

522.
The bark of small twigs of apple trees was chewed by some persons. I saw it done by persons who were in the habit of so doing. There is a probability that early settlers by necessity made use of barks and roots. I know of a man who would smoke dried wintergreen leaves mixed with dried pine needles in lieu of tobacco, when there was no tobacco available.

523.
"Sunday I am happy,
Monday full of joy;
Tuesday I am serving
What the devil can't destroy.

Wednesday and Thursday
I am walking in the light.
Friday is Heaven below
And so is Saturday night."

Horace Whitman of Woxall says it was spoken by an exhorter at a revival meeting.

524.
"Hutzel, pl. Hutzle" is used in Mont. Co. for a dried slice of pear, small variety.
Words used by Henry Summers of Green Lane

In Leb. Co., when I was a boy, I would be sent to the store to buy "peach hutzels," dried peaches. Lambert in his dictionary defines "Hutzel" as "dried peach". The fact that hybrid word "peach hutzels" was used indicates that "Hutzel" was applied to something different originally.

525.
In Leb. Co. a section of a freshly pared apple or of an orange is called "Schnutz." "Geb mer noch en Schnutz." [Give me another piece.]

526.
A pear, overly ripe or soft, is "masch." "Sie is gut awwer zu masch." [It's good but too ripe.] *Mont*

527. A note to No. 524.
During my time it was not unusual to find pear trees growing wild along fences, in deserted lots where once a cabin or house had stood. These trees were known as "wilde Bierebeem." They bore usually small fruit. Henry Summers always stated that it was of the fruit of these "wild" pear trees that "Hutzle" were made. This is to be noted. Dried peaches bought in stores were known as "peach hutzels."

528.
"Der Karfreidaag is der wichdichscht Daag im Yaahr, viel wichdicher wie der Sunndaag, so hot der Parre Leinbach uns Kinner gelannt in die Kinnerlehr." [Good Friday is the most important day in the year, much more important that Sunday. This is what Pastor Leinbach taught us in catechetical instruction.]
Jane Kilmer

529.
"Marye is Sunndaag. Marye schaffe mer net." Tomorrow is a holiday; tomorrow we won't work.
Mrs. Mary Koch, Egypt

"Sunndaag" [Sunday] has a general meaning of "holiday." Instead of saying, "Marye is en Feierdaag" [Tomorrow is a holiday], some say, "Marye is Sunndaag."

530.
"Es grebbt mich allimol as ich en seh." I am provoked (on account of the memory of some action) every time I see him. *Common use of "grebbe" [the English verb "grab"] in Mont*

531.
Proverb
"Geb em der Finger un er nemmt dir die ganz Hand." [Give him your finger and he'll take the entire hand.] *Common proverb*

532.
On the Millhouse lot on the Egypt cemetery is an interesting memorial. A box with a block of artificial flowers covered with glass. On the inside of the cover are are the photographs of all the persons buried on the plot. I suppose this should be understood as being prompted by the same feeling as the burial of baptismal certificates.

533.
"Ich wott ich waer im Himmel
Un du in Paradeis,
Un ich hett en wiesser Schimmel,
Un du en Kopp voll Leis."

[I wish I were in heaven
And you in paradise,
And I had a white horse
And you a head full of lice.]
Mrs. Hannah Issett

(All the items which I have gotten from James Jacoby and his sister Hannah Isset of Sumneytown have been very good.)
Commonly "paradise" in "Paradies" in the dialect.

534.
"Fechteck," a locality, small, where neighbors are quarrelsome. *Leh*

535.
"Hilly up and hilly down,
That's the way to Schaefferstown."
My grandfather, ca. 1900

536.
The Lutherans were called derisively, "Luttrischer Dickkopp" [fathead], pl. "Luttrischer Dickkepp."
Common

537.
The Reformeds were called in derision, "Reformiert, mit Dreck verschmiert." [smeared with dirt]
Common

538.
The term professor was often pronounced by children, "Brodfresser." *Schaefferstown*

539.
A small Bible was put in the hands of a corpse; usually such a one as the person living had read. *P. B.*

540.
On the Unionville cemetery is a tombstone with a sealed niche. Pumpernickle Bill senses that a photograph of the departed was placed therein.

541.
A member of the "Karicheroot" [church council], according to a widespread custom, selected his successor. "Ich hab niemand fer mei Blatz nemme." [I have no one to take my place] meant that he was willing to serve another term. This custom was well rooted. Reason? (A person had to be a deacon before he could become an elder.)

542.
At confirmation the collection plates are not passed to the members of the catechetical class, nor are the plates passed to members of the class on the day of their first communion. This was a well-established custom.

543.
At "die Vorbereiding" [Preparatory Service for Holy Communion], when I was a boy [in Schaefferstown] and in the first years of my ministry, no offering was taken.

544.
"Ich kann mei Hand schteh." I can take care of myself.
My wife; Jane Kilmer; a common expression at Myerstown

545.
"Ich kann mei Hand mache." I can get along with the matter. I can get along all right. *Schaefferstown*

546.
"Bleche Hannschaal,
Aldi Windmiehl,
Blos es Schtroh naus,
Holl die Kieh heem,
Yaag die Schof naus.
Waerscht net nuffgegraddelt,
Waerscht net runnergfalle,
Hettscht mei Schweschder gheiert,
Waerscht mei Schwoger warre!"

[Tin brain,
Old windmill,
Blow out the straw,
Fetch the cows home,
Chase out the sheep.
If you hadn't crawled up,
You wouldn't have fallen down,
If you had married my sister,
You'd be my brother-in-law!]
Horace Whitman, Woxall

547.
"Gruscht," a coming together of neighbors; a common meal and games; something in the nature of a sur-

prise party. Word used quite commonly in Mont Co by Horace Whitman, Hannah Issett and others.

548.
Proverb
"Yeder Haahne fecht's bescht uff sei eeye Mischthaufe." Each cock fights the best on his own dunghill (the manure pile in the barnyard). *Leb*
A person does his best work on his home ground.

549.
Of a consumptive: "Er guckt aus wie der lewendich Dod." [He looks like the living dead.] *Leb*

550.
Proverb
"Besser Unrecht gelidde wie Unrecht geduh." [Better to suffer an injustice than to impart an injustice.]

SIGNS OF DERISION
(ESPECIALLY AMONG BOYS)

551.
Thumb on the tip of the nose, fingers spread fanwise and sometimes wriggled. Said to mean, "Leck mich im Orsch." [Lick my fanny.] *Common at one time*

552.
Hands closed with index fingers extended. Stroking out along the left index finger with the right, almost as if whittling. Accompanied with "Pschie! Pschie!" *Common at one time*

553.
A boy will hold his two hands together so that the right thumb is on the left little finger and the right little finger will be on the left thumb. Then he will ask another boy to take hold of the right little finger and pull. As he does so the boy brings his left thumb to his nose and with the right hand drawn out, the thumb on the tip of left little finger, there is a double (No. 552) sign of derision. *Common at one time*

554.
"Wu halt's hie?" To what church do you belong? — "Ich halt naryets hie." I don't belong to any church. This is a common meaning of "hiehalde"; "naryets" = nowhere.

"SCHTREECH" (TRICKS)

555.
Pulling away a chair behind a person as he is sitting down.
Common in schools and at parties

556.
Putting a pin in a cushion or in a seat.
Common in schools and at parties

557.
Hanging a pigtail to the coat of a schoolteacher; to the coat of anyone. *Do*

558.
Inflating a pig's bladder, putting beforehand grains of corn into it and tying it onto the tail of a dog.
Rather common at one time

559.
Tying empty cans onto a dog's tail. *Do*

560.
Putting turpentine on dog's hind parts. This is known as "en Hund darbendiene." [to turpentine a dog] Nos. 558 - 560 were done to dogs that had become a nuisance.

561.
Tying two cats together at their tails. This is pure devilment, "Deiwelsschtreech."

562.
Fish do not bite when the moon is full, because they feed at night. *Common*

563.
Proverb
"Datt is ewwe widder der gross 'wann'." There, again, is that great "if." "Wann's net wege des gross 'wann' waer." [If it were not for that great "if."]
Common

564.
To catch fish, spit on the bait before casting into the water. *Very widespread*

565.
To catch fish, spit into the water before casting in the bait. This is done when fishing and the fish are not biting. *Not infrequently met with*

566.
If your shoes squeak, they have not been paid for. *Common*

567.
Small game will not be out of their holes, "net haus," when the moon is full, because it feeds during the night. *Common*

568.
If the hunting season is during a dry period, the rabbits will not be out, but in their holes.
Rather often heard

569.
A good rain during the hunting season will bring the rabbits out of their holes. *Rather common*

570.
Proverb
"Alles fer Friede." "Alles fer Friede halde." All things done for the sake of peace.
Used mostly by older people

571.
Proverb
"Mer kennt des net besser mache, wann's mer selwer mache deed." [One could not do this better if one had done it himself.] An expression which shows approval.
Common

[addendum]
"Der N— N— is zu die Maed gange." [N— N— went courting.] It was a "Gnecht" [hired man] from Schnecksville. "Noch re Zeit waar's Maedel in Druwwel un sie hen ausgemacht fer heiere." [After a time the girl was in trouble and they decided to get married.] "Er hot's seim Daadi saage welle un paar Daag eb die Hochzich saagt er's ihm." [He wanted to tell his father and a few days before the wedding he tells him.] "Pop" (or English "Pap"), "Samschdaag heirich." [Saturday I'm getting married.] His father looked at him in surprise and asked: "Muscht heiere?" [Must you get married?] He answered, "Ich MUSS net, awwer's is hatt notwennich!" [I don't HAVE to, but it's really necessary.] (I knew the man. As I remember, his name was Addison.)
Often heard around Egypt

Recitations for Christmas

572.
"Ich kann das ganze A B C,
Des grosse un des gleine.
Bis zwanzich zeh(!) ich in die Heh,
Un rickwarts bis zu eine.
Un singe kann ich as es schallt,
Un des is gaar net schwer,—?-
Bin noch ken siwwe Yaahre ale,—?-
Kann ich noch viel mehr.
(Sing) Alle Yaahre wieder
Kummt des Grischus Kind
Auf die Arde nieder,
Wu wir Menschen sind."

[I know the A B C's,
The large and the small.
I count up to twenty
And backwards to one.
I can sing till it echoes,
And this is not too hard.
I'm not yet 7 years old:
I can do much more.
(Sing) Every year again
The Christchild comes
Down to earth
Where we humans are.]

Recited by Mrs. Pierce Nothstein at Scheidy's Sunday School when she was a child.

573.
"Heit is Weihnacht,
O wie schee.
Ich hab sei Lebdaag
Noch nicht so gesehe,
Bin so glee un doch so bang,
Ich glaab as der Belznickel
Kummt eb lang."

[Today is Christmas,
Oh how beautiful!
In my lifetime
I have not seen such.
I'm so small and so frightened:
I believe Saint Nick
Will be coming soon.]
Do

574.
"Belznickel," with a buffalo robe tied around himself, would come on Second Christmas. He would be a catechist, asking the child about his behavior; asking him to say his prayers; striking an unruly boy; make him promise to behave (often advised by the parents what to say). "Belznickel" would hold out a present with one hand and when the child reached out for it, would strike the child sharply with his other hand; would scatter nuts and oranges on the floor and when the child bent down to pick them up, would strike the child with a rod. He gave the impression of one begrudgingly giving presents.
Leb

575.
Prayer for "Benznickel", a parody:

"Alle Auchen Kaesebrod,
Deiwel schlack der Belznickel dod."

[All eyes cheese bread,
Devil strike Santa dead!]

Pierce Nothstein, Carbon

Prayers

576.
"Abba liewer Vader. Aamen." [Father, dear father]
At mealtime.
Mrs. Pierce Nothstein

577.
"Diese Schpeise segne uns,
Gott der Vader, Gott der Sohn,
un Gott der Heiliche Geischt. Aamen."

[This food bless to our use,
God the Father, God the Son,
and God the Holy Spirit.]

At mealtime.
Do

578.
"Das Blut Jesus Christus macht uns rein vun allen Sinden. Aamen." [The blood of Jesus Christ makes us pure of all sins.] At mealtime.
Do

579.
Bedtime prayer
"Ich bin noch glein,
Mein Herz is rein,

Soll Yesus drin wohne
Un Yesus allein. Aamen."

[I am yet small,
My heart is pure,
Jesus shall dwell therein
And Jesus alone.] *Do*

580.
Bedtime prayer
"Liewer Gott, ich ruf zu dir
 Mach en frommes Kind aus mir. Aamen."

[Dear God, I call to Thee
 Make of me a pious child.] *Do*

581.
Bedtime prayer
"Oweds, wann ich schlofe geh,
Vazeh Engle mit mir geh.
Zwee zu Kopp,
Zwee zu Fuuss,
Zwee zu rechder Hand,
Zwee zu linker Hand.
Zwee, dass mich wecken,
Zwee, dass mich decken,
Zwee, dass mit mir noch Paradeis gehen.
Gott der Vader, Gott der Sohn,
Gott der heilische Geischt. Amen."

[Evenings when I go to bed,
Fourteen angels go with me.
Two at my head,
Two at my feet.
Two on the right hand,
Two on the left hand.
Two that wake me,
Two that cover me,
Two that go with me to paradise.
God the Father, God the Son,
God the Holy Ghost.] *Do*

582.
"Was em aagebore is, watt mer net leicht (hendich) los." [That which you're born with you don't get rid of easily.] *Leb*

583.
There is a frame barn beyond Schnecksville on Tamaqua Road in which the side boards have holes 1-2 inches and more in diameter bored in them. There are two or more to each board. The owner tells me that his mother, old Jemima Mickley, says that the boards were shipped by boat and were fastened together by pegs. There is a barn with similar holes above Romig's Mill. *Edwin Mickley*

584.
Riddle:
"Woll hinnich die Dier,
Woll fer die Dier,
Un Woll saagich dir,
Un Woll is es?
Was is sell?" — "Woll"

[Wool behind the door,
Wool before the door,
And wool I say to you,
And wool is it?
What is that? — Wool] *Pierce Nothstein*

585.
"Reetzel" [riddle]
"En Mann unne Gegleed, unne Aarm, laaft ins Wasser, leest Schtee un dutt sie in der Sack. Was is sell?" — "En Lieg"
[A man without clothing, without arms, walks into the water, picks up stones and puts them in a bag. What's that? — A lie.] *Do*

586.
"Was schteckt die Hosse naus un schtinkt?" — "Fiess" [What sticks out of the pants and stinks? — Feet] *Do*

587.
"Wann is en Mann en Mann? — Wann er alee is."
[When is a man a man? — When he's alone.] *Do*

588.
"Es waare 6 Brieder un ken Schweschdre, awwer yeders hot 2 Schweschdre ghat. Wie waar sell?" — "Yeders" was the name of a man. *Do*

589.
"Unser Maad hot Riewe gesse
Un hot sie net gebisse.
Geschder waar der 7 Daag
Un sie hot sie verschmisse."

[Our maid ate turnips
And she didn't chew them.
Yesterday was the 7th day
And she thew them away.] *Do*
[The word "verschmisse" is most likely a euphemism for "verschisse" (defecated)]

590.
If a house cat or dog licks his paws, there will be visitors. *Do*

591.
"Weschesel" — drying frame for clothes indoors in winter. *Do*
"Weschgaul" — the word used in Leb. Co.

592.
"Mammi, Mammi, Budderbrod,
 Schlag die Katz mit Lumbe dot."

[Mommy, mommy, butter bread,
 Kill the cat with rags.] *Myerstown*

593.
"Wie seid er [ihr]?" [How are you?] *Mont*
"Wie sin er [ihr]?" [How are you?] *Leh*

594.
Frank Steckel of Cementon, speaking of two persons, man and wife, both of very mean disposition, "Sis ken gudi Familye verdarwe warre, wu sie gheiert hen." [No good family was spoiled when they married.] Neither marrying otherwise would have founded a good family.

595.
If you shoot a cat with your gun, "verdarbscht die Flint" [you ruin your gun], that it ("die Flint macht nimmi dod") doesn't kill. To restore its killing powers, shoot a dog. *Sumneytown*

596.
To clean out a "hexed" gun, or "verbannt" gun, shoot a silver bullet through it. Some hunters believed that a woman could "hex" [bewitch]; that is, "es Feier nemme" [to take away its fire], so that the load would fall to the ground as soon as it left the barrel. *Sumneytown*

A woman could bewitch a gun by tucking under her belt the corner of her apron. "es Feier nemme" may go back to the flintlock; that is, it wouldn't strike fire.

597.
If a gun has been "verbannt" [bewitched], urinate through the barrel. *Do*

598.
Old gunners preferred rusty barrels as they would kill better. The shot would keep together better. *Jim Jacoby*

599.
"Der Winder watt so kalt wie der Summer warm waar." [The winter will be just as cold as the summer was warm.] *Egypt*

600.
"Der Winder watt so nass wie der Summer drucke waar." [The winter will be just as wet as the summer was dry.] *Do*

601.
Proverb
"En scheener Daag un en gudi Fraa sett mer net lowe bis Owed." [A beautiful day and a good woman should not be praised before evening.] *Green Lane*

602.
Proverb
"Die Narre un die Gsuffne schwetze die Waahret." [Fools and drunks speak the truth.]
Rather commonly heard

603.
Proverb
"En Gnarr, en Gsuffner un en Kind schwetze die Waahret." [A fool, a drunk and a child speak the truth.] *Not as frequently heard as No. 602; Mont*

604.
The body of a drowned person will rise to the surface on the 9th day. This is due to the bursting of the gall bladder. *"Sticks" Surface, Egypt*

605.
The body of a drowned person will come to the surface in three hours if a thunderstorm comes up. *Do*

606.
A drowning person will come to the surface three times before finally staying down.
Formerly a common belief, Do

607.
"Ich hab en Abbeditt as ich darich en Barig esse kennt." [I have such an appetite I could eat through a mountain.] *Dave Troxell*

608.
A rattlesnake will rattle three times before it strikes. *Common belief*

609.
"Mer hot ken Glick wann die Katze vum Haus weckgehn." [One has no luck if the cats leave the house.] (This seems to me to be a very interesting belief, bound up probably with "Hexerei" [witchcraft].)

LOCAL NAMES

610.
"Kiehweg" — road south of Souderton running alongside of the Allentown Road.

611.
"Dannpeik" — the turnpike from Reading to Lebanon. Name from the English. *So called in Leb*

612.
"Grawelpeik" (short English a) — pike from Collegeville to Green Lane. So called on account of the gravel used in building it.

613.
"Die Gross Schtross" — the King's Highway Colonial Road) leading from Zieglersville to Boyertown. It was wider than other country roads.

614.
"Die Glee Schtross" — the road leading from Zieglersville to Sassamensville. Not as wide as the "Gross Schtross."

615.

"die Schmalzgass," also merely "die Gass," the road from Sumneytown to Geryville. *Mont*

616.

"die Barigschtross" — There were three roads near Sumneytown that were called "Barigschtross." When they were spoken of in English, they were called "Ridge Road." *Mont*

617.

"die Deiwelslocherschtross" — the road leading from Green Lane to Maxatawny. *Leb*

618.

"die Graasich Leen" — When Schaefferstown was laid out by Alexander Schaeffer streets and bystreets were laid out. One of the small streets leading to the outlots became known locally as "die Graasich Leen," the grassy lane.

619.

"der Keschde Barig" — Chestnut Hill near Spinnerstown.

DIALECTAL PLACE-NAMES

621.[sic]

"Lang Schwamm" — Long Swamp, near Mertztown. Here swamp is used in the sense of meadow, "die Wiss" in Leb. Co.

622.

"Gross Schwamm" — Great Swamp, Spinnerstown, Pa.

623.

"der Schwamm" — "Falckner Schwamm," near Boyertown. When I was pastor at Keelor's Church, people would say, "Geschder waar ich im Schwamm." "Yesterday I was over at the Swamp churches." ("die Schwammer Kariche")

624.

"Haschdaal" [Deer Valley], a ravine in the South Mountain, west of Schaefferstown. *Leb*

625.

"Haschschtall" [Deer Stable], a rhododendron thicket near Walnut Spring in Leb. Co. The rhododendron is rare in the South Mountains, but there is a thicket up along the creek from Walnut Spring.

626.

"es Dor" — On the woodland road that runs in the South Mountain back to Walnut Spring, there used to be a gate. This was known as "es Dor."

627.

"Walnissbrunne," mountain spring, so called because a walnut tree stood by the side of the spring. It is located in the South Mountains, west of Schaefferstown. *Leb*

628.

"Neeyerwissli" [Negro Meadow]. This was a small clearing down in the hollow between "Walnissbrunne" and "Babble Schpring."

629.

"Babble Schpring," a spring near the road that leads from Cornwall to the Lebanon Pumping Station. So called on account of the poplar trees, Liriodendron tulipifera.

630.

"der Schofbarig" [Sheep Hill], low, hilly country, southeast of Schaefferstown. I suspect that the name "Schofbarig" was applied to this hilly country to distinguish from the higher South Mountain.

631.

"Grewwelbarig," the gravel hills northeast of Schaefferstown.

632.

"die Rot Brick," a bridge, painted red, on the Hammer Creek ("die Hammer Grick") on this side of the Lebanon Pumping Station. "Die Rot Brick" was a noted rendezvous for hunters and fishermen.

633.

"die Rot Karich," the Red Church near Orwigsburg; so called on account of its color.

634.

"es Saegloch" [Sawmill Hollow], a hollow in the "Sand Barig" [Sand Hill], south of Schaefferstown, in which a sawmill was located.

635.

"es Sandloch," a hollow in the "Sand Barig" [Sand Hill].

636.

"es Buxloch" [Laurel Hollow], a ravine in the "Sand Barig," where laurel grew plentifully.

637.

"der Sand Barig" [Sand Hill]. There is a sandy group of hills in southern Leb. Co. This is known as "der Sand Barig," to distinguish the area from the higher South Mountains to the west of Schaefferstown.

638.

"die Schnitz Grick" [Snitz Creek], a small creek in southern Leb. Co.

639.

"die Hammer Grick," the creek in southern Leb. Co., upon which the Lebanon Pumping Station is located. This was a favorite stream for fishing with the "Hammergaarn" [dip-net], which may have given the name to the creek.

640.

"Grabbeschteddel" [Crow Town], a small town in southern Leb. Co.

641.

"Haahneschteddel" [Hahnstown], a small town in Lanc. Co., east of Ephrata.

642.

"Hinkelschteddel" [Hinkletown], a small town in Lanc. Co., southeast of Ephrata.

643.

"Schtumbeschteddel" — Fredericksburg, Leb. Co.

644.

"Feierschteeschteddel," Flintville, a small hamlet between Schaefferstown and Iona.

645.

"Grubbeland." — This name still used for the land from Reistsville up to the city of Lebanon. I surmise that the name is due to the many roundish holes which dot the land.

646.

"Weisseecheland," White Oaks, Lanc. Co. "Ich will niwwer noch Weisseecheland." [I want to go over to White Oaks.]

A stretch of land was known by some natural characteristic: "Sandland" [sand land], "Weisseecheland" [white oaks land], "Druckeland" [dry land], "Barigland" [hill land], and from that I would conclude that "Grubbeland" [See No. 645] was due to some natural formation, rather than to the use of the "Grubbhack" [grubbing-hoe] to clear land.

647.

"Maryeland," Morgenland, Leh. Co.

648.

"Leddereckposchde," Leather Cornerpost. At hotels the hitching posts were covered with leather to prevent cribbing by the horses. This name may be due to such a post at a hotel by the same name.

649.

"Wollewwerschteddel," Mt. Aetna, Leb. Co. PG form ["Wollewwer"] of the name of the founder, Peter Wollweber?

650.

"Oxekopp" [Ox Head], a hotel on the hill on the Sumneytown-Geryville pike, where it crosses the "Barigschtross." [See No. 616]

651.

"Darrenascht" [Dry Branch], a hotel on the upper Ridge Road leading from Green Lane to Trumbauersville, about two miles from "Oxekopp" [See No. 650] on the "Barigschtross." [No. 616]

652.

"Grienebaam" [Green Tree], a hotel near Keelor's Church, Frederick, Mont. Co.

653.

"der Blankeweg" [Plank Road], the road from Cornwall to Lebanon. The name may be due to the fact that it was once covered with planks, a plank road.

654.

"der Schteetweg" [State Road] — the Lancaster pike coming from the east, now a part of the Lincoln Highway [Route 30]. It was very broad when first built. I do not know whether this was the name for the entire road or just for the portion approaching Lancaster city.   *I heard the name from Abe Wenger*

655.

"Rising Sun," a hotel, then a schoolhouse, in upper Leh. Co.

656.

"Gehlgaul," Yellow House, which is located between Boyertown and Reading. It is also known as "Gehle Haus" and "Gehle Wattshaus" [Yellow Inn]. These names were heard in Frederick, Mont. Co.

657.

"Blecherschteddel," a small hamlet south of Myerstown. The name is probably taken from a resident family.

658.

"Hexeschteddel" [Witch Town], a hamlet between Mickley's and Mechanicsville, Leh. Co. So called because at one time there was much "Hexerei" [witchcraft] carried on there.

659.

"Beint Schwamm" [Pine Swamp]. This area is remembered as farstretching swampland in the Poconos. The location seems to have been forgotten by people now living, though they still speak of the "Beint Schwamm," to which cattle were driven for summer pasturage.   *Egypt*

660.

"Meisschteddel" [Mousetown], a small hamlet near Sumneytown. When there was a group of houses set apart from the main town, the group often received a "Schpottnaame" [negative nickname].

661.

"New Jerusalem," a small hamlet near Salfordville.

662.

"der Yungebarig" [Yung or Young Hill], a hill in the public road between Green Lane and Red Hill. So called from a family living there.

663.

"der Karwersbarig," a hill between Sumneytown and Trumbauersville. So called from a family once living there.

664.

"die Schwamm Grick," an old name for the Unami Creek at Sumneytown. Most likely because it rose and flowed through swampy land. — The west branch of the Perkiomen Creek which enters the Perkiomen at Delphi is called "die Schwamm Grick," coming from Falkner Swamp.

665.

"Society Barig, Sciota Barig, Kuddelfleckbarig, Kuddelfleck Hall Barig" = a hill in Frederick Township, Mont. Co., near Keelor's Church. The original name was "Sciota Barig." Then a Sunday School building was erected on the hill, because the Lutheran congregation fought against having the Sunday School in Keelor's Church. On the Saturday night when the Sunday School building was to be dedicated the next day, the opponents of the Sunday School hung a "Kuddelfleck" [tripe] in the belfry. Thence the name "Kuddelfleckbarig." But the Sunday School Society gave its name also the the hill, whence the name "Society Barig" (English pronunciation of Society).

666.

"die Grundeechlekarich," a name for a church at Unionville, on account of the "Grundeechle" (ground acorn) growing near, Neffs, Pa.

667.

"die Aryelkarich" (Organ Church), the name given to the Egypt Church because it had the first organ among the country churches round about.

668.

"die Weiserkarich," a name given to the New Goshenhoppen Church in East Greenville, because it had been served by pastors Weiser, father and son, over a long period of years.

669.

"die Huwerskarich" [Hoover's Church]. This church, at Niantic or at Sassamensville, was so called because of the lengthy service of a pastor(?). The name was frequently used down in Frederick Township, though I do not remember that I ever heard an explanation of the name.

670.

"die Sexeckich Karich," a common name for the Lutheran Church out from Red Hill. — One day, when I lived at Green Lane, I asked a Stebanus (called "Schtefanus" in the dialect) girl, who was the maid in the home of Dr. Harvey Scholl, "Bischt Luttrisch?" [Are you Lutheran?] To which she answered, "Nee, sexeckich!" She meant that she was a member of the "Sexeckich Karich" [Six-cornered Church].

671.

If a gun "macht net dod" [doesn't kill], take vinegar and pour it into the barrel. Or pour vinegar over the shot. A gun with a shiny barrel was not regarded with favor. *A.A.Kleckner*

672.

To restore the "killing power" to a gun, shoot a ten cent piece of silver (pounded round) through the barrel. *Frank Sterner*

673.

Shooting a cat will bring "bad luck." *Do*

674.

To bring back the killing powers to a gun, shoot pieces of a rusty cut nail through the barrel. *Do*

675.

Proverb

"Sis en schlechdi Gluck as net an paar Hinklicher uffziehe kann." [It's a poor mother hen that cannot raise a few chicks.] This was said by Mrs. Snyder of Eagle Point, when she was left a widow with a large number of children. Her husband had committed suicide.

676.

Mrs. Masonheimer says, "Ich bin net imfindlich." She meant she was not easily impressed; to react quickly to something; to take up.

677.

"On the Fourth of July the corn stalks should be so high that one can hide a whisky bottle in the cornfield. So said my father," according to William Landis, superintendent of schools.

678.

When women sleep with their posteriors uncovered, then the cornstalks will grow. That is, when the weather becomes so warm that women sleep uncovered, the corn will grow. *Coplay*

679.

When women hang their legs out over the bed, the corn will grow. Corn grows when the nights are warm. *Francis Laubach, Ballietsville*

680.

"net zu Gnaade kumme" [to fail to thrive (grow)]. "Ich hab Zellrich geblanzt, awwer er is net zu Gnaade kumme." [I planted celery, but it didn't thrive.] *Mrs. Ed Wagner, Northampton*

681.

The family Bible should not be sold at a public sale. This brings bad luck. "Die Familye geht zu nix." "zu nix geh" has two meanings: (1) The family will die out; (2) The family will become worthless and penniless. *Rather common*

682.
A small lock of hair of a beloved one (often before burial) was cut off and placed in the family Bible. Four-leaved clovers were also placed in the Bible.

I suppose that I have been asked a half-dozen times to write family memoranda in family Bibles. This request may have been due to, "Ich kann net schee genunk schreiwe fer in die Biewel schreiwe," or because of the feeling that only the preacher was a fit person to write in the Bible.

683.
On some old barns in Leb. Co. "Dachfenschdre" [dormer windows] appear. When instead of having panes of glass, the windows were slatted, they were often called "Dachlaade." The hatchway to the roof of a house was also called "Dachlaade." — When the roofs of the big barns were repaired, reshingled in spots, a rope was thrown over the roof, fastened to the workman and held by another on the other side of the barn.

684.
"as mer heile kennt!" [that one could be moved to tears] "Die is so schee as mer heile kennt!" [Her beauty could move one to tears.] "Er hot sei Memm so wiescht behandelt as mer heile kennt!" [He abused his mother so that one could weep!] *Leb*

685.
When black powder was used, after several shots, particularly on a damp day, reddish lines would appear at the end of the barrel. This was looked upon as blood. Thence the belief, "Wann die Flint ken Blut ziegt, macht sie net dod." [If the gun doesn't draw blood, it won't kill.] This explains the beliefs about a rusty gun in Nos. 598, 671 and 674.

A.A.Kleckner, Egypt

686.
To keep the shot bunched for target or mark shooting, the shot were wound together with tow, with molasses or with thick grease. *Do*

687.
"nootschich" [amorous]. "Sie is der erscht nootschich." She is very amorous, open to free fondling. "Er hot sie mol gut genootscht." He spooned her vigorously, fondled her amorously.

"vernootscht," something that bears the marks of much handling. "Ich hett gern en Kuche ghat, awwer sie waare mer zu vernootscht." I would have liked to buy a cake in the store, but they had been handled too much.

Common terms
688.
Catch question
"Constantinople is a hard word. Can you spell it?"
The answer: I.T. *Common question among children*

689.
Catch question
"Nebuchadnessar, king of the Jews. If you spell it with two letters, I'll give you a pair of new shoes."
Answer: I.T. *Mrs. Orlando Wright*

690.
Catch question
"Kannscht Philip Schnawwel schpelle?" "Nee, wie geht's?" "PH - TH - I - LL (by letters) SCHNAUN SCHUN LI PHILIP SCHNAWWEL."
Orlando Wright

691.
"SCHNEE N A P Schnap (English short a), EB O LICKEL, OR-or Dickel O, K L (by letters) Liggel."
Mrs. Orlando Wright

P.G. NAMES OF CHURCHES
692.
"die Barig Karich," Hill Church near Annville, Pa.

693.
"die Barig Karich," Hill Church near Boyertown. Both Nos. 692 and 693 names from the location on a hill.

694.
"Keeley's Church," near Schwencksville. It was later discontinued. The Keeley family lived near the church.

695.
"Keelor's Church," Frederick, Pa. It was named for a hotelkeeper near the church.

696.
"die Schwamm Karich," the church at Falkner's Swamp.

697.
"die Schwamm Karich," Great Swamp Church near Spinnerstown.

698.
"die Langschwammer Karich," Long Swamp Church near Mertztown. Nos. 696, 697, 698, from localities called "Schwamm" in PG.

699.
"die Ziegels Karich," a church near Fogelsville, which had a tile roof on an earlier church building.

700.
"die Schmok Karich" [Smoke Church], a church near Hamburg.

701.
"die Blo Karich" [Blue Church], a church near Coopersburg, so called because it was painted blue.

702.

"die Eck Karich" [Corner Church], a church a short way from Robesonia, which stands at a crossroads.

703.

"die Blo Barig Karich" [Blue Mountain Church], Zion's Church at Strausstown, Pa.

704.

"die Leinbachs Karich," Tulpehocken Reformed [United Church of Christ] Church, east of Myerstown. So called because of the long pastorate of Rev. Leinbach.

705.

"die Lange Karich," Tulpehocken Lutheran Church near Stouchsburg. So named because of the long pastorate of Rev. Long.

706.

"die Schteene Karich," Stone Church, north of Northampton. It was so named when the first stone church was built.

707.

"die Schitze Karich," a Lutheran church near Spinnerstown, named after the Schitz family.

708.

"die Blug Karich," the Plow Church near Gouglersville, Pa.

709.

"die Bellemanns Karich," Belleman's Church near Leesport. It was named after the Belleman family. (Would Belleman be a Huguenot family name?)

710.

"die Heidelbaryer Karich," North Heidelberg Church near Bernville.

711.

"die Heedelbaryer Karich" [Heidelberg Church], a church near Slatington, Leh. Co.

712.

"die Keschdebaryer Karich," the Chestnut Hill Church near Spinnerstown.

713.

"die Inschinglenner Karich," the name applied to the Indianfield Lutheran Church near Telford.

714.

"die Inschingland Karich" [Indian Land Church], a church near Cherryville, Northampton Co.

715.

"die Richwell Karich," applied to either of the two Ridge Valley churches at Argus near Tylersport.

716.

"es Druckeland Karich," Dryland Church, Northampton Co.

717.

"die Hinnerschitz Karich," a church near Reading named after the Hinnerschitz family.

718.

"die Schpiese Karich," a church near Reading named after the Schpies family.

719.

"die Kimmerlings Karich," Kimmerling's Church near Avon, Pa.

720.

The meetinghouses of the Mennonites in Mont. Co. are known by place-names: "Schibbacher Versammlinghaus" [Skippack Meetinghouse], "Sollford Versammlinghaus," "Frangoni Versammlinghaus" [Franconic Meetinghouse]. The English term is meetinghouse. Not infrequently I heard: "Schibbacher Meetinghouse," "Sollford Meetinghouse," "Frangoni Meetinghouse."

721.

Even though the Mennonites do not call their meetinghouses "Kariche" [churches], nonetheless, they are often so called [by non-Mennonites]. "Er wuhnt net weit vun der Mennischde Karich." [He doesn't live far from the Mennonite church.] "Heit bin ich an die Dunker Karich verbei un's waar alles voll Fuhre." [Today I went by the Church of the Brethren and many horses and carriages were tied up there.]

722.

In saying, "I am going to church" we use the expressions, "Ich will in die Karich." "Ich will noch die Karich." The Mennonites say, "Ich will an die Versammling." *Mont*

723.

"Die Albrechtskarich" — the Albright Church at Kleinfeltersville, Pa., which is maintained as a memorial to the founder of the Evangelical denomination.

P.G. NAMES OF SCHOOLHOUSES
IN THE VICINITY OF SUMNEYTOWN

724.

"die Barigschtross Schul" — a school located on the "Ridge Road" near what was formerly "Darrenascht." See No. 651. The school no longer exists.

725.

"die Schwammgricker Schul," a schoolhouse on the Unami Creek [See No. 664], not far from the University of Pennsylvania camp. The school no longer exists.

726.
"die Diefgricker Schul," a schoolhouse on the Deep Creek, near Perkiomenville.

727.
"die Dreckloch Schul" is called in English "the Mud-hole School" near Perkiomenville. If I remember rightly, it was more respectfully referred to as "Hauck's School." Hauck is a family name.

728.
"die Freschlocher Schul," a school about a mile north of Green Lane, is called in English "Frog Hollow." It was also called "Buck's School" after the Buck family. In PG the words "Schul" and "Schulhaus" are used interchangeably.

729.
Proverb
"En yunger Buh un en yunger Hund welle alli Schtund." [A little boy and a little dog want to (urinate) every hour.] *Mrs. Raymond Remaley*

730.
"Wann's Graut net drauert, gebt's ken Kepp." [If the cabbage isn't in mourning, i.e. if it doesn't hang its head, there will be no cabbage heads.]
Thomas Hoffman, Egypt

731.
Riddle
"Patch upon patch, A hole in the middle. If you can guess that I'll give you a fiddle." — "A chimney."
Mrs. Orlando Wright, Egypt

732.
Spelling Constantinople: "C O N, Con, With an E, With an I, With a Constanti TI, With a tipple, With a topple, With a Constantinople." *Do*

733.
In Leh. Co. in the time of drought, it is said, "Waard bis die Allentaun Fair, no gebt's Rege." [Wait until the Allentown Fair, then it will rain.]

734.
At Sumneytown, Mont. Co., they said, "Wann der Yagowi sei Schwamm abmacht, no gebt's Rege." [When Jacoby mows his meadow, there will be rain.]

735.
At Schaefferstown they said, "Nau gebt's Rege, der Tom Brendle meht sei Wiss." [Now there'll be rain, Tom Brendle is mowing his meadow.]

736.
In Berks Co. they say, "Wann's Weisehaus celebration (English) is, gebt's ken Rege." [When the Orphans' Home at Womelsdorf has its annual celebration, there will be no rain.]

737.
Here and there I've heard, "Marye is es Weisehaus picnic, no gebt's uff der mehner Hand Rege." [Tomorrow is the Orphans' Home picnic, usually there is rain on that day.] There was a period of years when the annual picnic at the Womelsdorf orphanage was held without rain. This gave rise to No. 736. Then there was a period of years when the picnic fell on a rainy day. This gave rise to No. 737.

738.
"Wann die Zeiding gebt as mer Rege greechde un verfehlt's paarmol hinnenaner nooch, no gebt's en Drickning." [When the newspaper reports that we're getting rain and misses it a few times in a row, then there will be a drought.]

739.
Game
"Wie gfallt dir dei Gesellche?" The group forms a circle seated. This is an indoor game. One player in the middle of the circle goes from one to the other and asks, "Wie gfallt dir dei Gesellche?" [How do you like your little partner?] If the answer is "gut," the questioner passes on to the next one. If the answer is "net gut," the questioner asks, "Was verlangscht?" [What's your wish?] The answer is that so and so, one of the players, shall do so and so. The one in the middle then directs that the desire be carried out. This game, told to me by Robert Schaeffer of Northampton, formerly of Carbon Co., is like our game "Pleased or displeased?" A circle is formed. The player in the middle goes from person to person asking, "Pleased or displeased?" If the answer is "Pleased," the questioner passes on to the next player. If the answer is "Displeased," the question is asked, "What can I do for you?" The answer is usually a ridiculous request, "N— N— is to do this or that."

740.
Local rhyme:
"Der Isaac Wentz,
Der Isaac Wentz,
Der reit die Gens
Bis am Sem Schtrohl sei Middelfens."

[Isaac Wentz, Isaac Wentz,
He rides the geese
Up to Sam Strohl's middle fence.]

R.D. Schaeffer

741.
"Der Eesi Heini, Geht mit der Leweini." A boy by the name of Asa Hein is going with a girl Lovina. The rhyme was spoken "fer ausschpodde" [to make fun of]. *Deep Creek*

Children's Play
742.
One child says to another, "Look at the door." The other looks, whereupon the first says, "Half past four."

743.

(As in No. 742.) "Look at the blin(d) (window shade), Half past nine."

744.

(As in No. 742) "Look at the tree, Half past three."

745.

(As in No. 742) "Look at your finger, But you left a stinker."

746.

Children, when they passed a stinking object, like excrementa or a dead mouse, etc., would spit. The one who was the last to spit or who didn't spit at all was mocked by the others, "Du hoscht's geschluckt." [You swallowed it.]

From childhood
747.

"Here I stand, Big and stout, With my belly Full of sauerkraut." This was a favorite with young children, who standing with belly extended would proudly recite. *Do*

748.

"Daage un Nacht Rege" [day and night rain] — a PG name used in Leb. Co. for the spring equinoctial storms. The name came to be more broadly applied to rainstorms that came from the south and east and lasted a day and a night or days and night. "Des is der Daage un Nacht Rege." This is an expression I frequently heard up in Leb Co when a boy. I have not heard it since I left Leb Co. Of a long thunderstorm it was said, "Des dreht sich in en Daage un Nacht Rege." [This will turn itself into a day and night rain.]

The Harvest Home Service
749.

Every year at the end of the oats' harvest a thanksgiving service was held in our churches. This service was known as "die Ernkarich, die Erntkarich." The name "Erndefescht" was also sometimes heard, probably from the hymn, "Froh singt am frohen Erntefest." This latter name is no longer heard. The time for the service was the month of August. Now the service is practically always held in the month of September. At Old Goshenhoppen Church, Woxall, Pa., before 1900 the festival was held on a Thursday. Rev. C. R. Fetter, the Lutheran pastor at Old Goshenhoppen, tried to revive the weekday festival in the 1920's.

750.

The best examples of fruits and vegetables are brought into the church. At Egypt, Cementon, and Miller's [Reformed] churches there have been homemade bread and jellies. After the services the things brought into the church were given to the preacher. There were, however, some exceptions to this. At Miller's church some of the people are accustomed to take home what they bring to the church. (At the present time, 1945, these foods are taken to Phoebe Home.)

751.

At Harvest Home the benevolences of the congregation were chiefly contributed. The offering went for "Missionszwecke" or for "Wohltaetichkeiten." (That is, for the apportioned benevolences of the church at large.) In some of the older congregations, under the intense feeling that such offerings should be purely voluntary, the benevolent offering was held as a second collection; or it was held after the services as the congregation filed out of the doors.

FUNERALS
752.

When I entered the ministry and during the early part of my career as a minister, funerals almost without exception were held in the forenoon. At nine o'clock at the "Drauerhaus" [the house of mourning] and services later at the church. The favorite days for burial were Tuesday, Thursday and Sunday.

753.

Funerals on Sunday, "mit der Karich" [with the service] were looked upon as enjoying special favor. They grew in number until the churches took action against Sunday funerals "mit der Karich." Such funerals as are now held on Sunday are in the afternoon. Only when funerals began to be held in the afternoon were they again held on Sunday.

754.

An old-time funeral had thre parts: 1. The services at the house; 2. The services at the church; and 3. The services at the grave. The minister went to the house. Arriving at the house the minister went into the room where the relatives were gathered together and gave a short intimately comforting talk. This was known as "die Trostred." After this "Trostred," if he had not done so on a visit soon after hearing of the death, the preacher wrote up the "Leweslauf" [biography] of the deceased from baptismal and marriage certificates, which were ready at hand for him. This done he waited for the time to begin the services.

No matter what the announced time of beginning "am Haus" [at the house], the services were not to begin until all "die Freind" [parents, brothers, sisters, children] had arrived and taken their places among the relatives. "Der Vorsinger" [choir director] was there to sing. He did not bring any of the "Chor" [choir] along, but if he should happen to see among the people assembled some who were known to him as able singers, he would invite them to sing along. The songbook much preferred at the house services, when held in German, was "Der Saenger am Graab" [the singer at the grave].

On one occasion my colleague at Old Goshenhoppen Church, Rev. C. R. Fetter, was an hour and a half late for a funeral. There was considerable murmuring among the mourners, many of whom were in the yard anxiously looking for the coming of the "Parre" [pastor]. Finally he drove up to the gate. The hostler took hold of the horse. Fetter got out of his buggy. With a stolid face he asked, "Sin die Freind all do?" [Are all the relatives here?] "O ya!" several quickly answered. "Dann fange mir aa," [Then we'll begin.] said Fetter with a tone as if "die Freind" were holding up the funeral.

755.

My ministry began when English services were being introduced. Often I would conduct the services at the house in English and the services at the church in German. Later, when the relative strength of the English and the German changed, I had German at the house and English at the church.

756.

Many families in our union [Lutheran and Reformed] churches had affiliations with both the Lutheran and the Reformed congregations. The children were baptized by either one of the pastors, when one of the parents was Reformed and the other Lutheran. When the children were confirmed, they usually joined the faith of the father, sometimes that of the mother, but not often. Or the boys became members of the denomination to which the father belonged and the girls to that to which the mother belonged. Often the children were permitted to make the choice.

Rev. William Fox of Sumneytown was always anxious to have boys in his catechetical class. He didn't care whether he had many girls or not, for the community tradition was to have children follow the faith of the father and not that of the mother.

Now the order of services at the house was as follows:

Whole family of the same faith
Invocation
Song
Scripture Readings
Prayer
Song
Obituary
Sermon or address
Prayer
Song
Viewing of the corpse
Procession to the church

Union family
Invocation
Song
Scripture Reading
*Prayer
Song
Obituary
Sermon
*Sermon
*Prayer
Song
Viewing of the corpse

Procession to the church

Where all the members of a family belonged to one denomination, the pastor of the family conducted the funeral alone; but where there was a union family, the pastor of the deceased conducted the funeral and the pastor of the other members of the family assisted. The parts of the service marked with an * were taken by the assistant.

The first address was always looked on as the principal one. Where the officiating clergyman was assisted, sometimes one spoke in German and the other in English.

757.

The sermon-address at the house services was called "die Schtandsbreddich" (according to William Snyder, Egypt) in Leh. Co., because the coffin was taken out of doors and the preacher spoke standing at the side of the coffin. I am inclined to think that "Schtand" had reference to the person's station in life, as in the term "Eheschtand" [matrimony]. In Mont. Co. the house sermon-address was called "die Vermaahning" or "die Vermaahning am Haus." The sermon in the church in Mont. Co. was known as "die Hauptbreddich." Often, when the officiating clergyman was assisted, the assistant would take "die Vermaahning" and the officiating clergyman "die Hauptbreddich" (or "die Leichtbreddich").

758.

Funerals were sometimes "beschtellt fer nein Uhr am Haus, awwer der Parre un der Vorsinger waare beschtellt fer halwer Zehe." [set for 9 o'clock at the house, but the pastor and the songleader were expected to be there at 9:30.] This was due to the fact that ofttimes the "Freind" were dilatory in assembling. "Die Freind" included the near relatives, the parents, brothers and sisters, and children of the deceased. At times it was more inclusive, meaning those in the "Freindschaft" [relations]. In that case the nearest relatives were specifically called "die naegschde Freind."

Rev. C. R. Fetter, the Lutheran pastor at Old Goshenhoppen, was over an hour late for a funeral. There was considerable murmuring. When he finally came, he drove up to the gate of the yard, got out of his automobile and asked, "Sin die Freind all do?" [Are the relatives all here?] The bystanders answered, "Ya." Thereupon Fetter said, "Dann welle mir aafange." [Then we want to begin.] Here he cleverly used the custom of waiting for "die Freind" as an excuse for his tardiness. [See No. 754]

759.

I had a funeral at which on account of the small rooms in the house the coffin was placed in the yard and I stood on the porch, a small roofless platform, and gave the address. Prior to my time it was a frequent occurrence to place the coffin in the yard on account of the small house.

760.
At Keelor's Church, I was told, there was a funeral. The attendants were scattered all over the place. After the coffin had been brought into the yard, one went towards those that were out at the barn and called to them, "Kummet bei, nau hen sie der Hen (Henry) haus im Hof." [Let's gather. They now have Henry (the deceased) out in the yard.]

761.
At the conclusion of the house services the coffin was taken out and put into the hearse, "der Dodewaage," and the procession formed to go to the church. This procession was headed by the pastor, who set the pace for the procession. When near the church, the pastor drove faster, "so as er Zeit hett fer sei Fuhr weckduh, eb die Leicht keemt." [so that he would have time in order to put his team away before the funeral proper arrived] The tolling of the church bell announced the coming of the funeral. And the people who had come to the church for the services there, and had not been to the house, would gather together near the entrance. If any remained seated in the church, waiting for the coming of the funeral, they occupied seats in the rear or in the side tiers of pews.

The extent of the "Freindschaft," whether large or small, was usually well known and persons could readily tell about how much space would be required to seat the relatives. After those who had come with the procession had been seated —also such relatives as had not been at the house but had waited at the church to join the mourners—the rest of the assemblage followed into the church and there the services began. The order of service was like that at the house. The sermon was more formal, not such a discourse like at the house. Doctrinal truth was more emphasized.

762.
The corpse was placed in the vestibule of the church. Only in the case of a minister (Rev. George Lutz's funeral at Unionville) or an organist (Lawrence Acker's funeral at Egypt) have I seen the body taken into the church auditorium, up before the chancel. The above holds true where the church services were held before the burial.

At Schaefferstown the interment took place before the church service. When the coffin had been brought to the cemetery, it was uncovered for a last look. Then the commitment took place. At the words, "Earth to earth, ashes to ashes, dust to dust," the sexton cast upon the coffin three shovels of ground.

The church bell was tolled from the time the funeral cortege came into sight until it had gotten to the cemetery and the body had been interred. Thereupon it was rung continuously. At Schaefferstown, after the burial, the procession reformed on the cemetery and went to the church.

Frank Beidleman of Sumneytown committed suicide. It was customary to take the corpse to the church and place it in the vestibule. But it was not permitted to take the body of a suicide into the church, so we buried the body and then went to the church to hold services.

763.
When I was young, the pallbearers, "die Dreher," were chosen from persons of like age as the deceased and from among his close friends. It was considered an honor to be a "Dreher." No one would refuse and should, as rarely happened, one refuse on account of business or work, such a one was regarded as having committed an act worthy of divine punishment.

764.
It was looked upon as obligatory to help a friend's or a neighbor's family out in case of death. The neighbors would collect at the house in the evening of the day of death "fer ausmache wege der Leicht." [to make arrangements for the funeral] The women and some men would take upon themselves the work of "rischde," that is, the cleaning of the house and the preparing of the food for the meals on the day of the funeral. Young men would be called on to act as hostlers, taking care of the teams as the people gathered for the funeral at the house and unhitching and feeding the horses upon the return to the house after the interment. Then there were those who furnished conveyances for the mourners and particularly for the immediate family. "Ich hab an die Leicht gfaahre," meant that I furnished a conveyance and acted as a driver at the funeral.

765.
The food was commonly served cold together with warm coffee. The overseer of the kitchen and the dining room was known as the "Kichedribbel." When the nearest relatives had returned from the church, also the pastor, the "Kichedribbel"—the table having been set—would invite to the first table. First, he invited the pastor, then the nearest relatives. When the table was filled, the pastor prayed. All remained at the table until the last one had finished eating—all had finished. Only then would one rise to leave the table.

At a funeral which I conducted at a Mennonite home and at which two Mennonite preachers were present, at the meal, in recognition of their custom, I asked one of the Mennonite preachers to pray before the meal and the other after.

I knew two persons, who were local tramps, who attended all funerals miles around for the sake of the meals.

766.
The pallbearers, "Dreher," were the grave diggers. After the coffin was lowered, the grave diggers closed the grave. At Schaefferstown they preceded the procession from the graveyard to the church and formed on both sides of the entrance to the church, with their right hands to their hats as the mourners filed past two by two. The pallbearers wore black gloves which were furnished by the undertaker. At a church furneral at Egypt, after the mourners have been seated, the pallbearers are brought in and seated in the front of the church. At some churches they are seated before the mourners are seated.

In the viewing of the body, after the services and

when the body is taken into the church—at churches which I served in Mont. Co.—the family and the nearest relatives were first, thereafter the friends. In such instances, after all had passed the bier, the immediate family came back to the coffin for its closing. At the Egypt church the friends and then the immediate family last are brought to the coffin.

767.

Pallbearers were selected from friends and neighbors of the deceased. In the burial of a young man, young men were the pallbearers. In the case of a young child, young children were sometimes the pallbearers. Mourning was worn by all the near relatives: long veils by the women and black hats by the men. The widow would wear her veil for a long time after the funeral, when she went to church, the veil being pinned back. The men kept their hats on in church during all the services. In the procession and in the seating at the church, the mourners sat according to seniority: parent, children, brothers and sisters. Great care was taken that each relative should have the position in the procession and among the mourning group that tradition gave to him.

Our custom at regular church services is for all persons to rise up and remain standing for prayer. At a funeral all persons remain seated during prayer. In singing the congregation used to join in with the chorister, though in subdued voices. Now the choir sings and very few if any of the congregation join in the singing.

768.

Murderers and suicides were not buried on the church graveyard, but in some corner of the land upon which they lived or where there was no land available, they were buried outside the church graveyard wall. This prohibition obtained as long as the church graveyard was a common burial ground for the congregation. When lots were sold, the church lost its right to control burials, in part, to the lot owners. — At Unionville persons may not be buried on the church cemetery who are not members of the church.

During Rev. Dechant's ministry at Keelor's Church, Frederick, Mont. Co., there was a man, Howe by name, who had deserted from the Union Army in the Civil War. The United States marshall who was sent to apprehend him came upon him in the woods back of Perkiomenville. Howe fired upon the marshall and killed him. Later Howe was captured and hung, as I remember at Fort Henry (?). Howe had been a member of the Reformed Church at Keelor's and there were those persons, of his immediate family, who pressed for sepulture in the church graveyard. Dechant opposed such a burial. Howe was then buried in the woods back of Perkiomenville.

Rev. Dechant was much in favor of the Sunday School. The Lutherans of Keelor's Church under the leadership of John Gresh's father threw out into the street the books, chairs and desk, possessed by the Sunday School, that had been organized at the church. The opponents vented their rage against Dechant. On the Sunday after the Sunday School had been thrown out of the church, they gathered at the church. One by the name of Gresh threatened to beat up Dechant. Dechant looked him in the eye and said, "Schlagscht du hatt, wann du schlechscht?" [Would you hit hard if you were to strike me?] This so nonplussed Gresh that he slunk away. There was a man at Keelor's who had nailed a horseshoe to a cane. He went and took his stand at the side of Dechant, vowing that no one should lay hands upon his pastor, "uff sei Parre."

769.

Baptismal certificates, confirmation certificates, hymnals, the "Psalder" [psalter], Bibles and even family papers were buried with the corpse.

770.a.

It was quite widely believed that the hair and nails of a corpse kept on growing for a long time after burial.

770.b.

"in der Bux fatze" [to break wind in the laurel] is a common expression. Rev. W. O. Wolford tells me that it means "to throw a monkey wrench into something." "ken Fatz wert" — not worth a fart. It was much used by tavern loafers.

771.

"Siwwe Haar un ee Kiehschwanz" [Seven hairs and one cow's tail]. This expression was used in reference to persons distantly related. "Sin sie in die Freindschaft?" (Are they relatives?) — "Ya, siwwe Haar un ee Kiehschwanz!"

772.

"Himmelreich!" — an exclamation expressing surprise. It is used in Snyder Co., Leb. Co., and Berks Co.
Mrs. N— Hummel

773.

"Schneckehann, Seeschaal" — conch shell. *Egypt*

774.

"Es kummt ne noch eemol heem." "Es kummt ne noch heem." The time will come when what they are doing to another will be done to them. The same meaning is in the expression, "Sie ware zurick bezaahlt." They will in their turn suffer for the meanness which they are now showing.
Both often heard

775.

There are some 50 odd weather vanes on houses and barns in Egypt. A lightning rod is known as a "Gwidderrut, Gwidderrutschtang," though this latter name is more specifically used for the part of the lightning rod that runs from the roof to the ground. — The weather vane is known as the "Wedderfaahne" or merely as "Faahne."

776.

The weather vane is often named after its form, "Fisch," the form of a fish, "Haahne," a cock, "Peil," an arrow. Weather vanes were often placed on church spires and could be seen at a distance. Thus if an arrow was the weather vane on the church steeple, people in the community would refer to it as "der Peil."

"Es gebt anneschder Wedder; der Peil schteht fer Rege." [The weather is going to change; the arrow indicates rain.] "Der Peil weist fer Rege."

777.

An arrowhead is commonly known as "der Peil." In Leb. Co., however, when I was a boy, arrowheads were commonly called "Insching Peil, pl. Insching Peiler."

778.

"Er hot en Abbeditt as er darich en Barig esse kennt." [He has an appetite that he could eat through a mountain.]
Mrs. David Troxell

779.

When I was a boy, there were still two houses at Schaefferstown, which had divided front doors. The one stood on the corner where Calvin Groh built his house and was occupied by a Krieger family. The other stood opposite the Ream blacksmith shop. The upper wing of the door was open and the housewife would lean on the lower wing to speak to someone on the outside. Both were log houses.

780.

Isaac Smith told me that the old log houses had three window panes to a window. In the old houses the windows opened on hinges.

781.

The cellar doors in the house on our farm, the Alexander Schaeffer farm, had bars. They had two styles of staples.
A. Here the bar was pushed in and then back.
B. Here the bar was set in.

782.

James Jacoby of Sumneytown tells me that his people had the first coal oil lamp in Sumneytown. The evening they first lit it they had the shades of the room raised and a crowd of people gathered outside to see it. The time was in the 1860's.

783.

It was believed that if you blew out the light of a coal oil lamp by blowing down into the globe, you would blow the flame into the oil, and that the lamp would explode. The belief persists even today.
Mont, Leb

784.

To light the coal oil lamp a sliver was taken, set afire in the stove and then applied to the wick. Or paper was cut into this strips and rolled up spirally and used for lighters. ("lamplighter," "lighter")

785.

To fashion a "Mickewehrer," our English name was "fly-chaser," a newspaper was taken, fastened over a stick and cut into strips. It was used at the table when eating.

786.

"Mickegift" [fly poison] was a chemical paper which was put in a saucer. Water was poured upon it. It was used as a fly poison. Frequently seen at one time.

787.

"Mickebabier" was the common name for tanglefoot fly paper.

788.

"Mickedier" was the common name for a screen door.

789.

"Mickegscharr" was a fly net or fly harness that was put on over the regular harness to protect the horse against flies. It was made either of leather or of cord. In the latter case it was called "Mickegaarn." I am inclined to believe that the first fly nets were handmade, woven by hand as were the fish nets, hence "Gaarn." The name "Mickegaarn" was heard by me in Mont. Co. and was applied both to the leathern and the cord fly nets.

Excrementa

790.

Excrementa are known as "Dreck" [dirt] and sometimes from the shape [round], also as "Gnoddle" [turd].

"Dreck"

"Kiehdreck" [cow], "Geilsdreck" [horse], "Katzedreck" [cat], "Hunsdreck" [dog], "Seidreck" [hog], "Haschdreck" [deer], "Hinkeldreck" [chicken], "Scheissdreck" [excrementa of all kinds], "Dauwedreck" [pigeon], "Raddedreck" [rat], "Meisdreck" [mouse], "Mickedreck" [fly].

"Gnoddle"

"Geilsgnoddle," [horse], "Hunsgnoddle," [dog], "Schofgnoddle" [sheep], "Haschgnoddle" [deer].

791.

Excrementa when occuring in quantity or when collected for manure is termed "Mischt" [manure]: "Geilsmischt" [horse], "Kiehmischt" [cow], "Oxemischt" [ox], "Hinkelmischt" [chicken], "Seimischt" [hog] and "Haasemischt" [rabbit]. This last term is from rabbit "farms."

792.

"Mischthof," that part of the barnyard reserved for the collection of manure during the year; or the pile of manure itself. "Mischtpen," the manure yard in Mont. Co. with the meaning of "Mischthof."

"Mischthaufe," the manure pile. "Mischt schprehe," to scatter the manure in the fields.

"Mischtschpreher," the mechanical manure spreader; or the one who spreads the manure by hand.

"Mischtschlidde" — a sled used to take the manure from the stable to the manure heap. It was drawn by a horse. However, the wheelbarrow was usually employed. "Mischtgawwel" — a four-pronged fork used in working with manure. "Mischtwagge" — the farm wagon rigged up for hauling manure. Planks were laid on the frame of the wagon. They were termed "Mischtblanke." Two planks were placed on the side and were raised up as the load became higher. "Mischtbrieh" — the liquid manure which collects around rotten manure heaps.

793.

"mischde" — a verb. 1. to put dung on the land. "Die Woch will ich's Land mischde un die naegscht Woch bluge." [This week I want to manure the land and plow next week.] "Der Gaarde is gut gemischt." [The garden is well manured.] 2. to pass excrementa.

"Do hot der Hasch gemischt die letscht Nacht." [Here the deer defecated last night.] "Mei Gaul is grank; er kann nimmi mischde." [My horse is sick; he is unable to defecate.] Not infrequently the verb "mischde" is used in preference to the more common and vulgar "scheisse" in reference to animals.

794.

"ausmischde, die Schtell ausmischde," to take the dung out of the stables. This was done in the past on Saturday morning.

Old cemeteries
796. [sic]

The cemetery at the Old Goshenhoppen church was very wet and in rainy weather would collect in the open graves. They had a long-handled scoop with which they dipped out the water. When Shoemaker was janitor at Old Goshenhoppen and we had a funeral, he would come to me—in rainy or wet weather—and say, "Parre, when I leave the church while you are preaching, I do so to go out and dip the water out of the grave. Do not prolong the services or water will again collect in the grave!"

797.

In many old cemeteries the tombstones were fieldstones, "Feldschtee." They were crudely shapen. In cemeteries: at Schaefferstown we find limestone tombstones; at Old Goshenhoppen red shale stones; at Egypt and Unionville they are of slate. The initials of the dead were scratched on, with or without the date of death. These "Feldschtee" were trimmed off by some mason. In some old communities there were persons skiled in cutting tombstones, having learned the trade in Europe. (See the Stone Church.) First there were "Feldschtee," then "Sand-schtee" [sandstones], then marble and granite.

798.

The old cemeteries were not divided into plots. The place of burial was "der Roi noh" [in a row in sequence of death]. There seems, however, to have been a tacit understanding that room was to be reserved for a husband to lie alongside of his wife and vise versa. At Schaefferstown and at Egypt church cemeteries, there are burial places reserved for the burial of persons who have no lots. These are known as "die Commons."

799.

The symbol of the cross is almost wholly absent from our cemeteries. On tombstones are found: 1. at Schaefferstown, on early stones, skull and crossbones; 2. at Egypt, tulips and the six-point star; 3. at Unionville, tulips. The tombstone inscriptions run from the simple initials on early tombstones to a recital of the full name, date of birth, date of marriage, date of death, and the number of children. Sometimes the funeral text, a stanza from a hymn or a sentimental verse were added.

800.

At the open grave the hymn "Asleep in Jesus" has been the beloved hymn for generations. When German services were held, the favorite at the grave was "Nun bringen wir den Leib zur Ruh" [Now we bring the body to rest]. Other favorite funeral hymns were "Alle Menschen muessen sterben" [All men must die], "Wer weiss wie nah' ist mir mein Ende?" [Who knows how near my end?], "Jesus, meine Zuversicht" [Jesus, my comfort] and "Ich bin ein Kindlein arm und klein" [I am a child small and poor]. The hymns at the house and at the open grave were taken from the "Saenger am Grabe" [Singer at the grave], but the hymns in the church were taken from the church hymnal. Just as the hymnals differed, so the two services differed.

801.

At the Old Goshenhoppen Church there were two biers, called "Dodebaer," on which the coffins were placed and carried from the church to the grave. I was told that there was a time when the coffins were made without handles. The Old Goshenhoppen "Dodebaer" (note -ae- as in Lambert) had four handles and legs to stand on. It looked all the world like a wheelbarrow without the wheel and the front board and with handles at both ends, though longer.

802.

In my ministry I had several members (one of them Mrs. Caroline Jacoby of Sumneytown) who would kiss my hand. Members, older persons, addressed me as "ihr" (Sumneytown) and still do so (Egypt), instead of "du." Zacharias Gerhart of Green Lane always used "ihr" and "sie." "Hen ihr des schun gheert, Parre?" [Have you heard this, pastor?] "Welle sie mitfaahre, Parre?" [Would you like to drive along, pastor?] In the years of my ministry at Sumneytown, I was also addressed now and then as "Harr Parre" [German: "Herr Pfarrer"].

Seating in church

803.

In all the older churches the consistory sat in a body in the short pews to the left of the pulpit and chancel. The pews in which the consistory sat were known as "Eldeschder Schtiel" [Elders' chairs]. At Schaefferstown Reformed, at the Sumneytown church, at Keelor's church, at Old Goshenhoppen and at the Egypt church, the consistory sat to the left of the pulpit, i.e. on the left side of the pastor as he preaches.

At Egypt, when I came here in 1926, the trustees sat in the short pews to the right of the pulpit, to the right of the preacher as he faced the congregation. This preserved the distinction between the ordained consistory and the unordained trustees.

804.

The old married men sat in the gallery to the right of the preacher as he preached and faced the audience. The young and old unmarried men sat on the left gallery. At Sumneytown, at Keelor's, in the Old Goshenhoppen church and at Egypt this was the seating.

805.

The young unmarried girls sat under the gallery upon which the married men sat. This arrangement enabled the young unmarried men to see them. The older women sat under the gallery upon which the unmarried men sat. The central part [of the downstairs hall] was occupied by the married women. We must remember that in older times the men and women did not sit together in church. Later, when the men left the galleries and came down into the auditorium, they sat on the side of the church on which the consistory sat. This was true in the churches mentioned in No. 804.

806.

When I was young, it was not customary for the sexes to commune together. At a communion service, first, the pastor, then the consistory and the old men—such a former elders—, the married men, the single men, the old women, the middle-aged women, and finally the single women communed. The communicants did not come forward pew by pew, nor were they ushered out, but they came voluntarily, seeking to come forward with persons of like age and, if possible, of the same catechetical class.

807.

When my pastor, Rev. A. J. Bachman, distributed the bread and the wine, he would recite Biblical passages, stanzas of hymns, etc. Before the pronunciation of the benediction, he would give an "Ermaahning" [admonishment] to each table.

808.

Communing was known as "zum Nachtmol geh" or "es Nachtmol nemme" [to take Holy Communion]. "Wie viel sin zum Nachtmol gange?" [How many took communion?] The members came forward to the chancel railing. One service was known as a "Disch" [table].

"Heit am Nachtmol hen mer siwwe Disch ghat." [Today at Communion we had seven tables.] At Keelor's Church instead of "Disch" the word "Ring" was used. "Heit am Nachtmol hen mer siwwe Ring ghat." The favorite German communion hymn was "Ich komm jetzt als ein armer Gast." [I come now as a poor guest.]

The distribution of the bread and the wine at Holy Communion by the minister was called "es Nachtmol ausdeele, ausgewwe." In referring to private communion of a sick or feeble person, they said, "Der Parre hot re Nachtmol gebrocht." [The pastor brought her communion.] "Parre, hoscht schun all dei Nachtmeeler (Nachtmoler) gewwe?" [Have you given all the private communions?]

809.

Confirmed young girls and boys would wear their confirmation clothes to several subsequent communion services. When I was young, the traditional time for buying new clothes was just prior to the Holy Communion service.

810.

In singing German hymns, Rev. A. J. Bachman [Schaefferstown] would read the hymn through to the end, then repeat the first two lines of the first stanza. He would urge the congregation with the words, "Singet alle mit!" [All sing along!] The congregation would sing the first two lines and the organist would stop playing. Then Rev. Bachman would read the third line the congregation with the organ sang this line; so to the fourth line. The last two lines Bachman would read out as one and the congregation would sing them. This was known as "lining out" a hymn; in PG "ausleine." This way of singing was very impressive when smoothly carried out. The congregation sang only as much of the hymn as the preacher read out at one time.

When Rev. F. R. Shafer conducted services at Schaefferstown, he was unfamiliar with this manner of singing hymns. He announced "Hallelujah, schoener Morgen," [Hallelujah, beautiful morning] and read the first line. The congregation sang the line; the organist stopped playing and waited. Shafer did not know what was wrong and stood there at a loss what to do. Then a voice out of the congregation—my uncle, A. S. Brendle—called out the second line and the service proceeded, the organist playing right through the hymn.

New students for the ministry were not permitted to pronounce the benediction, so they would ask the blessing of the benediction in the form of a prayer. Shafer at that time was a student for the ministry. After the benediction the old preachers were accustomed to say, "Gehet hin in Friede." [Go forth in peace.] Shafer had planned to conclude the services with the same words after his benediction prayer, but he forgot them. He started, "Gehet hin in," paused and then added "Schtille." [stillness]

811.
In older times church services did not start promptly on the appointed time. Nonetheless, the preachers would always announce the services with "precies" [precisely]. "So der Herr gewill [sic], gedenken wir regelmaessiger Gottesdienst zu feiern an dieser Staette vier Wochen von heute morgens precies an zehn Uhr." [The Lord willing we plan to celebrate at this place the regular worship service four weeks from today in the morning precisely at 10 o'clock.]

812.
"Ring," a ring; a table of communicants. "ringle," to put a ring in a pig's snout to prevent it from rooting or digging up the sod. *Leb*

"ausringe" [to wring out]. "Die Wesch ausringe," to wring out the wash. The wash ringer is called "die Weschringer." It seems to me that both these words were taken over in late years from the English. The older people speak about "Wesch ausdrehe," which was done by hand, and not of "Wesch ausringe."

"die Bell ziege, pp. gezoge" — to ring the bell.

813.
"Sie hen ihm awwer der Jacket verhackt." They turned him and his plans down cold.
Common expression, especially in Mont and Leh

814.
"So arig wie siwwe Daag Regewedder." As dire as seven days of rainy weather. *Common expression*

EXPRESSIONS FOR WORTHLESSNESS
815.
"Ken drei Cent wert." [Not worth three cents] "Er hot ken 5 Cent zu seim Naame." [He hasn't 5 cents to his name.] *Common*

816.
"Ken Tschaa Duwack wert." [Not worth a chew of tobacco] *Quite common*

817.
"Ken hohle buhn wert." [Not worth a hollow bean] *Do, Leb*

818.
"Ken (roder) heller Cent wert." [Not worth a (red) cent] "Heller" — a coin. *Leb*

819.
"Ken Cent wert." [Not worth a cent] *Common*

820.
"Ken Vaddel wert zwische Brieder." [Not worth a quarter between brothers] *Occasionally heard*

821.
"Nix wert, wu die Haut ihn aaregt." [Not worth anything where the skin touches him] *Quite common*

822.
"Nix wert, wu mer ihn aaregt." [Worth nothing, wherever one touches him] *Do*

823.
"Himmelswelt!" [Heaven's world!], an exclamation. "Was in die Himmelswelt witt nau duh?" [What on earth do you want to do now?] "Was in Goddes Himmelswelt bischt am duh?" [What in God's creation are you doing?] "Himmelreich" [kingdom of heaven], an exclamation. "Himmelreich, waar des net gut?" [Ye gods, wasn't that good?]

824.
If a child is not born on the reckoned day, that is, if the birth is "delayed", then the child will be a boy.
Dr. Hertz, Lititz, Lanc

825.
In case the umbilical cord got sore, a piece of linen was taken, parched on both sides and wrapped around the cord with the neck turned downward. *Do*

826.
The Lititz Moravian Church bell is rung every day at 11:30. This custom, it is said, has existed for 140 years. — On account of the corpse house at the Moravian Church, the dead were never taken into the church.

At Schaefferstown, 12 miles north of Lititz, the church bell was rung every day at 11 o'clock (11 o'clock, as I remember). One week the bell of the Reformed Church was rung and the following week the bell of the Lutheran Church was rung. This served as a clock for the farmer in the field and for the worker in the factory. I do not know whether the custom is still continued. [John Hickernell, a lifelong resident of Schaefferstown, reports that it has been at least 50 years since this custom was discontinued.]

At Schaefferstown, no corpses were taken into the church. The interment took place before the church services.

827.
"Fluggelnescht," a flirt (in the milder sense); an adultress (in the harsher sense). A word used in Lanc. Co. *Willis Gibble, Lititz*

828.
"boose, pp. geboost," to do mischief; to do malicious mischief. A word used at Lititz by Willis Gibble on October 1, 1936. Found in Lambert on page 31.

829.
To practice marksmanship for deer, a buggy or wagon wheel was taken. A small board was nailed to it. It was rolled downhill and the board was fired at. The revolving wheel causing the board to rise and fall represented the bounding of a deer. Collected on October 1, 1936, from —- Richard of Catasauqua, formerly of Monroe Co. His mother was a Beidel.

SQUIRREL CALLS

830.
To call squirrels, imitating their calls, the forefinger was put in the mouth and pressed against the cheek and then blown. (I can't do this.) *Do*

831.
A.
Squirrel hunters would pick up a stone and throw it so that if fell on the other side of the tree. This would bring the squirrel around the tree and present a shot to the hunter.
B.
Some hunters took off their coats and hung them on the bushes. Then they moved cautiously around the tree. The squirrel would retreat upon seeing the coat.
C.
A dog trained to hunt squirrels is called an "Eechhaasehunt." Such a dog would track a squirel on the ground to a tree, then bark. It was something like a "coon" dog. My uncle, John Brendle, had one.
"der Eechhaas," the squirrel. This PG term for squirrel is not heard in the Perkiomen region around Green Lane or Sumneytown. The common PG term there is "Schwaerl;" "Rot Schwaerl" — red squirrel; "Groh Schwaerl" — gray squirrel.

832.
To call squirrels imitate their calls by kissing with an indraw the back of the hand, as if it were a sucking kiss. *Green Lane*

833.
To call squirrels take a walnut in the left palm and another in the right palm. Strike the walnut in the right hand rapidly over the walnut in the left hand. All these [830-833] are good imitations. *Lanc*

834.
A grouse when it rises, turns to the right or to the left. When it alights, it turns to the right or to the left. *Do as 830*

835.
A grouse will rise three times. On account of the small expanse of its wings, it becomes weary and can hardly rise the third time. Thus, if a hunter flushes a grouse three times, he will bet a good shot the third time. *Do*

836.
To hunt woodcocks, woodsnipes, one should walk into the woods a little way, stand still and then slowly look around. Walk a bit farther, stand still and look around slowly. The woodcock, "woodsnipe" (so he called the bird), catching the eye of the hunter, will flush as the hunter moves. *Do*

837.
Fishing rods were made of ironwood, with a fork at the end. The line was tied to the middle of the rod and wound around the fork. This enabled the fisherman to let out or retrieve the line by turning the rod. *Do*

838.
When the hunting season for deer was closed, they were hunted with silent dogs, that is, dogs that do not bark when trailing. These dogs wore sheep bells. *Do*

839.
Deer were very scarce in the 1890's. *Do*

840.
When a squirrel was treed, the hunter would hang his coat on a bush, then silently sneak around the tree. The squirrel would not move, seeing the coat. The hunter always shot for the head, looking for the ears. *Do*

841.
At Green Lane, when a squirrel was treed and it would keep itself on the opposite side of the tree, the hunters would throw a stone or roll it on the ground beyond the tree. This would cause the squirrel to come around and afforded the hunter a shot. *Green Lane*

842.
Hunters who were still hunting for squirrels would never sit so that they were on the side of the tree on which the hole was located, but always on the opposite side. They were of the opinion that a squirrel on coming out of the hole immediately goes to the other side of the tree. *Do*

843.
Suckers were speared by the light of a pine knot torch. *Do as 840*

844.
Shad were netted with a seine that was fastened at one end to the bank and dragged around in a half-circle. *Do*

845.
Richard saw a bald eagle swoop down and catch a big shad. As the eagle rose, the shad's tail was pointed toward the direction of flight. The eagle dropped the shad, dropped on it as it fell and caught it, so that it was turned head on. It might have been the the osprey. *Do*

846.
To locate a bee tree, a fire was built. After the embers had been burned, a honeycomb was thrown onto the fire. The odor attracted the bees. Honey was offered to them. Heavily laden they rose up and flew toward the bee tree. Their direction of flight was observed and followed. Another fire was built and the same procedure was followed until the bee tree was located. It was cut down in cold weather. *Do*

847.
To collect maple sap, holes were bored in the maple tree, sometimes three or four above one another. The

spouts were made of elderberry wood with the pith taken out. *Do*

848.
At one time, so my father says, maple sap was collected and boiled down into syrup in the lower part of Leb. Co. *Personal*

849.
Game

"Reef rolle." Rolling buggy wheels, hoops of barrels, discarded iron rims of wheels, was a common sport among children. *Do*

850.
Boys' game

"Skipping stones." Flattish stones were taken and thrown so as to strike the water on the flat side and then skip on. That boy was "champion" whose stone made the most skips. Especially at mill dams. *Do*

850.a.
Moses Dissinger preached near Adamstown in Lanc. Co. He was hot on the trail of — Brendel for conversion. Brendel and others played cards. Card playing was an abomination in the sight of Mose and so was cursing. Brendel came to the understanding with Mose that if he would say "Trump" three times on the pulpit, he, Brendel, would quit playing cards. If he would say "bei Gott!" three times on the pulpit, Brendel would buy Mose a new hat. Both agreed.

Mose preached as follows: If one passes a tavern at night as late as two o'clock in the morning, one hears nothing but "Trump! Trump! Trump!" And so on until towards the close of the sermon, when he said, "We must not forget that 'bei Gott sin mir gebore, bei Gott lewe mir un bei Gott gschtarwe mir!'" [with God we were born, with God we live and with God we die]
John Brendel, Denver

PRAYERS
851.
A night prayer:

"Jesu lieben ist besser
Als alles wissen."

[Loving Jesus is better
Than all knowledge]

Grandmother of Mrs. Harold Roth, Cementon,

852.
A night prayer:

"Ein gleines Kind, as beten kann,
Des hot der liewe Heiland gern."

[A small child, who can pray,
Is dearly loved by the Savior] *Do*

853.
Sung in the evening at family worship:

"Soll diese Nacht die letschde sei,
In dieser Jammerthaal,

So nimm mich, Harr, zu Himmel ein,
Zu auserwaehlder Schaar."

[Should this night be the last
In this vale of tears,

So take me, Lord, into heaven
To the chosen multitude.] *Do*

854.
Sung in the morning:

"Was mich auf dieser Welt betriebt,
Das wort (wehrt) eine kurze Seit,
Was aber meine Seele liebt,
Das bleibt in Ewichkeit."

[That which saddens me in this world,
That lasts a long time
What my soul loves however,
That lasts eternally.] *Do*

855.
Sung during the day:

"Meine Heimat ist nicht hier,
Meine Heimat ist nicht hier,
Ich weis eine bessre Heimat als dies,
Meine Heimat ist nicht hier."

[My home is not here,
My home is not here,
I know a better home than this,
My home is not here.] *Do*

856.
Sung during the day:

"Leiden missen wir auf Erden,
Leiden missen wir im Tod,
Aber wenn wir nieber kommen,
Ruhen wir im Jesu Schoss."

[We suffer on earth,
We must suffer in death,
But when we come over there,
We will rest in Jesus' lap.] *Do*

857.
Sung during the day:

"Ich wein, ich bet,
Ich schau den Himmel aa,
Ich bein [sic] ein armer Pilger hier,
Und geh noch Kaa-naa-aan."

[I weep, I pray,
I look toward the heavens,
I am a poor pilgrim here,
And go toward Canaan.]
Do

(It may be taken as almost certain that prayers and songs, which have High German words, go back to a printed source. It is noteworthy that in prayers an effort was made to use the Biblical German or the German of the pulpit.)

858.

Counting out rhyme:

"Eens, zwee, drei,
Zucker uff em Breih,
Salz uff em Schpeck,
Johann geht weck."

[One, two, three,
Sugar on the porridge,
Salt on the bacon,
John goes away.]

John Roth, Cementon

859.

"Mei Mammi backt Kuche,
Sie backt sie zu hatt,
Sie backt sie beim Dausend
Un gebt mir net satt.

Mammi, O Mammi,
Wann's widder so machscht,
So mach ich mei Bindel
Un saag, 'Gudi Nacht.'"

[My mommy bakes cakes,
She bakes them too hard,
She bakes them by the thousand
And doesn't give me enough of them.

Mammy, oh Mammy,
If you do this again,
I'll pack my bundle
And say, 'Good night!']
Do

"mei Bindel mache" — to make up my bundle to go on a journey.

860.

Williem Wieder of Cementon in telling why he did not go to church, said, "Ich warr beloge darich die ganz Woch un wann ich in die Karich geh, warr ich noch uff der heilich Sunndaag beloge." [I am lied to through the entire week and when I go to church, I am lied to on the holy Sunday.]
Do

861.

For earache, put an onion and sugar on a plate. Apply heat with a hot iron. Take the drop of liquor that results and put it into the affected ear.
Mrs. Lottie Strauss, Treichler's

862.

"Ehrenbreis," Veronica officinalis, is always green under the snow.
Do

863.

"Schprus" = hemlock. "Schprustee" is good for colds.
Elmer Walck, Long Run, near Weisport

864.

To get rid of warts, take white or black wool and tie off the wart. Take the first knot around the wart in the name of the Father, the second in the name of the Son and the third in the name of the Holy Ghost. Then take off the string and bury it under the eaves of the house.
Do as No. 862

865.

To cure ivy poisoning, lay open the Bible to a place where the names of the Holy Trinity appear, "wu die drei heechschde Naame sin," and place it thus opened under the pillow, so that the afflicted person will lie on the names of the Trinity.
Do

866.

To cure "Hatzschparr" [a digestive disorder], use the following: "N— N-(the name of the afflicted person), Hatzschparr, Aawax, weich aus den Ribbe, Wie Yesus Grischdus aus der Gribbe." [N. N., liver-growth, leave the ribs, as Jesus Christ left the manger.]
Do

867.

To cure "Hatzschparr" [See No. 866], "Lay the child with its head toward the sunrise. Pass your thumbs down front and out under the ribs back to the spine" and say, "Hatzschparr un Aagewax, weiche vun dem N— N— seine Ribbe, Wie unser Harr Yesus aus seiner Gribbe. Vater X, Sohn X, Heilicher Geist X." [Digestive disorder and liver-growth, Depart from N— N—'s ribs, As Jesus from the manger. Father X, Son X, Holy Ghost X.] Where the X appears, make a cross on the body.
*Mrs. Walck,
as she personally performed the "Brauch" [powwow].*

868.

The song, "Datt driwwe, datt drowwe, wu der Bellebaam schteht," is sung to the melody, "Where, oh where, has my little dog gone?"
Walck

869.

In Deep Run, worldly songs are called, "Schtroosselieder" [street songs].
Do

870.

Song [fragment]:

"Do waar ich emoll in Deitschland,
Do waar ich en aarmer Mann,
Do hen die Leit mir en Hinkel gschenkt,
Noh waar ich en reicher Mann.

[I once was in Germany,
Then I was a poor fellow
Then the folks gave me a chicken,
Then I was a rich man.

[Chorus]

[Cockle-doodle-doo is the name of my little chicken.]

"Gickerigie heest mei gleines Hinkelie." *Do*

871.
Mrs. Lottie Straus tells me that the version of "Billy Lyon" known to her began: "Do waar mer moll noch Redding." [Once we went to Reading] "Do waar mer," the plural with "waar," is not infrequently heard. "Do waar mer die anner Woch noch Harrisburg." [The other week we went to Harrisburg.]

872.
Counting out rhyme:

"Hicke, hacke Hollerschtock,
Wie viel Hanner hot der Bock?
Eins, zwei, drei,

[Hicke, hacke elderberry bush,
How many horns has the ram?
One, two, three,

Un du bischt frei."

And you are free.]

William Straus

873.
Counting out rhyme:

"Eens, zwee, drei odder vier,
Meedel, wann du danze witt,
Danz mit mir.
Finf, sex, siwwe odder acht,
Meedel, wann du heiere witt,
Heier diese Nacht."

[One, two three or four,
Maiden if you want to dance,
Dance with me.
Five, six, seven or eight,
Maiden if you want to marry,
Marry tonight.]

Mrs. Lottie Straus

874.
"Scharlatti, Scharlatti,
Geh mit uns ins Graas.
Do peift der Vogel,
Do dribbelt der Haas.

"Wie hoch is der Himmel,
Wie zwitzert die Schtern.
Was gleiche die Buwe
Die Maedcher so gern."

[Scharlatti, Scharlatti,
Come with me into the grass.
There the bird sings,
There the rabbit hops.

How high is the heaven,
How the star twinkles.
My, how the boys
Like the girls.] *Do*

875.
Raedsel [Riddle]
"Was waxt wann mer's fiedert un schtarbt, wann mer's drenkt?"

Walck

[What grows when one feeds it and dies when one gives it to drink?]
Fire.

876.
James Jacoby, wholly reliable, tells me that Mrs. C. R. Fetter, wife of Rev. C. R. Fetter of the Old Goshenhoppen Church, "brauchs" for "Blut schtille" [powwows to still the flow of blood]. This Jacoby, since 1913 and to date, 1936, has repeatedly told me.

877.
A woman sentenced to death by a judge was told by him that she could have her freedom if she would propound an unanswerable riddle in "drei Setze" [three sentences]. She compiled and gave the following:

"Uff em Ginni Ginni geh ich,
Uff em Ginni Ginni schteh ich,
Uff em Ginni Ginni bin ich frei."

"En Schweinche"

[On Ginni Ginni I walk,
On Ginni Ginni I stand,
On Ginni Ginni I am free.]

[a piglet]

Joe Fenstermacher

A SERIES GOTTEN FROM WILLIS GIBBLE OF LITITZ

Gibble is a Dunkard and these beliefs and ways are found according to him among them.

878.
A knife falling to the floor from the table while the family is eating means a male visitor will be coming; a falling fork means a female is coming.

Also from my wife

879.

If salt is spilled, bad luck will follow. To avoid bad luck take a pinch of salt and cast it over the shoulder.

880.

"Maryerot,
 Dreck im Kot."

[Red sky in the
 means rain.]

881.

"If the swallows fly high, the weather will be clear and dry."

882.

A ring around the moon foretells rain or snow. The number of stars within the ring indicate the number of days until rain or snow.

883.

"Drei kiehle Marye,
Bringe Reye unne Sarye."

[Three cool mornings
will bring rain with trouble.]

884.

"Wann der Reyevoggel (cuckoo) lockt, geb's Reye." [When the cuckoo calls there will be rain.]

885.

The turtle dove calls: "Gut Blut! gut Blut!" [Good blood! Good blood!]

886.

"Mannheim, Mannheim, du aarmi Schtadt,
Drucke Brod un des net satt."

[Manheim, you poor town,
Dry bread and still not enough.]

("Mannem" was often substituted for "Mannheim".)

887.

"Dannegaal, Dannegaal,
Where they eat potatoes shell and all!"

(Note the word "shell." In our English "shell" was and is to some extent used to denote the skins of potatoes, the pods of peas, of beans, etc. It is our English for the dialectal "Schaal" and used in its place.)

888.

"Was sauft un sauft un watt net voll?"
[What drinks and drinks and can't fill up?]

die alt Miehl" [the old mill]

889.

"Down in the meadow stands an old red bull,
He eats and eats and never gets full."

The old mill.

890.

Blow upon a dandelion seed head, one breath. The number of seeds that remain on the head show the number of years before your marriage.

891.

"Unser Vadder, wer du bischt,
Marye faahre mer widder Mischt.
Freidaag faahre mer die grosse Load,
Bis Samschdaag faahre der Schimmel dod."

[Our father, who you are,
Tomorrow we haul manure.
Friday we haul the big load,
Until Saturday the horse is dead.]

892.

"Heh Jeck, schteh uff,
Zieg die Schteeg aa.
Schpring die Hosse nunner,
Schteck die Kuh aa,
Die Ladann hot en Kalb."

[Hey Jake, get up,
Pull on the steps.
Run your pants down,
Ignite the cow,
The lantern has a calf.]

893.

"Bank," bench. This word is used by the Mennonites with the meaning "church board," in place of our [the former Reformed Church in which Brendle was a pastor for 50 years] "consistory."

"Die Bank saagt as des geye Gottesgesetz is." The church board says this is against the law of God.

894.

For sweeny: take a round stone and rub it over sweeny, saying:

"Fleisch, Mark un Bein,
Schwein nicht mehr wie dieser Stein."

Say the first part of the Lord's Prayer, up to "Give us this day." Make no crosses.

895.

"Phenaagel" — "I want to phenaagel in." I want to butt in. *Used at Lititz.*

896.

"Garwli" — a sheaf of wheat. When grain was cut and bound by hand, the sheaves were larger than the sheaves made by the binder. Hence the diminutive.

OMENS, "AAZEECHE", OF DEATH
[from Willis Gibble of Lititz, Pa.]

897.
If a fruit tree near the house blooms out of season—as in late fall.

898.
If a clock strikes tha has not been wound up for a long time.

899.
If a mirror breaks.

900.
If a dog wails at night after a wedding.

901.
If a bird flies at night against a window of a house, particularly when there is a sick person in the house.

All these omens have to do with the family or near relatives. Nr. 900 a dog belonging to the family and a wedding in the family.

902.
Children with blue arteries across the bridge of the nose will not live long.

903.
If a horse neighs at a funeral, while the horses stand hitched during the services at the house or at the church or in the procession, there will be a wedding.

904.
The Dunkard "Liewesmaal" (when spoken of in English, "love feast") was followed by the "Abendmaal" [Holy Communion]. The unleavened bread was baked by the deacons' wives and minister's wife in silence or with only necessary speaking.
Note the names "Liewesmaal" and "Abendmaal." Note also the baking of the unleavened bread in silence. I heard "Liewesmaal" used by persons who did not belong to the Dunkards [The Church of the Brethren].

905.
The kiss at the "Liewesmaal" was called [der] "heilige Kuss." The basin used to wash the feet was called "Fusszuwwer." Anointing was "gsalbt."

906.
The white headdress worn by the Dunkard women was known as "Gebethaupt," Among Mennonites of Montgomery County, Pa. it is called "Betkapp."

907.
The Mennonites call the pulpit "Breddicherschtul;" the Dunkards call it "Breddicherschtand." The latter name is due to the circumstance that for a long time the Dunkards were opposed to a raised pulpit and the preachers stood by the side of a table when preachig.
(Above is the Note 757 on the house funeral sermon being called "Schtandbreddich." Is there a relation here and is our name due to the cause given by Snyder? In our English we call a small table-like piece of furniture used to put on some object like the Bible, lamp, album, a "stand." Cf. "washstand." cf #914.

908.
In asking persons to pray at a meal the words commonly used by the Dunkards are:

A. "Nemm die Gelegeheit fer danke."
B. "Nemm die Freiheit fer danke."

In my own personal experience, when called on to pray at a meal in a private home, I was asked thus:

C. "Parre, sei frei." Compare this with B.
D. "Parre, saag Dank." Compare this with A.
E. "Parre, frog der Seye."

Note that in all these the word "bede" [to pray] is not used.

909.
Corpses were kept in an "Eisbax" during the summer; on a cooling board in the winter. Corpses were taken into the church, though not those of suicides. Suicides were buried in a corner of the farm or of the cemetery.

910.
The church harvest festival of the Dunkards was called "Erndegemee" (our "Erndkarich"). It was held in barns which were still full of unthreshed grain. It was held during the month of August.
The election of deacons was often held at the "Erndegemee." It was regarded as a special honor and also a special blessing for a farm, to have the "Erndegemee" within its borders.

911.
Grain when reaped with the cradle was allowed to lie on the ground to be rained on. This was supposed to facilitate threshing. This was called "reetse."
Cf. our saying: "Der Hawwer sucht sei Mehl uff em Feld." (Green Lane) [Oats looks for its flour in the field.]

912.
Gleaning was permitted. The farmer would thresh out the gleanings for the poor. One year a woman gathered 15 bushels of gleanings on the Christ Brubaker farm near Neffsville [a town south of Lititz].

[The end of the items from Willis Gibble of Lititz, Pa.]

913.
William Straus of Treichlers, Pa. tells me that the Wippoorwill is known as "Moivogel" in the Lehigh Valley.

914.

This morning, October 5, 1936, I visited Charles Snyder of Ballietsville. His wife was a daughter of David Miller, who was the son of Daniel Miller. The wife of Daniel Miller was a daughter of Jacob Lindaman and his wife, Elizabeth Newhardt. Daniel Miller was baptized by the Rev. Gobrecht. There are some fine baptismal certificates in the family.

I asked Snyder about the "Redder" [wheels] on the barns. I told him that I had heard say that they were a protection against witches. He started to explain that they were put on in front of the mows "fer alli Unreinigkeit weck zu halde" [to keep away all impurity]. I asked him how this could be accomplished. He, drawing a circle in the air with his forefinger, said: "Es geht rum un is zu un hot ken End odder Blatz wu sie aagreife kenne. Un sie misse en Blatz hawwe wu sie Halt draa nemme kenne." [It goes around and is closed and has no end or place where they can take hold.]

This is the first person who told me that the barn signs had an occult meaning.

Present at the time were his wife, his daughter, Mrs. Sidney Wotring and his granddaughter Marie.

Later note: On December 1, 1936, Charles Snyder tells me that his father came over from Germany as a young boy. He married a Sauerwein girl.

Snyder was a carpenter by trade and this belief may have come to him through association with other carpenters. I do not see how it came to him from his father, i.e. from Germany. It was a "thing" that would come up in the carpenter trade. I believe that there was a tradition, perhaps not widespread, that the barn signs had the significance attributed to them by Snyder.

GREETINGS

915.

A person meeting another in the morning commonly says:

"Gude Mariye" or "Gudde Marye" with a nod of his head. The answer is commonly the same as the greeting, though an older generation replied: "Danke."

916.

A person meeting another during the day or in the afternoon would say "Scheener Daag" or "Guden Taach," although the latter was infrequent. I heard "Guden Taach" when it was addressed to me by persons who used "ihr" and "sie."

917.

A person greeting another "Hot ihm die Zeit gebodde." [bade him the time] Not to acknowledge the greeting was an affront. "Ich hab ihm die Zeit gebodde un er hot sich net bedankt (hot mer ken Anwatt gewwe) un nau guck ich en nimme aa." [I bade him the time of the day and he did not return the greeting (gave me no answer) and now I no longer look at him.]

918.

In Lebanon County a general greeting was: "Wie geht's?" [How are you?] with a nod of the head. To this the answer was:
  A. "So zimmlich." [So so.]
  B. "Zimmlich gut." [Rather well.]
  C. "Nix zu braecke." [Nothing to brag about.]
  D. "So, wie mer's dreibt." [Just as one makes it.]
  E. "So langsam." [Slowly.]
  F. (humorously) "Uff zwee Beh." [On two legs.]
  G. "Nix zu bralle." [Nothing to brag about.]
  H. "Nix zu kicke." [Nothing to kick about.]
  I. "Ganz gut, danke." [Quite well, thank you.]

919.

In the evening the greeting is "Gudenowed," "Gutnowed" or "Guddenowed." The answer is the same as in Nr. 915.

920.

When taking leave of another, one would say:
  A. "Adyee," "Hadyee." [From the French "adieu"] This was rather commonly used in certain sections.
  B. "Gude Nacht," when taking leave at night time.
  C. "Mer sehn (sehne) nanner widder." [We'll be seeing each other.]
  D. "Ich seh dich widder iwwerdemm." [I'll be seeing you soon.]
  E. "Good-bye."
  F. "Ich seh dich heit iwwer acht Daag." [I'll see you a week from today.]
  G. "Loss es gut sei." [I wish you well.]

921.

A person entering a group may greet the group as follows:

"Gutnowed bei einander." [Good evening to all.]
"Wie geht's bei einander?" [How are all of you?]
The above lists do not exhaust the number of greetings.

922.

Mrs. Polly Schaeffer of Cementon, Lehigh Co., says that it was customary to say when you gave a rose to someone: "Ich geb dir en Liewesgruss." [I give you a greeting of love.]

923.

"Er is ken Schuss Pulwer wert." Not worth a shot of powder. "Schuss" refers to the amount of powder used to load a gun(?).

924.

"Es is die Mieh net wert." Not worth the trouble.

925.

"Mer kann sei Gleiches (Leb. Co.) net finne."
"Mer kann seines Gleiches (Mont. Co.) net finne."
One cannot find his likeness (one like him) anywhere.

926.

"Hoscht du schun zu Mariye gesse?" Have you had breakfast?

"Hoscht du schun zu Owed gesse?" Have you had supper?

"Hoscht du schun zu Nacht gesse?" Have you had supper?

All are common.

"Wu hoscht Middaag gesse?" Where did you eat dinner?

927.

Names:

"Mariye-esse"	Breakfast.
"Middaag-esse, Middaag"	Dinner.
"Owedesse, Nachtesse"	Supper.
"Nein Uhr Schtick"	Nine o'clock lunch.
"Vier Uhr Schtick"	Four o'clock lunch.

All except the last still heard.

928.

"Sie saage als: 'Die Parre hedde nix wie Kinner un Bicher.'" [One hears it said: Preachers have nothing but children and books.]   *Myerstown*

929.

"Drei-schtechich uff der Boddem naus." The meaning is something that is indefinite.   *Widely used*

A SERIES HEARD FROM MRS. ED. WAGNER AND HER DAUGHTER, MINNIE NAGEL, OF NORTHAMPTON

930.

When flowering plants, flowers, in the yard or garden bloom out of season, there will be a death in the near relationship.   *Common belief*

931.

A visitor coming in at the back door and leaving by the front door takes away the "Glick" [luck] of the house. (The visitor should leave the house the way he came in.)

932.

For whooping cough, "Blohhuschde," get some hair from a child that never saw its father (not necessarily a posthumous child) and hang the hair on the body and wear it.

923.

To assist a child in teething hang around its neck the "Hannzaah," eyetooth, of a pig.

934.

For teething, take the bloody brain of a wild rabbit and pass over the gums of the child. (Here there seems to be a relationship between the brain, "Hann," and the teeth.)

935.

(There is a belief among older people that the eyeteeth, "Hannzeh," touch the brain, "noch em Hann gehne.")

936.

(In Lebanon County, if a person enters a home at one door and passes out at another door, that person will not take away the luck of the house, if he sits down before going out.)

937.

For teething, rub the gum with the white of an egg, immediately after the child is brought back from its first visit.

938.

For earache, cut out pegs of fat, "Schpeckzabbe," from a "Schunke" [ham], heat and put into the ear. "Schunke" [ham], heat and put into the ear.

939.

For earache, boil "Hubbe," hops, and let the steam enter the ear through a funnel, "Drechder."

940.

For smallpox, hang a packet of camphor, "Gamber," and "Deiwelsdreck" [asafetida] around the neck.

941.

Wash hair with sage tea to prevent it from turning grey.

942.

A child born on Wednesday will not live long.

943.

In "Blut schtille" [to stop blood] the patient need not be in the presence of the "Braucher" [powwower]. (One must visualize the bleeding person as if one were in his presence.) Repeat Ezekiel, Chapter 16, Verse 6 [And when I passed by thee, and saw thee polluted in thine own blood, I said unto thee when thou wast in thy blood, Live; Yea, I said unto thee when thou wast in thy blood, Live.] using the name of the person in place of "thee" and keep on repeating until the blood ceases to flow. (The coagulation of the blood was unknown to common people and therefore a mystery.)

This was done by Mrs. Wagner's mother when a neighbor came and told her that another was bleeding. Mrs. Wagner's mother kept repeating Ezekiel 16, 6 until the other had returned home.

944.

One who falls ill on Sunday and takes to bed, will not live long.

945.

One is not to get up from a sickbed on Wednesday. There will be a relapse.

946.
Ice between Christmas and New Year foretells "viel Obscht" [much fruit] the next year.

947.
A postponed wedding is unlucky.

948.
It is unlucky if two persons, children, in the same family marry in one and the same year.

949.
"Wann mer unmechdich watt, sett mer die Fiess uff die Kautsch duh." [If someone becomes unconscious, put their feet on the couch.] This seems ridiculous, that in case of unconsciousness one is to put his feet on the couch, but here "mer" is for the High German "man," the impersonal.

950.
Do not wash on Wednesday, "en Unglicksdaag." [unlucky day]

951.
"Wann die Gwidde bliehe, watt's kiehl." [When the quinces bloom, it will become cool.]

952.
"Ausgangs Moi odder Middels Moi geb's noch 3 kalde Daage. Des sin die Harre Daage." [At the end of May or in the middle of May there are three additional cold days. These are the Lords' days.] (Brockhaus, *Handbuch des Wissens,* "gestrenge Herren, Eisheilige Eismaenner, die Tage vum 11-13 Mai (Mamerties, Pankratius, Servatius) an denen in West und Mitteleuropa haeufig Nachtfroeste mit ihren Schaedigungen der jungen Pflanzenwelt eintreten, weshalb diese Tage besonders gefuerchtet sind.")

Mrs. Wagner said that she received her knowledge of the "Harre Daage" from the mother of Wilbur Moyer of Egypt. (I knew her.) Thus while she was certain of the significance of the "Harre Daage," she was not certain as to the time of their occurence. "Ausgangs Moi" would be towards the end of May.

953.
Water from the first snow in March is good for sore eyes. This water does not become foul.

954.
A child looking in the mirror soon after birth will become proud.

955.
If a baby's upper teeth appear first (growing down)—before the lower ones, the child will not live long. "Sie waxe ins Graab." [They grow into the grave.]

956.
Children should not eat chicken at their birthday dinner. It is bad luck.

957.
"Wer immer in die Karich. Do is ebbes letz.
Wer gaar net in die Karich geht. Do is ebbes letz.
Wer alsemol in die Karich geht. Der is recht."

[When one always goes to church, something is wrong.
When one never goes to church, something is wrong.
When one goes to church occasionally, that's right.]
(Not infrequently heard in Egypt, Northampton and Lowhill.)

958.
A man sentenced to be hung protested his innocence. He had been convicted of murder on the evidence that he was caught carrying the body of a murdered person in a bag to the river. He explained that he had been walking along the road; that a man came along with a bundle; that the man asked him to take the bundle and cast it into the river, and that he had done so. And on the gallows he said: "I am innocent and this will show my innocence. After I am hanged a black cloud will appear "un's watt so arig regere as es Wasser eich in die Schuh laaft." [and it will rain so hard that the water will run into your shoes.] — "Un so hot's aa." [And so it did.]

This is an old story.   *O.P. Leh, Egypt*

(This belongs to a group of stories which tell of signs that show a person to have been put to death innocently.)

959.
If a person's front teeth are far apart (there are spaces between them), "hen die Eldre ghurt." (The parents committed fornication or adultery.) If the upper teeth are spaced, the father committed fornication. If the lower teeth are spaced, it was the mother.
Rev. William Helfrich, Bath, in the year 1927

960.
A child that teeths early will not walk early, and vice versa   *Common belief*

961.
A child that talks early will not walk early.
Not infrequently heard

962.
Swallows come on April 15 and leave on August 15.
Only heard at Egypt

963.
It is sinful to kill swallows and robins. (Also to rob their nests.)
Quite common belief Lebanon County

964.
The nest of a swallow in a barn is a protection against fire and against lightning.   *Rather common*

965.

"Wann der Regevoggel ruft, geb's Rege." [When the cuckoo calls, there will be rain.]

966.

The use of the word "Pieces": "Ich geb ken Pieces drum was es gebt." "Ich geb ken Pieces drum wie's gebt."

[I don't care what happens.]

The word is quite frequently heard and in a way that would lead one to suspect that it doesn't come from the English.

967.

"Kunschtschtick" as used in the dialect does not mean so much an artistic as a clever piece of work.

THERE WILL BE A THUNDERSTORM, A RAINSTORM:
(all from Lebanon County)

968.

When pigs run around in the pen, "Seipenn."

969.

When cows come to the bars before the usual time for stabling for milking.

970.

A cat washes its face.

971.

Flies come to the screened windows or doors.

972.

If a cumulus cloud appears just above the horizon in the west in the morning, there will be a rain "eb der Daag verbei is" or "uff die Nacht." [before the day is over or in the night]

973.

If a hen preens its feathers, there will be rain.

When flies bite viciously. (That is not only the house flies, "Schtechmicke," but also the horse flies, "Geilsmicke.")

974.

When a dog eats grass.

975.

When water jars, "der Wassergruck," [sg.] sweat, there will be rain. Such jars as are set in the cooling cellar.

976.

Weather changes at full moon, "voll Licht."

977.

Annie Garloff, near Myerstown, when asked why she didn't marry, she being an old maid, answered:

"So lang as ich leenich bin, hawwich yuscht mei eegner Druwwel. Wann ich heier, hawwich mei Mann un mei Kinner ihrer Druwwel noch dazu."

[As long as I am single, I have only my own troubles. If I marry, I have the troubles of my husband and my children in addition.]

978.

"absolutt," an adverb, means very necessary, needful. *Leb*

"Mer sedde absolutt Rege hawwe; es is so drucke as es schtaabt wann mer blugt." [We should have rain by all means; it's so dry that the dust flies when one plows.]

979.

The English word "caution" is used with the sense of something extraordinary. "Es waar en Caution wie er gedobt hot." [It was most unusual the way he blustered.] "Er kann schaffe as es en Caution is." [He can work unusually hard.] *Leb*

980.

Rheumatism means rain. "Des hawwich als net geglaabt, awwer nau wann ich Rummadis grick, wees ich as mer Rege griege." [I didn't use to believe it, but now when I get rheumatism I know that we'll get rain.] *Egypt*

981.

When limbs that had been broken years back ache, there will be rain. Also of limbs that have been paralyzed and have regained some of their vitality. "Wann ich Schmatze grick in mei laahme Hand, noh kummt en Rege." [When I get pain in my lame hand, then rain is coming.] *Still common*

982.

"Eb mer Rege griege, fiehl ich immer as wann ich ken Lewe hett." [Before we get rain, I always feel listless, as if I had no life.] *Egypt*

"Wann ich so lass fiehl, noh meen ich watt Rege am kumme." [When I feel so listless, then I think rain is coming.] *Leb*

983.

When the dishes on the table at any of the meals of the day are eaten clean, there will be a change in the weather. *Very common*

984.

The direction which the first storm of the year takes, will be the way that all storms will go. If it passes to the north of a town, all the storms will pass to the north of the town, i.e. all the storms that summer. *Green Lane*

985.

Heavy fur on wild and domestic animals means a severe winter. *Common*

986.

When muskrats build large houses in the fall, there will be a severe winter. *Jonas Hiltebeitel, Green Lane*

987.
High weeds in the fall foretell deep snow during the following winter.   *Green Lane*

988.
In cutting down trees, usually those that were hollow, in the fall for firewood for the winter, if large caches of nuts collected by squirrels were found, that meant a severe winter.   *Leb*

989.
Squirrels can distinguish between good nuts and bad nuts and will not collect any bad nuts for their winter supply.   *Mont*

990.
In the fall caterpillars black at both ends and brown in the middle foretell a winter severe in the beginning and at the end, but mild in the middle. A caterpillar brown at both ends and black in the middle means a winter mild in the beginning and at the end, but severe in the middle. (The latter condition I believe is imaginary.)

Some have it that the amount of black, the extent of black at the ends, tells the extent of the winter. Thus I have been told that caterpillars have been seen that were almost wholly black. "Des gebt en hadder Winder!" [There will be a hard winter!]

When there was more black at the front than at the tail, the beginning of winter would be severe and long; vice versa also held.

The caterpillar is the larva of *Isia isabella*.

991.
"Graad so viel Rege as mer hen in Summer, graad so viel Schnee griege mir in Winder." [Exactly as much rain as we have in summer we will get in winter.]

992.
If the smoke coming from the chimneys and from locomotives hugs the ground, there will be rain.
   Very common

993.
The first frost of the fall and late summer will come six weeks after the katydids begin to cry.
   Henry Summers, Green Lane

994.
"Sunneblicker,
Hoischpritzer."   *P. B.*

Said when the sun shines intermittently between clouds in the summer.

995.
When in a cloudy sky the sun shines through the clouds and the beams are visible as they extend to the earth, we say: "Die Sunn ziegt Wasser." That means there will soon be a storm. The sun draws water into the clouds so that they may become filled and let it drop. Another expression for the same phenomena is: "Die Sunn ziegt Schtraahle." [The sun is drawing beams.]

996.
When the whistle of a distant locomotive or the rumble of a distant train—not usually heard—is heard, there will be rain. "Die Luft kummt fer Rege." [The air indicates that there will be rain.] This is usually a "Landrege."

997.
Proverb

"Mer kann net lewe vum Wind." [One cannot live from the wind.] This was said by the Rev. C.E. Held of Sumneytown, Montgomery County, when the congregation was dilatory in paying his salary.

998.
Proverb

"Wu is der Mose hiegange wu er drei Yaahr alt waar?" [Where did Moses go when he was three years old?]—"Ins Vierde." [Into the fourth.]   *Egypt*

999.
Riddle

"Wu waar der Mose wu's Licht ausgange is?" [Where was Moses when the light went out?]—"Im Dunkle." [In the dark.]   *Common*

1000.
Expression

"Des is iwwer die Weis." This is beyond all bounds. This is "out of reason."   *Not infrequently heard*

"Weis" here seems to come from the German "Weise."

1001.
Expression

"Des is aus der Weis." It seems to come from German "Weise." The meaning is the same as 1000: extraordinarily, not according to what is warranted. "Er hot schun paar Mol so Schtreech gmacht, awwer des is aus der Weis." He has before this done things that were out of place, but this is going too far.

1002.
[Die] "Weis" is the melody of a hymn or song.
   Common word

1003.
Expression

"Do gehne die Katz die Haar aus." [Now the cat's losing its hair.]

This expression is used when one is in a difficult situation, i.e. "up against it."

1004.
Expression

"Do muss mer aahalde fer gut Wedder." [Here one has to hold on for good weather.] Here one must hope that all luck is on his side.   *Common expression, Leb*

1005.
Riddle

"Wie schreibt mer 12 as es wennicher is as 12?"
[How does one write 12 so that it's less than 12?] *Egypt*

1006.

A "Harschel, Haschel" in the almanac means rough, stormy weather; a "Landrege" of several days duration. *Leb*

[Sir William Herschel. Original name, Friedrich Wilhelm. 1738-1822. German-born English astronomer.]

1007.
Riddle

"Was fer Esel kann mer net reide?" [What kind of an donkey can one not ride?]—"En Hannesel." [Hornet.] *Old Goshenhoppen Church*

1008.
Riddle

"Was fer Esel kann mer net reide?" [See 1007.] "En Kelleresel." [A sow bug, wood louse.] *Egypt*

1009.
Riddle

"Was fer Esel kann mer net reide?" [See 1007.] "Dich!" [You!] *Egypt*

A SERIES HEARD IN GRACE REFORMED CHURCH, NORTHAMPTON, PA.

1010.

"Eens, zwee, drei,
Maad, holl Wei.
Paff, sauf raus!
Du bischt haus."

[One, two, three,
Maid, fetch wine.
Preacher, drink up!
You are out!]

1011.

Rapidly spoken and then asked, "What is that?"

"Graabadzi, Brauneezi, Bohndarzi, Dumedu."
(Grabb baade, Brau Neez, Bohne darre, Do meh du.)

A man was mowing with the scythe in a meadow and another was spreading the mown grass. As he mowed he saw a crow wading in the water, a woman sewing with brown thread and another woman drying beans.

He repeated the above rapidly and ended up with "Do meh du!"—"Here, you mow!" while holding out the scythe to his companion. His companion did not comprehend what he was saying and of course did not understand that he was to take a turn at mowing.

*Mrs. Mantana Mitman,
735 Lincoln Avenue, Northampton*

1012.

Rapidly spoken:

"Mee der Affaa is die laamend dei."
(Meh, du Aff aa un die laahm End is dei.)

"Aff" in explaining the words was said to be the name of a person; and one person exhorting another to mow, promised him a lame duck. Probably "Aff" is to be taken as meaning "monkey."

Mrs. Bobscht, Northampton

Bumbernickle Bill has a version:

"Meht der Offe aa is die laahm End dei."
Will Strauss, Treichler's

1012.a.

In the song "Zu Ulla":

"Mundaag -	Wescherei,
Dinschdaag -	Bigglerei,
Mittwoch -	Flickerei,
Dunnerschdaag -	Butzerei,
Freidaag -	Backerei,
Samschdaag -	Schparickerei,
Sunndaag -	Ruherei."

[Monday -	Washing,
Tuesday -	Ironing,
Wednesday -	Mending,
Thursday -	Cleaning,
Friday -	Baking,
Saturday -	Courting,
Sunday -	Resting.]

The great day for courting was Saturday. I know of instances where young men went on Saturday evening and stayed until Monday morning. On Sunday they helped to milk the cows and do the chores.

[End of series.]

1013.

"Do kummt der Yaeger ridden,
Er gloppt so laut ans Dierli
Mit sei goldner Ring.
Rei loss ich dich nicht kommen,
So reide numme hie wu du hergekommen bischt.
Du darfscht net bei mir bleiwe,
Weil du schunscht net bei mir bischt."

[Here comes the hunter ariding,
He raps loudly at the door
With his golden ring.
I'll not permit you to come in,
So ride back whence you've come.
You may not stay with me,
Because you were never here before.]

Lottie Strauss, Treichler's

1014.
Riddle
"Mer geht an ee Loch nei un an zwee Lecher naus, noh is mer erscht recht drin?" [One goes into one hole and out two others; then you're really in.]—A pair of trousers. *Norman Xander, Ruchsville*

1015.
Game
In playing "Hide and Seek" that player who was able to become free would yell: "Pump!" three times: "Pump, pump, pump!"
This was known as "abgepumpt." *Charles Snyder*

1016.
Game
"Long Town." Play to the first base. The runner had to be hit by the ball. *Do*

1017.
Game
"Copenhagen." Players grasp a rope. One in the center tries to catch anyone who lets go of the rope. *Do*

1018.
Part of the "Bucklich Mennli" song:

"Wann ich in mei Gaarde geh,
Fer mei Zwiwwle butze,
Kummt en glee Mennli rei
Un fangt aa zu brutze."

[When I enter my garden,
To clean my onions,
The little man comes in
And begins to cry.]

*At Dodder's Eck
above Mauch Chunk*

1019.
"Zu Yula":

"Mundaags is die Wescherei,
Yula hie, Yula hei.
Geht die ganze Woch verbei
(Or: Watt die ganze Woch net frei)
Mit ihre Wescherei."

[Monday is washday,
Yula hie, Yula hei.
The entire week goes by
(Or: The entire week is not free of)
With its washing.]

Refrain:

"Wer gut lewe will,
Esse, drinke, saufe will,
Der geht zu der Yula hie."

[He who wants to live well,
Wants to eat, drink and pour it down,
He goes over to Yula's place.] *Do*

1020.
"Ich kann ball nimmi faahre,
Mei Wagge is so schwer,
Mei Geilche sin so maage,
Mei Geldsack is so leer."

[I can hardly travel,
My wagon is so heavy,
My horses so thin,
My purse so empty.]

*I was in Dodder's Eck
in company with John S*

1021.
Riddle
"Was is der Unnerschitt zwische en Parre un en Schtaagefens?" [What is the difference between a minister and a worm fence?]—"Der Parre schwetzt vum Himmel un der Schtaagefens weist noch em Himmel." [The minister speaks of heaven and the worm fence shows the way, points toward heaven.] *Egypt*

1022.
Riddle
"Wann mer en Kuh Sundaags in en Feld yaagt, wann kann mer sie rausyaage, so as mer sie net uff en Daag rausyaagt?" [When one chases a cow into a field, when can one chase her out so that one doesn't chase her out on a day?]—"Mittwochs." [On a Wednesday.] *Egypt*

1023.
In the hymn "Ermunter euch, ihr Frommen," Nr. 248 in the hymnal published at Cleveland, in the possession of O.P. Leh, occur the lines:

"Es hat sich auf gemachet,
Der Braeutigam mit Pracht.
Die Thuer ist aufgeschlossen,
Die Hochzeit ist bereit."

[The bridegroom has
prepared himself with splendor.
The gate is open wide,
The wedding is ready.]

1024.
"Unser Vaader Besemschtiel,
Bed die ganze Woch net viel.
Mundaag mariyets fang ich aa,
Denk die ganze Woch net draa."

[Our father broomstick,
Prays the entire week little.
Monday morning I begin,
Don't think of it all week.]

*Mrs. Rosa Dasheimer,
Efforts*

1025.
Today, October 26, 1936, I went with John Schupp to the section above Kresgeville, Efforts, "Dodder's Eck," the country where he was born and spent his youth. He told me that when he was 14 (!) years old he was asked by a neighbor's girl, "Bella" for Isabella, after "so en Zammegelaaf mit re heem geh." [to go along home with her after a get-together.] He went along. When he got there, he found the father and the mother sitting by the stove. The old man with his shoes off warming his feet. After a while the old man yelled to the mother, who was deaf: "Mam, Ich denk mer gehne nuff." The woman nodded and both started up the stairs. He paused at the door of the stairway and said: "Ich denk dir dutt nix as dir net duh kennt uff die Kautsch odder uff der Bodde. Dir besser geht nuff ins Bett wu dir waarm sei kennt," and went on up. [I guess you won't be doing anything that you could not do on the couch or on the floor. You'd better go up to bed where you can be warm.] After a while the girl who was a little younger—not much, a few months or so, and well built ("gut gebaut"), said: "Gehscht mit nuff?" [Will you go along up?] He want along "fer sehne wie des Ding geht—des waar der Gebrauch." [to see how this thing went—this was the custom] As they passed through the room of the parents to the room beyond—"Datt hen die Alde gelege so breed ausnanner in ihrem Bett." [There the old folks lay spread across their bed.]

"Mir hen uns ausgeduh un sin ins Bett. Un sie waar "game." Sie hot schier net waarde kenne.....Noh bin ich eigschlofe un's waar vier Uhr eb ich wacke warre bin. Un wu ich heemkumme bin, hot der Daadi mich marickwaddich gedrosche. Awwer mer is viel mit eldre Buwe un Meed rumgschprunge un mer hot ewwe duh welle wie sie."

[We undressed and got into bed. And she was game. She could hardly wait..... Then I fell asleep and it was four o'clock before I woke up. And when I came home, my dad gave me a terrible beating. But one ran around much with the older boys and girls and one wanted to do what they were doing.]

"Die Bella hot die Kieh ghiet so as sie net fattlaafe deede ins Holz un ich bin zu re gange. Der Busch waar graad dabei—-well mer is aa ebbes vum me Schtick Vieh."

[Bella tended the cows so that they wouldn't run into the woods and I went to see her. The woods were right there—well, we are a kind of an animal.]

1026.
John Schupp does not believe that his father was truthful when he said that he courted (with bundling) his wife four years without improper actions. Nor does he believe that of any other couple. "Sis net gsaat, wann's nix draus gebt, as nix geduh waar." [It's not said that when nothing results that nothing was done.]

1027.
John Schupp says: "Wu awwer moll zuviel Buwe zurickgange sin uff die Meed" [When too many boys went back on their word] ("zurickgange") because a promise was usually asked and usually given "fer heiere wann's ebbes gebt." [to marry if something happened] "sin die Meed so warre as mer nix duh hot kenne mit ne—net so viel as unnich der Frack lange." [the girls got so one couldn't do anything with them—not as much as reaching under their dress.]

1028.
Upon sneezing one should always say, "Danke." [Thank you.]
John Shupp

1029.
If you have been ill, sneezing is a sign that you are becoming better. When you can't sneeze, you are becoming worse.
Do

1030.
Sneezing is a sign that a cold is either coming or going.
Not infrequently heard

1031.
Eels catch fish and eat them after the manner of snakes. They usually go after large fish, trout, 10—12 inches long. After catching they lie on some large flat stone to devour their catch.
John Shupp

1032.
Eels are readily caught after a thunder storm when the water is dirty. Hooks should be baited with bloody meat.
Do

1033.
"Was im Fleesch is, geht net aus die Gnoche." (The nature you inherited you will always keep.]
Do

1034.
Word: "Glofderholz," cord wood. Common word.

1035.
Word: "arrieyre," to argue. "Do waare sie am arrieyre un sin doch zu kem Beschluss kumme." [Here they were arguing and didn't come to any conclusion.]
Do

1036.
"Die eent is blind,
Die anner laahm,
Un die Dridde (Dritt, Leb. Co.) hot ken Zaah im Maul."

"Fer was gehscht du net zu die Meed?"
"Sis nix. Die eent is blind, die anner, etc."

[The one is blind,
The other is lame,
And the third hasn't a tooth in her mouth.]

[Why don't you go courting?]
[It's not worthwhile...]

These words were used by my father and others.

1037.
The choruses which are repeated over and over at revivals and at camp meetngs are widely known as "Rounds." *Willis Gibble, Lititz*

1038.
Prest. Smith, the cashier of our bank, tells me (I also observed the same down at Keelor's Church) that down at the Hill Church, when they are ready to eat pie, they turn the plate around and eat the pie from the back of the plate. Before doing so the plate is eaten clean and wiped clean with bread.

1038.a.
Of dessert it was said: "owwe druff hen mer noch Minspie ghat." [on top we had mince pie.] Dessert was something "owwe druff."

1039.
Proverb
"Er wees so wennich (vun de Sach) wie en Sau vun Sunndaag." [He understands as much (about the matter) as a pig about Sunday.] *Monroe*

1040.
Proverb
"Er wees so wennich (vun de Sach) wie en Kuh (or Gaul) vun Sunndaag." [He understands as much (about the matter) as a cow (or horse) about Sunday.] *Leb*

1041.
Some older farmers were accustomed to give their livestock an extra portion of feed on Sunday. In the case of horses it was explained, "Sie hen mehner Zeit fer esse Sunndaags wie in die Woch." [They have more time to eat Sundays than in the week.] (Though probably also in honor of the day. So also at Christmas.)

1042.
"Lichtmess,
Schpinne vergess."

[Candlemas, February 2,
Forget your spinning.] *Common*

1043.
John Schupp tells me that "die Schwalme Lecher" [swallow holes in the barn] were made so that birds had a place of refuge in winter.

1044.
Robert Werley, of our bank, tells me that Burton Werley, a tavern loafer, went to help a farmer haul and spread manure. At night the farmer, his wife and Werley slept in one bed, the woman lying between the men. This was done at the farmer's request. For four nights the slept in this way and every night he and the farmer alternately and successively "hen die Fraa hergnumme." [took their turns with the wife] When he left he received no pay. (There is ground for credence of the story, for the persons with whom Werley would have intimate associations would be such as were moneyless and conventionless.)

1045.
Proverb
"Eeyelob schtinkt." [Self-praise stinks.] *Leb*

1046.
Songs and ballads are known as "Leibschticker" [favorite tunes] in Monroe County. When I was out with John Schupp, he would ask people whether they remembered any "Leibschticker."

1047.
Adam Hiester of Strausstown tells me that songs and ballads were known as "Schelmenlieder" [rogish songs] in his locality. That this name bacame current through the denunciations of the ministers, who dubbed the songs of tavern and street as "Schelmenlieder."

1048.
"Datt kumme die siwwe Wind zamme." [There the seven winds meet.] This is spoken of a very windy or of a cold windy hollow. *Leb, Mont*

1049.
"Unnich em Wedder." [Under the weather.] "Er is e wennich unnich em Wedder." [He is a bit under the weather.] An expression meaning that one is sick; that one is slightly ill; that one is indoors on account of sickness. *Often heard*

1050.

"Hinkel, Haahne, Fleddermaus,
Gratz die Katz die Aage raus."

[Chicken, rooster, butterfly,
Scratch the cat's eyes out.]

Willis Gibble, Lititz

1051.
Word: "Wild Vieh," small game, rabbits, squirrels, pheasants, etc. *Egypt*

1052.
Word: "Schtichdunkel," dark as pitch.
"Sticks" Zerfass, Egypt

1053.
On November 9, 1936, Henry Troxell of Ruchsville tells me that the barn decorations (so called barn signs) were "howweled out" to the depth of inch. He thought that this was done by the carpenters so that the painting of the figures might be facilitated. He said that the whole figure (sign) was worked out. This of the barn on his farm and also of a barn on the Trojan Powder Co. farms.

1054.
Henry Troxell knew of no occult significance attributed to the barn signs. To protect the barn from evil machinations, "writings" were put in the stables below.

1055.
It is believed to mean good fortune to have swallows build in the barn, as that would protect the barn from lightning. [Cf. 1043.] *Henry Troxell*

1056.
"Bumbernickle Bill" some time ago told me of a barn down country that had worked out signs, but he attributed the "working out" to the action of the paint.

1057.
"So iwwerzwarg wie en auslennischer Kalenner." As cross-grained as a foreign calendar. Said of a person hard to get along with or to reason with. *Leh, P. B.*

1058.
"So wie die Hesse im Kesselgaarde." [Like the Hessians in the kettle garden.] There seems to me to be a story back of this expression. Meaning a mixed-up way of doing things. *Do*

1059.
If you shoot a cat (or kill a cat), thereafter you cannot "shoot straight" with that gun. Note the expression "shoot straight." *Mantz, Miller's Church*

1060.
In a funeral the corpse is to be taken out of the house feet first, or else the dead will come back. *P. B.*

1061.
Proverb
"Kaaft is kaaft" or "Verkaaft is verkaaft." [Bought is bought or sold is sold.] A bargain is a bargain. There was a time when goods that were bought could not be returned and exchanged.
Both Mont

1062.
If, in washing dishes you wet your apron, your husband will be a drunkard. *Mrs. Hummel*

1063.
Abraham Wenger of Egypt, who comes from the Dunkards of Lancaster County, an uncle of Willis Gibble of Lititz, see above, has given me the following on Berks County:

A.
"In Berks sin die Leit so dumm, sie schlachde die Kieh fer die Kelwer abgwehne." [In Berks County the people are so stupid they butcher the cows to wean the calves.]

1064.
B.
"In Berks do sin die Leit so dumm, sie schwefle die Ieme fer der Hunnich griege." [In Berks County the people are so stupid they asphyxiate (with sulpher fumes) the bees in order to get the honey.]

1065.
C.
"In Berks Kaundi do heest's fedde Oxe un dumme Leit." [In Berks County they speak of fatted oxen and stupid people.]

1066.
D.
"Die Berks Kaundi Leit sin so dumm, sie losse's Licht brenne fer die Schwefelhelche [sic] schpaare." [The Berks County people are so stupid the let the light burn in order to save matches.]

1067.
"Die Schwowe waare so dumm, sie hen en Karich gebaut unne Fenschdre un noh hen's Licht (die Helling) neidraage welle in Seck." [The Suabians (a term of ridicule) were so stupid they built a church without windows and then wanted to carry in the light (illumination) in bags.] *Leh*

1068.
"Die Blohbariyer Leit sin so dumm, wann sie en Seischtall baue, mache sie gleene Lecher fer die gleene Sei un grosse Lecher fer die grosse Sei." [The Blue Mountain folk are so stupid that when they build a pigsty they make small holes for the small pigs and big holes for the big pigs.] *Northampton*

1069.
There was a tradition at Lancaster when I was a student there in the seminary that Dr. Philip Schaff swapped a fat hog for a suckling pig because the hole from the pen to the stall was too small for his hog.

1070.
A tradition at Schaefferstown reported that the brother of N- was so "hoch gelannt" [highly educated] that every morning before he put on his shoes he would look them over to see how much had been worn away from the soles the day before and was thus able to tell how long they could still be worn.

1071.
"Wann mer en Leeb Brod unnerewwerschich hielegt, heile die Engel im Himmel." [When one places a loaf of bread upside-down, the angels in heaven weep.] *Laury's Grange*

1072.
Proverb
"Frisch geronne is halwer gewonne." [To begin a race in good condition is half won.] *Will Strauss*

1073.
If you hang a mirror upside-down, there will be a death in the family. *P. B.*

1074.
Proverb

"Frisch gewogt is halwer gewunne." [To venture with courage is half the battle.] Cf. 1072. *Leb*

1075.
When we played croquet, my father—to cause us to miss when we struck for the stake—would take his forefinger, wet it with spittle and make a cross on the top of the stake.

1076.
Near Muddy Creek [just south of Adamstown in Lancaster County] is a cane maker. The board on which the cane is bent is called "die Hex." The "Hex" on the board itself is the knob around which the wood is bent to form the handle of the cane.

*N- Young,
near Muddy Creek Church,
November 11, 1936*

1077.
Spoken at Christmas at Stiles Sunday School in 1901 by A. E. Hassler:

"Ich bin der Daadi Riggel,
Ich bin noch glee.
Wann ich greesser bin,
Saag ich noch meh."

[I am Daddy Riggel,
I am still small.
Once I am bigger,
I will say more.]

1078.
"Wann me uff em Hund sei Schwanz drett (dred), gauzt er." [If you step on a dog's tail, he barks.] ("drett" is a Lancaster County form)

Meaning: Suppose a preacher should in a sermon vehemently condemn hidden vices and after the services were over, someone should express dissatisfaction with the kind of sermons that were being preached, another sensing that the critic had the very hidden vices which had been condemned and because of them was critical of the preaching, might say: "Wann mer uff em Hund sei Schwanz dred, gauzt er."

1079.
Word: "Bautz" — hobgoblin. When I was a child, I often heard children put to silence with the threat: "Der Bautz gickt dich!" [The hobgoblin will get you!] *Leb*

1080.
In Egypt the word "Buckelbautz" is used. Is this for "bucklich Bautz"? Cf. 1079.

1081.
Riddle

"Was geht am (ans) Wasser un losst sei Bauch daheem?" [What goes to the water and leaves its stomach at home?]—"En Fedderdeck." [A featherbed.]
Ray Worman, Egypt

1082.
Proverb

"Aus Menschehaut muss es Geld gemacht warre." [Money has to be made from the hides of human being.]
Mrs. Rayond Remaley

1083.
Verses on the zodiacal signs given by Willoughby Troxell, the "Gensegnoche Mann," so known locally on account of his goosebone weather predictions.

"Der Wiederbock schteht,
Die Kinner sin bees,
Der Leeb, der brillt,
Die Woog, die gilt,
Der Schitz, der schiesst,
Der Wassermann giesst,
Der Fisch, der schwimmt,
Der Schteebock schpringt,
Der Schkarpian schticht,
Die Yungfraa schpricht,
Der Grebs, der glemmt,
Der Ox, der brennt."

[The ??? stands,
The children are angry,
The lion roars,
The scales count,
The archer shoots,
The waterman pours,
The fish swims,
The ram jumps,
The scorpion sticks,
The virgin speaks,
The crab pinches,
The ox burns.]

In recitation the last word of each line is stressed. I have noted two ways of reciting the zodiacal lines:

(a) Der Grebs, der glemmt,
(b) Der Ox, der brennt.

1084.
Plant potatoes in the "Woog," then they will become weighty. *Mrs. Raymond Remaley*

1085.
Do not plant onions in the "Schitz" or "sie schiesse," they will shoot up into seed heads. This of onion sets in spring planting. *Do*

1086.
Plant cucumber seed in the "Wasserman," then they will not become small, dry and "runzlich" [wrinkled]. ("Sie warre wessrich." [They will become "watery."] *Do*

1087.
Plant cabbage in the "Schteebock," then the heads will become hard and solid. ("net los"[not loose], "net uffschpringe" [not open up])   *Do*

1088.
Plant flowers (seed or plants) in the "Yungfraa" [the sign of the virgin], then they will blossom profusely.   *Do*

1089.
Plant vines in the "Grebs" [the sign of cancer], then they will bring forth many vines.   *Do*

1090.
To a boy called Jeremiah, in derision we called:
"Jeremiah, blow the fiah,
Puff, puff, puff."   *Childhood memory*

1091.
Word: "Laade." I have heard the plural as "Laade" and also as "Leede."
Expression: "Henk dich an der Laade!" means "Get busy!" or "Put your shoulder to the wheel."
   Sumneytown

1092.
A story heard in Lancaster County about 1910 by C. W. Unger and told to me on December 14, 1936:
A young preacher was asked to preach in a country charge. He came into the field on a Saturday afternoon and stopped off at the home of one of the deacons. There were only two beds in the house and when night came the young preacher was told that he had to sleep with the daughter, a comely maiden. It being the only course open to gain a night's rest before the work of the next day, he reluctantly assented. "Du weescht wie dich zu bedraage." [You know how to behave.] said the deacon. For safety's sake a chair was put between the sleepers. The preacher observed all the proprieties.
The next morning the young man preached at the church nearest to the deacon's home and returned home with the deacon for dinner. In the afternoon he was to preach at a more distant church. Because he did not know the shortest way, the daughter was sent along to guide him until he would come to the direct road to the church. He rode and she walked along.
As they went along they came to a field where beautiful flowers were growing. The girl admired them very much and the young preacher gallantly dismounted, giving her the reins of the horse, climbed over the fence, gathered a bouquet and gave it to the maiden. She took the bouquet, thanked him and then "ihn wennich scheel aageguckt [looked at him archly] and said: "Ich seh du kannscht dich besser iwwer en Schteefens schaffe wie iwwer en Schtul." [I see you can get over a stone fence better than over a chair.]

1093.
Irwin Frantz tells me that his father when angry would say:

"Schtann piecium,
Do waar ich so dumm wie en Rieslumm."

1094.
Consumptives will pass away when the leaves fall from the white oak tree in the fall of the year.
   B. B.
"Lungeauszehring" — consumption of the lungs.

1095.
Consumptives will pass away when the leaves appear on the trees in the spring of the year.   *Leb*

1096.
Consumptives will pass away either in the spring when the leaves appear on the trees or in the fall when the leaves drop from the trees.   *Sumneytown*

1097.
Words used to express urinating:
"Wasser losse" — "Ich geh nimmi gern vun Heem; ich muss mei Wasser zu oft losse." [I don't like to leave the house; I have to urinate too often.] Much used by old people.

1098.
"pisse" is used when speaking of or to children, though also used of adults. To a child: "Muscht pisse?"

1099.
"brunse" is used mostly of adults, though also of children.

1100.
"seeche" is looked on as cruder. It is used by some when the bladder is heavily loaded. Used also of horses.

1101.
"tintelliere" = to urinate.   *P. B.*

1102.
Voiding the bowels:
"puppe" is mostly used when speaking to or of small children. Children's language. Excrementa of children is called: "Pupp."

1103.
"scheisse" is used of adults. Excrementa is "Scheissdreck."

1104.
"en Tschabb schaffe" — "Ich muss en Tschabb schaffe." This is a rather common way of saying: "I must ease myself."

1105.
"naus misse" — "Ich muss naus." I must ease myself. Originally it may have meant "to go out of the house to void the bowels," but now it has come to mean simply to void the bowels. It may mean either

urination or a passage of the bowels or both. Children and some adults used to refer to urination as "doing Number 1," and to a bowel passage as "doing Number 2." The English expression with like meaning, "I must go out," is widely used.

1106.

Other expressions: "Ich muss noch em Toilet." [I must go to the toilet.]

"Ich will ins Priwwi." [I want to go to the privy (outhouse).]

"Ich muss uff der Haffe." [I have to go on the pot.]

1107.

Dr. Minner of Egypt tells me there is a day in the fall of the year known as "Gensedaag" [goose day], upon which one must eat a goose in order that one may be lucky the whole year round. He says he heard it among the Pennsylvania Dutch.

1108.

N- Billig of Egypt tells me that "Gensedaag" [Cf. 1107.] is "Nicodiemus Daag," October 19.

1109.

Old Rev. Tom Leinbach, pastor at Bernville, Strausstown, etc. around 1900, was accustomed to go from Womelsdorf, his home, on Saturdays to his farther congregations, do what pastoral work was demanded and then stay overnight for the next morning service. Well, one Saturday "hot der Parre uffgschtellt fer die Nacht bei eens vun seine Vorschteher, der en scheeni yungi luschdiche Fraa ghat hot. Nochdem as sie aardlich in die Nacht nei geblaudert hen, sin sie ins Bett. Der Parre erscht in sei Schtubb, der Mann un sei Fraa in die Schtubb danewe. Der Parre hot net eischlofe kenne. So geye Middernacht schteht er uff, ruft sei Vorschteher: "Ich glaab's ebbes letz is mit meim Gaul. Ich heer en. Ich glaab as er vielleicht daschdaich is. Werdscht so gut un gingscht naus un deedscht en drenke un wann er ken Hoi hot, em wennich neischtecke." [the pastor spent the night with one of his deacons who had a merry young wife. After they chatted well into the night they went to bed. First the pastor into his room, the man and his wife into the next room. The pastor was unable to fall asleep. So toward midnight he got up, called to his deacon: "I think there's something wrong with my horse. I hear him. Perhaps he's thirsty. Would you be so good and go out and give him some water and if he has no hay, give him some.] Gewiss deed er. [Certainly he would (replied the deacon).] Der gedrei Vorschteher is naus. ... Wu er zerick kumme is, saagt er zum Parre, "Dei Gaul waar net weiders daschdrich." Der Parre hot sich awwer arig bedankt as er nausgange waar." [The faithful deacon went out. ... When he came back, he said to the pastor, "Your horse wasn't especially thirsty." The pastor was was most grateful that the deacon had gone out to check on his horse.]

Rev. Amandus Leiby,
who succeeded Leinbach

1110.

Names for the diamond-shaped square, etc. opening in the gable of barns:

"Luftloch" [air hole] This name is quite common. For ventilation.

1111.

"Schwalmeloch" [swallow hole] To provide an opening so that the swallows can enter the barn and build their nests there. This is a common explanation.

1112.

"Dunschloch" [vapor hole] For ventilation. In the walls of the old stone barns there were perpendicular openings, say 20 inches high on the outside and 18 inches wide on the inside and approximately two inches wide. What were they called? One notes them in brick barns where the designs make checkerboard openings. Is the name "Dunschloch" or "Rischtloch?"

1113.

"Rischloch" is the name given by "Bumbernickel Bill." (I do not see the meaning of "Risch.") (Undoubtedly the builders of stone barns took lighting and ventilation into consideration. The perpendicular openings mentioned in 1112 were, as told to me, for lighting the mows of the barn, which were at the ends of the barn.)

1114.

Words: "Newwelich," adjective, "foggy."

"dufdich," adjective. A thin wreath of fog rising up from the ground in summertime. "Do is es dufdich." [It's foggy here.]

1115.

The Newhards living between Egypt and Ormrod have an old cherry tree that bears blossoms but no fruit. They were repeatedly advised to beat up or shoot up the tree on New Year's Day—in the morning without speaking.

On New Year's morning the son George rose early, went out, climbed into the top of the tree and started in beating it up. While he was doing this, his brother-in-law, William Solt, came out and shot into the trunk of the tree. Thereupon the silence was broken by George.

1115.a.

In the family there was old Mrs. Newhard. There was also in the house her daughter Hattie who was married to a William Solt and her brother George Newhard. It was around Christmas that the two men were talking about the barrenness of the cherry tree. Then old Mrs. Newhard said to the boys: "Ferwas geht ihr net draa un garebt der Baam uff Neiyaahr—die Nescht in der Gibbel—unne gschwetzt odder ferwas schiesst ihr net in der Baam? Awwer es muss ruhich sei." [Why don't you go to it and beat the tree on New Year's—the branches at the top—without speaking or why don't you shoot into the tree? But there must be silence.] On New Year's morning one of the boys got a rod and climbed the tree and threshed the branches. Then unkown to him the other came out with a revolver and fired three times into the trunk. Whereupon the one in the tree gave a yell and quickly came down. "Sie hen der ganze Daag rumghockt un gegrummelt." [They sat around the whole day and grumbled.]

1116.

Dr. Minner says that a Mrs. Ressler said to him: "Heit is Gansdaag. Ich denk du hoscht aa en Gans heit." [Today is goose day. I imagine you'll also have a goose today.] The doctor does not know which day it was. Our older people regarded a goose dinner as preferable to a turkey dinner.

Old Mrs. Louis Kohler, wealthy and intelligent, always had a goose dinner at Thanksgiving and at Christmas.

1117.

Today Charles Snyder (Cf. Nr. 914.) died. During his illness I had visited him and asked him who had told him about the barn signs. He answered that he had heard about them from "die Alde" [the old folks] I did not inquire further, for when a man is sick, it is inopportune to ask him about "so dumme Sache." [such dumb stuff]

1118.

Word: "Landsgschpiel" — games of the countryside. This word was used by Henry Schaeffer, Egypt, Pa.

LANDSGSCHPIEL

1119.

"Fingerziehe." Two persons hook the middle finger of the right hand to see which can draw the other.
Leh, Leb, Mont

1120.

Lifting weights with the middle finger to see who can lift the greatest weight. *Do*

1121.

"Schtrubbkatz ziehe." A rope or band was placed around the heads or necks of two persons to see which could pull the other, i.e. which had the stronger neck and head. *Henry Schaeffer*

1122.

"Besemschtiel." Two players sit on the floor with legs extended and shoes against each other. A broom is taken and held where the feet meet. The players bend forward, grasp the broomstick and then seek to draw the opponent upright. This can only be done if the legs do not buckle. This was widely played at one time.

1123.

Jumping backward upon a chair, off again, on again. *Henry Schaeffer*

1124.

Sitting on the floor, rising up on one leg and holding out a chair at the leg with one hand. *Leh*

1125.

To walk the top rail of a post fence to see who could walk the fartherst without jumping off. *Common*

1126.

Holding a broomstick with both hands and jumping over it without letting go. *Common at one time*

Jumping backwards over the broomstick without letting go.

1127.

Laying hands on top rail of post fence and vaulting across. *Do*

1128.

Seeing who could jump fartherest over a creek with a running jump, "Aarann" — the run before jumping. *Do*

1129.

Standing on the head and striking the heels together. *Common*

1130.

Holding up one leg and jumping with the other to see how far one could jump.

1131.

To see which one could hold out the greater weight at arm's length.

1132.

Sucking a straw full of water and then blowing it out upon another.

1133.

In playing Nr. 1126, before jumping one would say:

"Jack, be nimble, Jack, be quick,
Jack, jump over the candlestick."

1134.

Sliding down the strawstack.

1135.

"Hummler Nescht aushewe, pp. ausghowe" — to rob a bumblebee's nest.

1136.

Catching fish with bare hands under the "Ufer" [bank]. One lay down on the bank and brought his hands together under the "Ufer" trapping the fish.

1137.

Two persons face each other. They bring up their hands and interlock their fingers. They attempt to force the fingers back and bring the opponent to his knees.

(All of these "Landsgschpiel" were frequent pastimes of the country youth.)

1138.
Children would drink newly made cider out of barrels with the aid of straws. They also drank maple sap out of bored holes with the use of straws.

1139.
Word: "glaawe." "Gehscht mit in die Karich?"—"Ich glaab net." Will you go along to church?—I shall not. I suppose not.—A negative answer. One hears it in our English: "I believe not." "Ich denk net" has the same meaning, i.e. a negative answer to an invitation.

1140.
Verbatim from a letter written by William Brown, Klingerstown, Pa.:

"Dart drunne in them Wissa grous,
 Ous thou grick dart souft thou Hous,
 In thou grick dart schwimma the fish
 Lustich war noch ledich is."

"Madle won mere Kinna greya
 Misse mere the Weyga tiega
 Miss singa high o bye
 Gay und koch em Kind thou brye."

"Inn them Shicle is as Male
 Inn them Keller is the Milich
 Geh un rear thes briley eye
 Setses iwer fire mey (ney?)"

"Endlich kuncht se rouse ge-rantz
 Gel du hust thou brye far brandt
 Ich dank ich mus dich larnd Koche
 Soufa Konst do gonse Wocha."

"Do Kump the rous um halver fier
 Uf am dish an gleccle beer
 Gay tca nuf tzum fiddle dum
 Fardz Kind ums Milcha rum."

[Down there in the meadow grass,
 The rabbit drinks from the creek,
 In the creek there swim the fish
 Happy is he who is unmarried.]

[Maiden, when we have children
 We'll have to rock the cradle.
 We'll have to sing: High-o-bye!
 Go and cook the child some pap.]

[In the dish there is flour,
 In the cellar there is milk.
 Go and stir the pap
 And set it on the fire.]

[Finally you can scratch it out(?)
 Didn't you burn the pap?
 I guess I'll have to teach you cooking
 You can drink weeks on end.]

[Here comes out at 3:30
 On the table a glass of beer.
 Go up to fiddle dum,
 So the child has milk(?).]

Despite the spelling one can get a good understanding of the dialectal pronunciation of Snyder-Northumberland counties.

1141.
Word: "uffmundere," to cheer someone up. "Der N- is milsich un ich muss ihn alli Daag uffmundere." [N- is melancholic and I have to cheer him up every day.] To raise up fallen spirits. *Leb*

1142.
"So viel Daag as der erscht Schnee leit, so viel Schnee geb's darich der Winder." As many days as the first snow remains on the ground there will be snowfalls through the winter.] *Mont*

1143.
Proverb
"Unsereens muss es Wedder ewwe nemme wie es kummt." [The likes of us have to take the weather as it comes.] *Do*

1144.
Proverb
"Es Wedder basst net yeder Mensch." [Weather does not please everyone.] *Common*

1145.
Proverb
"Es Wedder kann mer net verennere." [One can't change the weather.] *Do*

1146.
Proverb
"Es gebt ken Wedder as alli-ebber basst." [There is no weather that pleases everyone.] *Do*

1147.
Proverb
"Wann die Mensche es Wedder mache deede, waer niemand zufridde." [If human beings were to make the weather, no one would be satisfied.] *Common*

Nr. 1143-1147 do not exhaust the forms of the thought that it is useless to complain about the weather.

1148.
An anecdote I often hear in the past:

A farmer who was unable to raise good crops went "zum Prieschder" [to the priest] and asked him to pray that he might have good crops. He received the answer, "Do badde Bede nix; do muss Mischt bei!" [Here prayers are of no avail; manure is the answer.] "Do batt Bidde un Bede nix; do muss Mischt bei!"

[Here asking and praying are of no avail; manure is the answer.]

1149.
To ascertain whether there will be floods with the going away of a heavy snowfall, take a ball of snow and hold it over a lit candle. If there is no dropping of water as the snowball melts, the snow will disappear without floods. If the melting causes drops of water, here will be floods. *Robert Werley, Egypt*

1150.
"En guder Dau is so gut wie Rege." [A good dew is as good as rain.] Heard during prolonged dry weather at Egypt.

1151.
Storms, thunderstorms, coming after days of hot dry weather, will be severe. *Common*

1152.
A dry summer foretells a wet winter. *Common*

1153.
A cold winter foretells a hot summer. *Common*

1154.
A dry winter foretells a wet summer.

1155.
A slow moving thunderstorm is dangerous, i.e. lightning will strike. *Common*

1156.
A low storm is very dangerous, i.e. lightning will strike. *Mont*

1157.
The shorter the time between the flash of lightning and the clap of thunder, the nearer the stroke. If you can count up to five before the thunder, the stroke is a mile away.

1158.
"Hitzwedderleeche," "heat lightning," is lightning on the horizon seen in the evening or at night without hearing thunder. *Leb*

1159.
"A storm before seven,
Clear before eleven."

1160.
If there is a thunderstorm before seven o'clock in the morning, there will be seven storms that day. *Leb*

1161.
A thunderstorm brings with it a change in the direction of the wind. "Wann der Wind sich moll dreht, is der Schtarm glei do." [When the wind turns, the storm will soon be here.]

1162.
A "Windschtarm" is what appears to be a thunderstorm but which passes over with little thunder, hardly any rain but with great wind.

1163.
"Wann die Schneegens siddlich fliege, geb's kalt Wedder." [When the wild geese fly south, there will be cold weather.]

1164.
"Wann die Schneegens naddlich fliege, geb's waarem Wedder." [When the wild geese fly north, there will be warm weather.]

1165.
"Wann en Bauer verhungert, is es sei eegni Schuld." [When a farmer starves, it's his own fault.] *Leb, Mont*

1166.
Proverb
"Wie mer am Esse is, so is mer am Schaffe." [As one eats, so one works.] *Mont*

1167.
Proverb
"Wer langsam is am Esse is langsam am Schaffe." [Cf. 1166.] *Leb*

1168.
Proverb
"Wer net schafft, soll net esse, saagt die Biewel." [He who does not work, should not eat, says the Bible.] *Leb*
"Wer net schaffe will, soll aa net esse, secht die Biewel." *Mont*

1169.
Proverb
"Wie mer in der Busch greischt, so kumm's aus em Busch raus." [As one calls into the woods, so it comes back out.] *Mrs. Morris Lindenmuth, Egypt*

1170.
"Zu gleene Kinner un yunge Hund sett mer schee schwetze." [One should speak kindly to children and young dogs.] *Mrs. Orlando Wright, Egypt*

1171.
"Wann die Marie nass iwwer der Barig geht, kummt sie drucke zerick." [When Mary goes over the mountain wet, she'll come back dry.] *Common*

1172.
"Katze Breddich un lange Brotwascht." [A short sermon and a long sausage.] This I often heard during my pastorate in Montgomery County. "Parre, ich gleich en katzi Breddich un en lange Brotwascht." The meaning which I got out of it was, "On Sunday I like a short church service and a long dinner." I do not recall having heard the expression in Lebanon County.

1173.
"Mer kann immer ebbes Neies lanne." [One can always learn something new.] *Common*

1174.
"Mer kann ebbes lanne vum dummschde Mann." [One can learn something from the most ignorant man.] *Not infrequent*

1175.
"En Weibsmensch as ihre Bett macht mariyets is fleissich; middaags, mied; oweds, faul." [A woman who makes her bed in the morning is diligent; at noon, tired; in the evening, lazy.]

1176.
"Alli Yahr macht en guder Bauer en Dausend Daaler un en Kind." [Every year a good farmer makes $1,000 and a child.] *Gus Renninger, Falkner Swamp [He had a large family.]*

1177.
Of a sermon: "Katz und gut." The preachers of a former generation were accustomed to preach long sermons. "Sie hen sich so oft widderholt." [They repeated themselves so often.] A more recent generation preached shorter sermons. "Mer saagt was mer zu saage hot un noh mit faddich." [One says what one has to say and then have finished with it.] *Often heard*

1178.
The expression "Langsam un deitlich" may have meant originally "slowly and distinctly," but now it has come to mean "without haste and in an orderly manner."

I was called to conduct a funeral at Eschbach's Crossing about 13 miles away from the Old Goshenhoppen Church. When I got to the house, the man told me: "Parre, des soll langsam un deitlich hergeh." [Pastor, the service is to be conducted without haste and in an orderly manner.] Services at the house were to begin at 9 o'clock. We had lunch before the services and lunch after the services. The services at the church were set for 2 p.m.

At the time I felt that the family thought a funeral "wu Zeit gemacht is" [where time was made] looked as though the mourners were trying to get rid of the departed as quickly as possible, while a "slow" funeral showed that they wanted to keep the departed as long as they could.

1179.
"Zobb an dei eegni Naas." Pull at your own nose. Mind your own business. *Common*

1180.
"En yeders hot genunk mit sich selwert." [Each person has enough trouble of his own.] *Common*

1181.
"Wann en Fraa fehlt, fehlt's iwweraal." [When there's no woman in the house, in the family, there's something missing everywhere.] *Common*

1182.
"Sis yuscht ee Muss in der Welt un sell is: 'Du muscht schtarwe.'" [There's only one must in the world and that is: You must die.] This is spoken when someone says to another: "Du muscht so un so duh!" [You must do so and so.]

1183.
"Driebsaal uff Node [sic] geblose,
Mach en Lied un sing's!"

[Suffering in addition to pain:
Write a song and sing it!]

This was said when someone had sorrow or grief that was magnified. *Ed Bolig, Sumneytown*

1184.
"O Yammer in der grosse Kammer,
O Triebsaal in der gleene."

[Trouble in the large room,
Suffering in the small one.] *Do*

1185.
"Eens uff em Dach griege" [to get one on the roof] is used to express the belief that one got a setback.

"Parre, wie ich an dei Gaarde verbei gange bin, hawwich gsehne as dei Buhne ganz gehl waare. Noh hawwich gedenkt, do hot der Parre mol eens uff sei Dach grickt." [Pastor, when I went by your garden, I saw that your beans were all yellow. Then I thought to myself, here the pastor suffered a setback.] (The beans were yellow from the frost.) *My neighbor*

1186.
"Der Wind legt sich enwedder am Sunnunner odder am Sunnuff." [The wind will subside either at sundown or sunrise.] *N- Hatzell*

A SERIES OF VERY INTERESTING RHYMES
from Charles Easterly
between Vera Cruz and Lanark
gotten by
Bumbernickel Bill
December 26, 1936

1187.
"Sauf, Bruder, sauf,
Es geht alles drauf."

[Drink, brother, drink,
All's going down the hatch.]

1188.
"Maryerot
Bedeit Dreck un Kot."

[Red in the morning sky
means dirt and mud.]

1190. [sic]
"Am Eens kumme die Trains,
Am Zwee losst mer sie geh.
Am Drei kumme sie rei,
Am Viere dutt mer sie rumfiehre.
Am Fimfe dutt mer sie pschimfe,
Am Sexe kumme die Hexe.
Am Siwwe warre sie weckgedriwwe,
Am Achde dutt mer's Bett bedrachde.
Am Neine dutt mer's Bett bescheine,
Am Zehe dutt mer sich rumdrehe.
Am Elfe dutt mer sich helfe,
Am Zwelfe kumme die Welfe."

[At 1 the trains come,
At 2 one lets them go.
At 3 they come in,
At 4 one leads them about.
At 5 one scolds them,
At 6 the witches come.
At 7 they are chased away,
At 8 one observes the bed.
At 9 one lights up the bed,
At 10 one turns around.
At 11 one helps oneself,
At 12 the wolves come.]

1191.
"Ich un du
Un noch en Buh
Un der (Bruder) Peeder Seipel,
Hen verrissene Hosse aa
Un raus henkt der Beidel."

[You and I
And another boy
And (brother) Peter Seipel,
Are wearing torn pants
And out hangs the purse.]

["Beidel," literally, "a small bag," also has the meaning "scrotum."]

1192.
"Ich wott ich waer en Parre,
Odder wott ich waer net warre."

[I wish I were a pastor,
Or wish I had never become one.]

1193.
"Sauergraut un Schpeck,
Macht die alde Weiwer fett."

[Sauerkraut and bacon,
Makes the old women fat.]

1194.
"Drucke Brod,
Macht em die Backe rot."

[Dry bread
Makes the cheeks red.]

1195.
"Fer denke
Kann em niemand henke."

[For thinking ones thoughts
No one can be hanged.]

1196.
"1, 2, 3, 4,
Meedel, wann du danze witt,
Danz mit mir.
5, 6, 7, 8,
Meedel, wann du bei mir schlofe witt,
Waard bis die Nacht."

[Maiden, if you want to dance,
Dance with me.]

[Maiden, if you want to sleep
with me wait till night.]

1197.
"Katz un dick,
Is aa en Schtick."
(Macht aa en Schtick)

[Short and thick,
Is also a piece.]
(Makes a piece also.)

1198.
"Dinn un lang,
Macht aa en Schtang."

[Thin and long,
Also makes a pole.]

1199.
[The text to a popular folksong.]

[Mother:]
"Schpinn, schpinn, mei liewe Dochder,
No kaaf ich dir en Hund.

[Spin, spin, my dear daughter,
Then I'll buy you a dog.]

[Daughter:]
a.

[Ya, ya, mei liewe Mammi,]
awwer der net zu rund.

[Yes, yes, my dear mother,
but not too round.]

b.
Schpinn, schpinn, mei liewe Dochder,
No kaaf ich dir en Schof. [a sheep]

[Ya, ya, mei liewe Mammi,]
awwer eens as net schloft.
[but not one that sleeps.]

c.
Schpinn, schpinn, mei liewe Dochder,
No kaaf ich dir en Bett. [a bed]

[Ya, ya, mei liewe Mammi,]
awwer aa die Deck.
[but also the cover.]

d.
Schpinn, schpinn, mei liewi Dochder,
No kaaf ich dir en Kind. [a child]

[Nee, nee, mei liewe Mammi,]
Nee, liewer en Rind.
[No, rather an heifer.]

e.
Schpinn, schpinn, mei liewe Dochder,
No kaaf ich dir en Schatz. [an apron]

[Ya, ya, mei liewi Mammi,]
Awwer der net zu katz.
[But not too short.]

f.
Schpinn, schpinn, mei liewe Docher,
Ich kaaf dir en Schtang. [a pole]

[Ya, ya, mei liewe Mammi,]
Awwer der net zu lang.
[But not too long.]

g.
Schpinn, schpinn, mei liewe Dochder,
Ich kaaf dir en Disch. [a table]

[Ya, ya, mei liewe Mammi,]
Awwer aa mit me Fisch.
[But with a fish.]

h.
Schpinn, schpinn, mei liewe Dochder,
No kaaf ich dir en Unnerrock. [a petticoat]

[Ya, ya, mei liewe Mammi,]
Awwer enner mit me Tock.
[But one with a tuck.]

i.
Schpinn, schpinn, mei liewe Dochder,
No kaaf ich dir en Shanty.

[Nee, nee, mei liewe Mammi,]
Nee, liewer en Brandy.

j.
Schpinn, schpinn, mei liewe Dochder,
No kaaf ich dir en Bauerei. [a farm]

[Nee, nee, mei liewe Mammi,]
Nee, liewer en Brennerei.
[No, rather a distillery.]

k.
Schpinn, schpinn, mei liewe Dochder,
No kaaf ich dir en Eeg. [a harrow]

[Nee, nee, mei liewe Mammi,]
Nee, liewer en Seeg.
[No, rather a saw.]

l.
Schpinn, schpinn, mei liewe Dochder,
No kaaf ich dir en Schtiel. [a handle]

[Ya, ya, mei liewe Mammi,]
Awwer recht viel.
[But very many.]

m.
Schpinn, schpinn, mei liewe Dochder,
No kaaf ich dir Hosse. [pants]

[Ya, ya, mei liewi Mammi,]
Awwer die net verschosse.
[but not all shot up.]

n.
Schpinn, schpinn, mei liewe Dochder,
No kaaf ich dir en Rind. [a heifer]

[Ya, ya, mei liewe Mammi,]
awwer net zu gschwind.
[but not too quick.]

o.
Schpinn, schpinn, mei liewi Dochder,
No kaaf ich dir en Schank. [a cupboard]

[Nee, nee, mei liewe Mammi,]
Nee, liewer en Bank.
[No, rather a bench.]

p.
Schpinn, schpinn, mei liewe Dochder,
No kaaf ich dir en Hemm. [a shirt]

[Ya, ya, mei liewi Mammi,]
Awwer net zu eng.
[But not too narrow.]

q.
Schpinn, schpinn, mei liewe Dochder,
No kaaf ich dir en Seil. [awe]

[Nee, nee, mei liewe Mammi,]
Nee, liewer en Feil.
[No, rather a file.]

r.
Schpinn, schpinn, mei liewe Dochder,
No kaaf ich dir en Bascht. [a brush]

[Nee, nee, mei liewe Mammi,]
Nee, liewer en Nasccht.
[No, rather a branch.]

s.
Schpinn, schpinn, mei liewe Dochder,
No kaaf ich dir en Kalb. [a calf]

[Ya, ya, mei liewe Mammi,]
Awwer net zu alt.
[But not too old.]

t.
Schpinn, schpinn, mei liewe Dochder,
No kaaf ich dir en Scheier. [a barn]

[Ya, ya, mei liewe Mammi,]
Awwer recht deier.
[But very expensive.]

u.
Schpinn, schpinn, mei liewe Dochder,
No kaaf ich dir en Schibb. [a spade]

[Nee, nee, mei liewe Mammi,]
Nee, liewer en Sibb.
[No, rather a sieve.]

(Here we see an extreme example of folk versification. The almost endless versification that can be carried on by facile minds to a rhythm. Here we see also the birth of variations to folksongs.)

1200.
"Wer's erscht riecht,
Aus dem griecht's."

[He who smells it the first,
From him you'll get it.]

1201.
"Hoi is deier,
In die Scheier."

[Hay is expensive,
In the barn.]

1202.
"En Raad,
Is net graad."

[A wheel,
Is not straight.]

1203.
"Yammer in die Kammer."

[Suffering in the room.]

1204.
"Im Moi esst mer die Boi."

[In May one eats the pies.]

1205.
"Geh weck odder ich schlack dich in der Dreck."

[Go away or I'll knock you in the dirt.]

1206.
"Bier uff Wei,
das loscht du sei."

[Beer after wine, let that be.]

1207.
"Awwer Wei uff Bier,
das rot ich dir."

[But wine after beer, that I recommend.]

1208.
"Der Dude guckt gut in der Hut."

[The dude looks well in the hat.]

1209.
"Weide Schuh dricke net,
Enge Schuh fidde net."

[Wide shoes do not pinch,
Narrow shoes do not fit.]

1210.
"Geld zwingt die Welt."

[Money rules the world.]

1211.
"Grank mit der Naas im (Brot)Schank."

[Sick with the nose in the cupboard.]

1212.
"Hund, halt dei Mund."

[Dog, be quiet.]

1213.
"Wann mer der Esel nennt,
Kummt er gerennt."

[When one speaks of the donkey,
He comes arunning.]

1214.a.
"Yung un dumm."

[Young and inexperienced.]

1214.b.
"Unser Aldi draagt ihr Ding im Karwel."

[Our old woman carries her thing in a basket.]

1215.
"Do leit der Schneider beim Seider."

[Here Snyder lies by his cider.]

1216.
A game
"Police, Gickeregies, schtinkiche Fiess."

[Police, cock-a-doodle-doos, stinky feet.]

The above was spoken to the person who was "it." Those caught were penned in the woodshed-coal house on the school grounds.

1217.
"Do schteh ich im Eck un schneid Schpeck,
Wer mich liebt, der hollt mich weck."

[Here I stand in the corner and
and cut bacon, He who loves me takes me away.]

1218.
"Im Brunne hot mer's gfunne."

[In the well it was found.]

1219.
"Im Matz losst mer die Fatz."

[In March one breaks wind.]

1220.
"Im Auguscht esst mer die Gruscht."

[In August one eats crust.]

1221.
"Am Drei esst mer's Breih."

[At three one eats pap.]

1222.
"Grumm un graad macht en Raad."

[Crooked and straight makes a wheel.]

1223.
Game
Hold something over his head and ask: "Was gilt des Band in meiner Hand?" [Of what use is this band in my hand?]—"Sie odder er?" [She or he?] "Er." [He.]—"Was soll er duh?" [What shall he do?]

1224.
"Wann ich muss, geb's ken Verdruss."

[If I must, there'll be no fuss.]

1225.
"Rund im Grund."

[Round in the ground.]

1226.
"Karbet macht Arwet."

[Carpet makes work.]

Otherwise heard by me

1227.
"Alt un kalt."

[Old and cold.]

1228.
"Im Febuaar is alles waahr."

[In February all is true.]

1229.
"Wann?—Sis ken Pann."

[When?—It's no pan.]

1230.
"Wann is ken Pann
 En Kiehfutz ken Ariyel
 Odder wottscht immer druff rum drudle?"

[When is no pan
 A cow's rear no organ
 Or would you always doodle around?]

1231.
"Vun Kopp zu Mund,
 Vun Mund zu Grund."

[From head to mouth,
 From mouth to ground.]

1232.
"Was?—En alt Fass."

[What?—An old barrel.]

1233.
"Schmidt, du muscht mit!"

[Smith, you must come along.]

1234.
"Wie ich yung un leddich waar,
Do waar die Lieb so gross.
Wie ich alt un gheiert waar,
Do waar der Deiwel los."

[When I was young and single,
Love was so great.
When I was ald and married,
The devil was on the loose.]

1235.
"Gesundheit! Soll dir wohl duh,
Wann's drunne bleibt."

[To your health! May it do you well, if it stays down.]

1236.
"Am Achde losst mer's grache."

[At eight let it crack.]

1237.
"Dinn un rund, geht zu Grund."

[Thin and round goes to naught.]

1238.
"Grank uff die Bank."

[Sick on the bench.]

1239.
"Gschosse is net gedroffe."

[Fired is not hit.]

1240.
"Wolle, loss es rolle."

[Wolle, let it roll.]

1241.
"Schneck im Dreck."

[Snail in the dirt.]

1242.
"En Faus owwedraus."

[Meaning of "Faus" unclear.]

1243.
"En Maus im Haus."

[A mouse in the house.]

1244.
"Im Gaarde muss mer waarde."

[One must wait in the garden.]

1245.
"Grosser Fresser, glenner Scheffer."

[Big eater, little worker.]

1246.
"Die Schof sin im Hof."

[The sheep are in the yard.]

1247.
"Im Feld mach mer's Geld."

[In the field one makes money.]

1248.
"Ich in die Kich."

[I in the kitchen.]

1249.
"Sach uff em Dach."

[Things on the roof.]

1250.
"Heller im Keller."

[Brighter in the cellar.]

1251.
"Drunne gezwunge."

[Forced down there.]

1252.
"Howwe gebliwwe."

[Remained up here.]

1253.
"Drunne gebliwwe."

[Stayed down there.]

1254.
"Wo?—En Boh."

[Where?—A beau.]

1255.
"Drunne gebunne."

[Tied down there.]

1256.
"Wittmann, Drittmann, Fittmann."

[Widower, third man, fit man.]

1257.
"Die Maaryeschtund hot Gold im Mund,
Wer die verseimt, der bleibt en Lumb."

[The morning hour has gold in in the mouth, He who misses it remains a rag.]

1258.
"Draus aus em Haus."

[Outside of the house.]

1259.
"Bett im Eck, Lady, geh weck."

[Bed in the corner, lady, go away.]

1260.
"Fleesch macht bees."

[Meat makes angry.]

1261.
"Wie heller, wie schneller."

[The brighter, the faster.]

1262.
"Wann net gehscht, dann schtehscht."

[If you don't go, you'll be standing.]

1263.
"Der Widder (Zodiacal sign) is der Vadder awwer net der Lieder."

[Aries is the father but not the leader.]

1264.
"Wer sich ernehre will mit Fische un Yaage,
Der muss verrissene Gleeder draage."

[He who wants to live by fishing
and hunting must wear torn clothing.]

1265.
"Wie geht's?—Hinnich der Dier schteht's."

[How are things?—It's standing behind the door.]

1266.
"Ich hab net gheiert fer en Mann yuscht fer Fun."

[I have not married to have a husband; I've married just for fun.]

1267.
"Die Maad am Raad."

[The maid at the wheel.]

1268.
"Ich un du un noch en Buh,
Noh kummt en Kuh dazu."

[You and I and another boy,
Then there comes a cow.]

1269.
"En Maad im Paad."

[A maid on the path.]

1270.
"Es Haus is draus."

[The house is outside.]

1271.
"Schof im Schlof."

[Sheep that are asleep.]

1272.
"Der Haahne hot ken Faahne."

[The rooster has no flag.]

1273.
"Die Schtee sin glee."

[The stones are small.]

1274.
"Der Blank is grank mit der Naas im Schank."

[Blank is sick with his nose in the cupboard.]

1275.
"Hund im Grund."

[Hound in the ground.]

1276.
"Im Bett wert mer net fett."

[You don't get fat in bed.]

1277.
"Wann mer in der Gadember Woch schlacht, verderbt's Fleesch."

[If you butcher during Ember Week [cf. 1359] the meat will spoil.]

1278.
"Wer gut schmiert, der gut fiehrt,
Wer zu gut schmiert, der in die Helle nei fiehrt."

[He who greases well, will lead well
He who greases too well, will lead you to hell.]

1279.
"Der John, net fer grank awwer fer Fun, hot die Kann in die Hand."

[John, not for sick but for fun, has the can in his hand.]

1280.
"Der Franky in die Shanty is net fer Candy awwer fer Brandy."

[Franky in the shanty is not for candy but for brandy.]

1281.
"Der glee Tscheck mit der Seck."

[Little Jeck with the bags.]

1282.

"Sis mir verleed mit's Pannebeckers Meed,
Un abaddich mit der Kate
Sie hockt uff die Schteeg."

[I'm sad about Pannebecker's
daughters and especially about
Kate; she sits on the steps.]

(This group is most interesting. We have here evidence of a rhyme plus the older foot rhyme. These should be carefully studied.)

A GROUP OF WEATHER LORE
copied from letters from D. E. Lick,
Fredericksburg,
to
Bumbernickel Bill
December, 1936

1283.
"Schpot Herbscht wann der Wind nooch me Landrege unne rum kummt, vun Mariye zu Middaag, zu Owed, windert's noch net ei, wann er awwer owwe rum zu Norde geht wert's aahaltend kalt." [In late autumn when after a land rain the wind moves about from the east to the south to the west, winter will not yet set in; if the wind, however, comes from the north, it will get cold and stay cold.]

1284.
"Wann der Wind im Schornschtee odder am Hauseck heilt, geb's wiescht Wedder." [When the wind howls in the chimney or around the house, there'll be bad weather.]

1285.
"Wann der Haahne oweds greht wann er uffhockt, bleibt's Wedder noch wie es is; wann er awwer uff der Schtang greht vor Halbnacht, geb's Rege neechtlich." [When the rooster crows in the evening as he's going to roost, the weather will remain as it is but if he crows on the roost before midnight, there will be rain at night.]

1286.
"Wann die Grabbe uff Drubbe gehne, gebt's Rege im Summer im Winder Rege odder Schnee." [When the crows fly in flocks, there'll be rain in summer; in the winter rain or snow.]

1287.
"Wann die Grabbe so faul 'har, har, har' locke, wert's waermer." [When the crows call "har, har, har" in a lazy manner, it will get warmer.]

1288.
"Wann die Hinkel arig abfaertre [sic] am Lege in eem Daag im Herbscht odder Winder, waert's viel kelder der naegschde Daag." [When the chickens moult a great deal while laying on a day in autumn or winter, it will be much colder the next day.]

1289.
"Wann der Bodde uffgeht im Chrischtmonet, geht er alli Monet uff seller Winder." [If the ground thaws in December, it will thaw every month that winter.]

1290.
"Mer soll bei Leiwe nix nehe un nix nagele uff der Himmelfaahrdaag. Wann mir en Gleed neht odder flickt uff seller Daag, ziegt's Gwidder gern aa. Wann mer nagelt, schlaagt's Gwidder seller Summer ei eenich aryets wu der Schall vum Nagele hiefaahrt." [By no means would one sew or nail on Ascension Day. If one sews or mends a dress on that day, one will attract lightning. If one nails anything, that summer lightning will strike any place where the sound of the nailing has been heard.]

A woman who had sewn on Ascension Day suddenly recollected the day—as a storm arose—and took the garment and threw it out on the bakeoven.

1291.
"Deel Leit glaawe as es Gwidder en Schtee waer, en Gwidderschtee. Der Gwidderschtee, wie mer wisse, is was es gebt wann's Gwidder in me Baam odder ebbes so dreft un schmelzt der Sand im Bodde zamme uff en Glumbe." [Some people believe that thunder is a stone, a 'thunder-stone.' The thunder-stone, as one knows, is what results when the lightning strikes a tree or something like that and melts the sand in the ground resulting in a lump.] (Lick believes in the occurence of such stones.) "Die menschde Leit hen en Glaawe as es waere "heese" un 'kalde' Gwidderschtreech." [Most people believe that there is a "hot" and a "cold" thunderbolt.]

1292.
"Es gebt Rege wann der Regevogel peift." [There will be rain when the plover calls.]

1293.
"Es gebt Rege wann's Baddersli (!) peift." [when the quail calls.]

1294.
"Es gebt Rege wann die Katz Graas fresst." [when the cat eats grass.]

1295.
"Es gebt Rege wann der Hund Graas fresst." [when the dog eats grass.]

1296.
"Es gebt Rege wann die Schwemm ruffwaxe iwwer Nacht." [when the mushrooms grow from the ground overnight.]

1297.
"Es gebt Rege wann die Regewerm Heife Grund ruffbringe iwwer Nacht." [when the earthworms build up piles of earth overnight.]

1298.
"Es gebt ball Rege wann die Holzarwet im Haus odder es hilzich Hausrot im Haus gracht." [There will soon be rain when the woodwork in the house or the wooden furniture in the house cracks.]

1299.
"Es gebt ball Rege wann die Leit ungewehnlich viel faahre uff der Schtrooss." [when there are unusually many people driving on the roads.]

1300.
"Es gebt ball Rege wann mer alli Sadde Yacht heert vun weidem." [when one hears all sorts of noise in the distance.]

1301.
"Es gebt ball Rege wann die Sunn odder der Mond en Ring hot." [when the sun or the moon has a ring.]

1302.
"Es gebt ball Rege wann der Rauwevogel 'Kuk-ku-kuk, Kuk-ku-kuk' lockt, is es Zeit fer's Hoi reiholle, wann mer's net nass hawwe will." [when a bird of prey calls "kuk-ku-kuk, Kuk-ku-kuk," it's time to bring in hay if one doesn't want it to get wet.]

1303.
"Es gebt ball Rege wann's Freschli peift uff em Baam." [when the spring peepers pipe in the tree.]

1304.
"Wann der Laubfrosch (Hyla versicolor) uff me Baam greischt im Daag, gebt's Gwidderrege." [When the tree-toad calls in a tree during the day, there will be a thunderstorm.]

1305.a.
"Es gebt ball Rege wann mer en Schlang dodschlaagt un hengt sie uff en Fens." [There will soon be rain when one kills a snake and hangs it on a fence.]

1305.b.
"Es gebt ball Rege wann die Schlange haus leie daags un mer losst sie zufridde." [when the snakes are lying outside during the day and one lets them be.]

1306.
"Es gebt ball Rege wann's net daut." [when no dew falls.]

1307.
"Es gebt ball Rege wann's Moos uff's Wasser kummt." [when algae forms on the water.]

1308.
"Es gebt ball Rege wann der Mischthaufe im Scheierhof schtinkt." [when the manure pile in the barnyard smells.]

1309.
"Es gebt ball Rege wann die Luft noch Bisskatze schtinkt." [when the air smells like polecats.]

1310.
"Es gebt ball Rege wann die Bullfragge blaerre." [when the bullfrogs call.]

1311.
"Es gebt ball Rege wann der Glee welk watt und hengt die Bledder." [when the clover becomes wilted and the leaves droop.]

1312.
"Es gebt ball Rege wann en Grug mit Wasser odder en eisne Bump schwitzt im Summer." [when a pitcher with water or an iron pump sweats in summer.]

1313.
"Es gebt ball Rege wann's Maryerot weit geye Owed ziegt." [when the red glow in the morning sky extends toward the west.]

1314.
"Maryerrot, Dreck un Kot." [Red glow in the morning means dirt and mud.]

1315.
"Wann die Schwalme negscht (not far overhaed?) uff en rum schwewe, bedeit's en Regeschtarm." [When the swallows float about overhead, it means rain.]

1316.
"Es gebt ball Rege wann der Schmok vum Schanschde runner uff der Bodde fallt." be rain when the smoke from the chimney returns to the ground.]

1317.
"Es gebt ball Rege wann die Windwerwel naerdlich gehn." [when the whirlwinds move to the north.]

1318.
"Es gebt ball Rege wann die Sunn glaar, hell silwerich scheint." [when the sun shines brightly and appears silvery.]

1319.
"Es gebt ball Rege wann die Sunn Wasser ziegt." [when the sun draws water.]

1320.
"Es gebt ball Rege wann der Mond am Neilicht mit der Haerner unnerschich schteht—noddich leert er aus." [when the new moon stands with the horns down.]

1321.
"Es gebt ball Rege wann's Owedrot unne rum geye Mariye ziegt." [when the glow in the evening sky draws toward the south.]

1322.
"Drei Reife hinnich ennanner." [Three frosts in a row.]

Zeeche fer schee odder drucke Wedder
[Signs for lovely or dry weather]

1323.
"Wann die Sunn feierich rot scheint." [When the sun appears fire red.]

1324.
"Schwer Dau im Summer." [Heavy dew in summer.]

1325.
"Wann's frieh mariyets regert odder drepselt yuscht so en Bissel dann un wann darich der Daag, geb's drucke Wedder." [When it rains early in the morning or a bit now and then during the day in small drops, there will be dry weather.]

1326.
"Wann die Luft vun sudde ziegt darich der Daag un vun Nadde darich die Nacht." [When the air comes from the south during the day and from the north during the night there will be dry weather.]

1327.
"Wann der Mond am Neilicht uff em Rick leit un hot der alt Mond in der Aerem." [There will be dry weather when the new moon lies on its back and has the old moon in its arms.]

1328.
"Owedrot, Mariye schee." [Red glow in the evening, lovely weather in the morning.]

Zeeche fer windich Wedder
[Signs for windy weather]

1329.
"Wann die zaahme Gens fliege, watt's windich." [When the domestic geese fly, it'll be windy.]

1330.
"Wann's Rindvieh schpringt un fecht, watt's schtaermich." [When the cattle jump about and fight, it'll be stormy.]

1331.
"Wann der Gillerei greischt, watt's windich un kelder." [When the killdeer calls, it'll turn windy and colder.]

1332.
"Wann's Feier brummt im Offe, watt's windich." [When the fire hums in the stove, it'll turn windy.]

1333.
"Wann die Katz uff em Kobb leit, gebt's Schtaerm." [When the cat lies on its head, it will storm.]

Verschiedene Wedderglaawe un Wedderschprich
[Various weather beliefs and weather sayings]

1334.
"Neiyaahrs Maryerot macht viel Not." [New Year's red in the morning means much suffering.]

1335.
"Newwel im Yenner bringt Reife im Moi." [Fog in January brings frost in May.]

1336.
"Wann's Graas im Yenner waxt, waxt's schlecht darich's ganz Yaahr." [When the grass grows in January, it will grow poorly the entire year.]

1337.
"Wann der Dachs sei Schadde seht im Lichtmess Marye, dann geht er widder in's Loch un bleibt noch sex Woche drin. Wann Lichtmess Marye awwer drieb is, dann bleibt der Dachs haus un's watt noch enanner Friehyaahr." [When the groundhog sees his shadow on the morning of February 2, he will again go into his hole and remain there for six weeks. But if the morning of February 2 is overcast, the groundhog will remain outside and there will be another spring.]

1338.
"Matheus brecht Eis,
Hot's kens, macht's Eis."

[On St. Matthew's Day the ice
will break; if there's none ice will form.]

1340.[sic]
"'Der Horning schiddelt's Horn,' so saagt mer wann der Munet rau Wedder hot am Aafang. Wann er awwer wiescht Wedder hot am End, dann saagt mer als: 'Der Horning schiddelt der Schwanz.'" ["February is shaking its horn," says one when there's raw weather at the beginning of the month. When the weather is bad at the end of the month one says: "February is shaking its tail."]

1341.
"En druckner Matz, en nasser Abrill un en kiehler Moi, bringt viel Frucht un Hoi." [A dry March, a wet April and a cool May, bring much grain and hay.]

"Matzebliet is net gut,
Abrillebliet is halb gut,
Moibliet is ganz gut."

[Blossoms in March are not good,
Blossoms in April are half good,
Blossoms in May are very good.]

1343.
"Wann's regert uff der Karfreidaag, badde die Rege nix seller ganz Summer." [If it rains on Good Friday, the rains that summer will be of no avail.]

1344.
"Wann die Marieye drucke niwwer geht, kummt sie nass riwwer. Geht sie nass niwwer, kummt sie drucke riwwer. Die Meening is das die Mariye en Wolk waer un gingt iwwer der Barig uff der zwett Yuli un keemt widder zurick uff der fuffzeht Auguscht." [When Mary goes dry, she will come back wet. If she goes over wet, she will come back dry. The meaning is that Mary is a cloud and goes over the mountain on the second of July and comes back again on the fifteenth of August.] (This same explanation was given by my grandfather when he was at home with us [in Schaefferstown]. It was tantamount to saying that if a northwest wind blew on July second, a southeast wind would blow on August 15.) [Cf. Nr. 1171.]

1345.
"Griene Grischdaag, weisse Oschdre.
Weisse Grischdaag, griene Oschdre."

[Green Christmas, white Easter.
White Christmas, green Easter.]

1346.
"Die heeschde Daage vum Summer bringe gern die kelschde Daage vum Winder sex Munet danooch." [The hottest days in summer are apt to produce the coldest days of winter six months later.]

1347.
"Wann der Warmet un Ungraut hoch waxt im Summer, geb's gern diefer Schnee im negschde Winder." [When ragweed and other weeds grow high in the summer, there is apt to be deep snow the next winter.]

1348.
"Wann's Laab lang uff die Beem henke bleibt, geb's en langer hadder Winder." [When the leaves remain long on the trees (in the fall), there will be a long hard winter.]

1349.
"Wann's Welschkann Bascht dick is uff die Kolwe, geb's en hadder Winder." [When the husk is thick around the corncob, there will be a hard winter.]

1350.
"Wann's viel Niss un Ebbel hot, geb's en hadder Winder. Noert misse die Eechhaase viel Fuder hawwe." [When nuts and apples are plentiful in the fall, there will be a hard winter. Then the squirrels much have much food.]

1351.
"Wann's in der erscht Schnee regert, dann regert's gern in alli Schnee seller Winder." [If it rains on the first snow, then it will be apt to rain on all the snows that winter.]

1352.
"Wann die wilde Gens herbschts fliege, waert's kalt un gebt Schnee; wann sie friehyaahrs fliege, waert's waarm un gebt Rege." [When the wild geese fly in the fall, it will turn cold and snow; when they fly in the spring, it will turn warm and rain.]

1353.
"Wann die Sonn odder der Mond en Ring hot, geb's Rege odder Schnee." [When the sun or the moon have a ring, it will rain or snow.]

1354.
"Wann der Mond en Ring hot mit Schtanne drin, so viel Daage gebt's wie Schtanne im Ring sin bis der negscht Schnee fallt." [When the moon has a ring around it with stars within the ring, as many stars as there within the ring there will be days before the next snow falls.]

1355.
"Wann der Mond en Hof hot, Sommer odder Winder, geb's wiescht Wedder." [When the moon has a "court", a ring, summer or winter, there'll be bad weather.]

1356.
"Wann en Newesonn odder Wedderzeeche am Himmel schteht, bedeit's wiescht Wedder." [When a double sun or a weather omen appears in the sky, it means bad weather.]

1357.
"Wann's glatt Eis gebt im alde Yaahr, gebt's viel Ebbel der negscht Summer. Der schwerer's Eis uff die Beem, so das die Nescht enanner reide, desto mehner Ebbel." [When there's glazed ice on the ground and on the trees in the old year, there will be many apples the next summer. The heavier the ice is on the trees, so that the branches ride each other, the more apples.]

1358.
"Wie der letscht Freidaag im Munet, só is der ganz negscht Munet." [The following month is just like the last Friday in the preceding month.]

1359.
"Wie der Daag waar im Quatember, der Quatember Daag, der Daag noch em Quatember, so die drei negschde Munet." [As the weather is on the day before Ember Day, on Ember Day and on the day after Ember Day, so the weather will be the next three months.] [Ember days: Three days out of each calendar season reserved for prayer and fasting by some Christian churches, observed on the Wednesday, Friday and Saturday after the first Sunday of Lent, after Whitsunday, after September 14 and and after Decmeber 13.]

1360.
"Wann's regert vor der siwwe Uhr, regert's siwwe Mol seller Daag." [If it rains before seven o'clock, it will rain seven times that day.]

1361.
"Friehe Maryerege un alde Weiwerdenz wehre net lang." [Early morning rains and old women's dances don't last long.]

1362.
"Wann's Neilicht im Schtier kummt, geb's en Weil rauh Wedder un wann's im Summer is." [If the new moon occurs in the sign of Taurus, there will be a period of rough weather even if it's summertime.]

1363.
"Wann's regerisch is un's hellt nachts uff, halt's Wedder net lang." [If there has been rainy weather and it clears at night, the clear weather will not last long.]

1364.
"Wann die Wolke am Himmel kipperich waerre, gebt's ball Rege." [When a mackerel sky develops, there will soon be rain.]

1365.
"Wann en Herschel im Kalenner schteht (conjunction of Herschel and the moon), geb's um selli Zeit rauh Wedder." [When there's a Herschel in the almanac, there will be rough weather at that time.][Cf. Nr. 1006]

1366.
"Wann en Eishaus im Kalenner schteht (quartile 90 degrees of planets from the sun), geb's rauh kalt Wedder selli Zeit." [When an icehouse appears in the almanac, there will be rough cold weather at that time.]

1367.
"Wann die Wolke gucke wie gewennt Hoi (wavy cloudiness), geb's ganz negschtlich Rege." [When the clouds look like tedded hay, there will be rain very soon.]

1368.
"Wann die Sonn drieb unnergeht Sonndaag oweds, gebt's Rege vorm Mittwoch. Wann sie drieb unnergeht Mittwoch, gebt's Rege vorm Sonndaag." [When the sun sets in a clouded sky Sunday evenings, there will be rain before Wednesday. When the sun sets in an overcast sky on Wednesday, there will be rain before Sunday.]

1369.
"Wann die Sonn aaryets hell uffgeht un schluppt glei hinnich en Wolk, geb's seller Daag Rege." [When the sun rises clearly and soon slips behind a cloud, there will be rain that day.]

1370.
"Wann en laafender Brunne odder en Krickli drucke is im drucke Wedder un fangt widder aa zu laafe unni as es geregert hot, geb's negschtlich Rege." [When a flowing spring or a small run is dry in dry weather and begins again to run without rain, there will be rain soon.]

1371.
"Wann die Hinkel sich uff die Fens hocke bei drieb Wedder, waert's glei hell." [When the chickens sit on the fence in overcast weather, it will soon clear.]

1372.
"Wann die Sei Schtroh draage fer Neschder mache, waert's kelder." [When the pigs gather straw to make nests, it will get colder.]

1373.
"Wann der Wind unnerei kummt (east to south to west) odder wann er mit der Sonn geht, gebt's ken Rege. Wann er awwer widder zurick geht oweds, so das er widder von Marye kummt, dann is der Rege negscht." [When the wind comes from below or when it goes with the sun, there'll be no rain. But when it comes back in the evening, so that it again comes from the east, the rain is near.]

(Here in the originals appears the notation copied from letters of Lick to Bumbernickel Bill in December of 1936. The spelling is partly Lick's, partly mine.)

1374.
"Es gebt ball Rege wann die Lufthutsche greische." [There will soon be rain when the loons call.] (Also: Lufthutschle.)(This should follow 1305. Note the name for loons.)　　　　　　　　　　D.E.Lick

A GROUP FROM MRS. HOBART REINSMITH,
Bath, Pennsylvania
per
Bumbernickel Bill

1375.
"Wann der Haahne greht in der Nacht, is es schee der negscht Daag." [When the rooster crows at night, the weather will be fine the next day.]

1376.
"So weit as die Sunn in die Scheier uff Grundsau Daag scheint, so weit blosst der Wind der Schnee noch nei." [As far as the sun shines into the barn on Groundhog Day, the wind will blow the snow into the barn.]

1377.
"Wann die Katz mit ihrem Buckel ans Feier hockt, geb's Schnee. Wann sie sich in die Heh (upon a chair)[hockt], dann geb's Rege." [When the cat sits with her back to the fire, there'll be snow. When she sits up (on a chair), there'll be rain.]

1378.
"Wann die Gens uff em Eis schtehne uff der Elfde November, laafe sie in Dreck uff Grischdaag." [When the geese stand on ice on the eleventh of November, they will be walking in dirt, mud, on Christmas.]

1379.
"Wann die Schpinn ihre Weschlein iwwer die Schtrooss schpannt, geb's aa Rege." [When the spider stetches her washline over the road, there will also be rain.]

1380.
"Wann die Grabbe arig fliege un greische, geb's Schtarem." [When the crows fly around excitedly and call, there will be storm.]

1381.
"Wann die Schtanne so arig glitzere, geb's kalt Wedder." [When the stars glitter brightly, there will be cold weather.]

1382.
"Wann's regert fer der Siwwe, hell's uff bis Elfe. Wann's regert noch der Siwwe, regert's bis Zwelfe." [If it rains before seven o'clock, it will clear before eleven. If it rains after seven, it will rain before twelve o'clock.]

1383.
"Wann's friehyaahrs uff's Wasser regert, scheint die Sunn seller Daag nach." [If it rains on the water in spring, the sun will shine again that day.]

1384.
"Wann's friehyaahrs dunnert, watt's widder kalt schpotyaahrs, widder waarm," [If it thunders in spring, it will again get cold; if this happens in fall, it will turn warm.]

A GROUP FROM JOHN R. ACKER,
1552 Washington Street,
Allentown, Pennsylvania
per
Bumbernickel Bill

1385.
"Wann der Moond en grosser Ring hot, schtelle die Schtanne drin so viel Schtanne so lang noch bis es Schnee gebt." (Note "schtelle die Schtanne.") [When the moon has a large ring around it, the stars within the ring tell how long it will be until it snows.]

1386.
"Die haarich Rauwe, wann sie ganz schwatz sin, geb's en kalder Winder; mehner gehl net so kalt." [When the hairy caterpillars are entirely black, there will be a cold winter, when they are more yellow, not so cold.]

1387.
"Wann die Warrem net so dief im Boddem sin, geb's aa net so kalt Wedder." [When the worms are not so deep in the earth, the weather won't be so cold.]

1388.
"Wann die Schneegens siddlich fliege, kannscht dich druff verlosse, as es arig kalt watt." [When the wild geese fly south, you can depend on it that it will become very cold.]

1389.
"Wann en Mann gsuffe heemkummt, geb's aa die merscht's(!) Zeit Schtarem." [When a husband comes home intoxicated, a storm usually results.]

1390.
"Wann die Katz hinne uff ihrem Kobb leit, werd's aa windich un schtarmich." [When the cat lies back on its head, the weather will turn windy and stormy.]

1391.
"Wann die Hinkel frieh mause, dann dutt's frieh eiwindere." [When the chickens molt early, winter will come early.]

1392.
"Wann Haahne so grehe darich die Nacht, dann geb's aa wiescht Wedder." [When roosters crow during the night, there will be bad weather ahead.]

1393.
"Wann die Weibsleit so schpringe, dann geb's aa wiescht Wedder." [When the womenfolk run about, there will be bad weather.]

1394.
"Wann die Schwalme nidder fliege, geb's Rege; hoch, schee Wedder." [When the swallows fly low, there'll be rain; when they fly high, there'll be good weather.]

1395.
"Wann die Kinner griddlich sin, geb's wiescht Wedder." [When the children are fretful, there will be bad weather.]

1396.
"Wann die Beem's Laab lang halde, geb's en langer un kalder Winder." [When the trees long keep their leaves, there will be a long and cold winter.]

1397.
"Wann die Esel im Schpotyaahr ihre Ohre nunnerhenke, bedeit's viel Schnee. Sie duhne sell so as der Schnee net in ihre Ohre geyaagt watt." [When the mules hang their ears in the fall of the year, it means much snow. They hang their ears so that the snow is not driven into their ears.]

1398.
"Wann am Supper(!)disch schier gaar alles, odder alles, uffgesse is, geb's schee Wedder." [When at the supper table almost everything or everything is eaten up, there will be good weather.]

1399.
"Wann die Kieh arig blarre, geb's Rege." [When the cows bellow, there'll be rain.]

1400.
"Wann die Grabbe arig fliege, watt's windich un kalt." [When the crows fly about, it will be windy and cold.]

1401.
"Der Schtoy waar der eenzigscht Mann" [Stoy was the only man] that could cure hydrophobia. They came to him from all distances with persons bound with ropes and chains; and he cured them. He was the only one who could cure "mad" persons. But now 'Schtoy' is dead and his cure is lost. If one had his cure, one could become wealthy."
This was told to me by my father

1402.
Painted barn decorations appear quite frequently on barns on the Lancaster Co. side of the South Mountain all the way up to Brickerville.

1403.
Not only is the bite of a "mad" animal "gifdich" [poisonous], but the very foam, "Schaum," which drips from its mouth, if coming in contact with the human body is dangerous. It causes madness.

1404.
"Wie mer's Yaahr aafangt, so geht's darich's Yaahr." [As one begins the year, so it will be throughout the year.]

1405.
As the first day of the week, so the week will be—a good day, a good week; a bad day, a bad week.

1406.
It is better to receive money on the first day of the week, Monday, than to disburse money. *Green Lane*

(Usually introduced: "The Jews like to receive money, etc." Monday is not the first day for the Jews.)

1407.
The first twelve days of January symbolize the twelve months of the year. The general weather conditions of each of the twelve days foretells the general weather of the corresponding month.

In an account book of 1830 I found a weather record of the first twelve days of the year. This would show that it is an old belief.

1408.
"Donnere iwwer's darre Wald,
Es schtarwe viel Leit yung un alt."

[Thunder over the dry forest,
Many people are dying, young and old.]

1409.
"Sauergraut is erscht gut, wann's siwwet Mol uffgeweremt is." [Sauerkraut is not really good until it has been warmed up seven times.]

1410.
"Sauergraut is bully,
I tell you, it is fine.
I think I ought to know it,
For I eat it all the time."
Anthony, Strausstown

1411.
"Wann die Daage zunemme, nemmt die Kelt zu." [When the days get longer, the cold increases.]
Not infrequently heard

1412.
"Wie lenger die Daage, wie greesser die Kelt." [The longer the days, the greater the cold.] *Not infrequent*

1413.
"Ebber as in Yenner gebore is, kann sehne was d un ich net sehne kenne." [One who has been born in January is able to see that which you and I cannot see]

1414.
When only girls have been born into a family and the parents desire a boy, the last girl born is to receive the name of the mother in baptism and the next child will be a boy.

If boys have been born into a family and no girl, then the last boy born is to be baptized with the name of the father and the next child will be a girl.
Mrs. Sydney Wotring

1415.
To change the sex, when there has been a succession of babies of the same sex in a family, "loss die Elder Bletz wexle im Bett." [let the parents exchange places in bed]

1417.[sic]
If February comes in like a lamb, it will go out like a lion.
(This is curiously applied to February.)

1418.
"Lichtmess, Schpinne vergess!" [Candlemas, February 2, forget your spinning!] *Common in Mo*

1419.
"Grundaxedaag" [Groundhog Day] = February

(Here in Lebanon County, when I was a boy, the groundhog was rare.)

1420.
"Daxdaag" [Groundhog Day] — February 2.
Northampton, L

1421.
"Grundsaudaag" [Groundhog Day] has become common for February 2, mostly through the "Grundsau" Lodge. Elmer Fehnel, however, tells me that the name was used alongside of "Daxdaag" in Northampton County.

1422.
"Mer sett schlachde wann der Mund zunemmt." [One should butcher when the moon is waxing.]
Not infrequent

1423.
"So viel Newwel in Hanning, so viel Froscht in Moi." [There will be as much frost in May as there is fog in February.] *Ed Bolig, Sumneytown*

1424.
"Frieh donnere, frieh sommere." [Early thunder, early summer.] *Old Mrs. Kleckner, Egypt*

1425.
"Die Ros is rot,
Der Himmel is bloh.
Geb mer en Boss,
No bin ich froh."

[The rose is red,
The sky is blue.
Give me a kiss,
Then I'm pleased.]
Cal Reed, Sumneytown

(Perhaps modeled after Nr. 1426.)
Probably original with him.

1426.
A suitor calling on the father of his sweetheart said:

"Fer des bin ich kumme,
Fer des bin ich do.
Nau geb mer die Betz,
Noh bin ich froh."

[For this I have come,
For this I am here.
Now give me Betty,
Then I'm pleased.] *Do*

1427.
"Uff Eschepuddeldaag dutt mer Esch uff die Kieh fer Gsundheet." [On Ash Wednesday one puts ashes on the cows for their good health.] *Old custom*

1428.
Thursday after "Faasnacht" [Shrove Tuesday] is "Weschlumbedaag." [washrag day]
Personal memory, Leb

1429.
"En scheener Daag un en gudi Fraa sett mer net lowe bis Owed." [A lovely day and a good wife should not be praised before evening.] *Rather common*

1430.
"Was is die Welt so schee!
Daags ruh ich un nachs(!) schlof ich."

[How lovely is the world!
By day I rest and by night I sleep.] *Leb*

1431.
"Matteis macht odder bricht Eis." [St. Matthew's Day makes or melts ice.] *Isaac Smith, Green Lane*

1432.
A thunderstorm in March is dangerous to pregnant women. It will (!) cause the death of a pregnant woman. (Source unknown)

1433.
A father can bring up 99 children, but 99 children cannot take care of one father. *Leb, Leh*

1434.
If a tablecloth falls to the floor, there will be hungry visitors. *Mrs. James Jacoby, Sumneytown*

1435.
Proverb
"Was moll waar, watt widder." [That which was, will be again.] *Not infrequent*

1436.
"Wer eemol gschtohle hot, schtehlt widder." [He who has stolen once, will steal again.] ("Wann die Gelegeheit do is.") [If the opportunity presents itself.] This and Nr. 1435 were not infrequently heard in the past. I have heard neither of recent years.)

1437.
"Wann mer die Fresch dreimol heert, is Friehyaahr do." [When one hears the spring peepers three times, spring is here.] *Jacob Gable, heard at old Goshenhoppen church*

1438.
"Wu ich yung waar, hen mer gmeent es waer en langsamer Bauer, as sei Hawwer net gseht grickt hot in Matz. Nau is es gut wann mer en naus grickt in Abrill." [When I was young, we were of the opinion that a farmer was slow if he didn't sow his oats until March. Now it's satisfactory if one gets it planted in April.] *Isaac Smith, Green Lane*

1439.
"In Matz gehne die Kinnergrankheede rum. Der Matzwind draagt sie rum." [In March the diseases of childhood make the rounds. The March wind carries them.] This is the belief that measles, mumps, whooping cough, etc. are carried around by the winds in March because they seemingly are everywhere. (They come and go at will.)

1440.
Women are accustomed to plant "sweet peas" on St. Patricks Day. *Mont, Leh*

1441.
"Matzeschtaab, Abrillelaab." [March dust, April leaves.] *Ed Bolig, Sumneytown*

1442.
On March 31 plant cabbage. This is "Dettlaus Daag" and no lice [i.e., bugs will bother the cabbage]. (The dialect word, "Leis," lice, is the inclusive designation for small insects, "Ungeziffer.")
Mrs. Clem Musselman, Egypt

1443.
Plant cabbage on April 10. "Deel Leit blanze Graut uff der zehet Abrill." [Some people plant cabbage on the tenth of April.] *Do*

1444.
When the silver maple leaves are turned so as to show the underside, there will be rain. *Sumneytown*

1445.
In some families of Myerstown, Lebanon County, the Christmas tree was kept standing with its decorations until Easter. *Recollection of my wife*

1446.
A four-leaved clover gotten from another will bring no good luck. One giving it away will lose what good luck may have been his. *Leb*

1447.
The first milk of a fresh cow, particularly a heifer, was milked into the ground or poured away.
At one time general

1448.
"Uff der erscht Abrill schickt mer die Narre hie wu mer will." [On the first of April one sends the fools where one will.] *Dan Moser, Anise, Mont*

1449.
"Der Abrill dutt em Moi's Kann weise." [April shows May rye.] *Egypt*

1450.
"Zwiwwleschnee" — the onion snow. Onions are set out soon after the grund is open. Usually there is a melting snow after the onions have been set out. This snow, supposedly the last in spring, is known as the "Zwiwwleschnee." "Mer hen der Zwiwwleschnee noch net ghat." [We haven't had the onion snow yet.]
Widely used

1451.
A snow falling in late spring, that melts away soon after it has fallen, is called frequently "en Dreckschnee." [a dirt snow]

1452.
When large snowflakes fall with a west wind, we say here in the Whitehalls, "Die Heedelbaryer robbe Gens." [The Heidelbergers are plucking geese.] *Egypt*

1453.
"Friehyaahr is net do bis die Oschderoier gesse sin." [Spring is not here until the Easter eggs have been eaten.] *Hen Brown, Laurys*

1454.
"Uff Griedunnerschdaag sett mer ebbes Grienes esse fer Gsundheet." [On Maundy Thursday one should eat something green for ones health.]
Widely heard

1455.
"Wann die Auferschtehung frieh kummt, hen mer en frieh Friehyaahr." [When the resurrection comes early, there will be an early spring.]
Frank Ashton, Green Lane

1456.
"Fer Gsundheit hen die alde Baricks Kaundy Leit die hattgekochde Oschderoier gesse mitsamt der Schaale." [For good health the old Berks County folks ate the Easter eggs together with the shells.]
David Werner, Myerstown

1457.
"En blindi Sau find aa emols en Eechel." [A blind hog will sometimes find an acorn.] A person finding something, a solution, something lost, a way out- others also along—will say the above. *Quite common*

1458.
"Wie der Baam geboge watt, so waxt er." [As the tree is bent, so it will grow.] *Occasionally heard*

1460.
"Wie mer der Baam biegt, so waxt er." [As one bends the tree, so it will grow.] *Do*

1461.
"Der Offe dutt mer net weck bis die Logess Beem bliehe." [You don't put the stove away (for the warm season) until the locust trees bloom.] The stove in the sitting room was set up in the fall and taken down in the spring, usually at house-cleaning time. There often came in May or June a period of cold rainy weather when the men would seek comfort in the kitchen—the stove being removed from the sitting room—to the annoyance of the women.
My grandmother used the saying.

1462.
"En guder Baas is so viel wert wie zwee Schaffleit." [A good boss is worth as much as two workers.] *Leb*

1463.
George Newhard tells me that he drove two rows of cut spikes into his unfruitful cherry tree to bring it to bear. He believes that it doesn't bear because it was planted in the "Blumme Zeeche." [in the sign of Virgo]

1464.
Sweet cider was to be preserved for the winter "im unnergehnde Muund" [during the waning of the moon], when the moon was down, so that it doesn't ferment, i.e. rise up. (Sweet cider was preserved by bringing it to a slight boil and then bottling it. It was known as "abgekocht Seider." [boiled cider]
Rev. Sidney Smith, Northampton

1465.
The first milk of a fresh cow was to be given to the cow herself. *Mrs. Sidney Wotring*

1466.a.
"So lang as die Bledder net recht gedreht sin noch me Schtarem, geb's meh Rege." [As long as the leaves have not returned to their normal position after a storm, there will be more rain.] With a storm the leaves of plants in the garden are turned so as to show the underside. This means until the leaves have come back to their normal position. *Do*

1466.b.
"En aldi Kuh watt net satt un verhunst en yunger Bull." [An old cow is not easily satisfied and ruins a young bull.]

1467.
Coal oil, castor oil, "en Schtick Schpeck" [a piece of bacon] are all good applications for corns. The "Schpeck" is to be tied on. *Do*
("Schpeck" — a piece of fat from a ham or from a piece of bacon.)

1468.
A person born on the first day of May will not live long. *Do*
(This is probably a survival of a forgotten Walpurgis night belief.)

1469.
May 3 is "der Buhnedaag." [bean day]
Mrs. Clem. Musselman, Egypt

1470.
"Feichder Moi, viel Frucht un Hoi." [A damp May brings much grain and hay.] *Egypt*

1471.
Ed Bolig of Sumneytown told me that the month of May was called "der rollich Moi" [the month when young people are "in heat"] by people when he was young. The origin of many a wedding seems to have been in the month of May.

1472.
"Uff Himmelferdaag geb's gern Gwiddre." [On Ascension Day thunderstorns are apt to come up.] *Common*

1473.
"Wann me Ende-Oier setzt uff Himmelferdaag, geb's scheckiche Ende." [If one sets duck eggs on Ascension Day, variegated ducks will result.]

1474.
"Uff Himmelferdaag hawwich gheiert, awwer ich deed nimmi. Es is zu oft in die Heh gfaahre." [I married on Ascension Day, but I would never again. It rose up too often.] (Double meaning)
Mrs. E.M., Egypt

1475.
"Mittwoch is en Unglicksdaag; do sett mer net wesche." [Wednesday is an unlucky day; one should not wash on that day.] *Common*

1476.
"Uff en Gademberdaag sett mer net wesche." [On an Ember day one should do no washing.]
Mrs. Joe Kern, Egypt

1477.
"Uff der 15 Moi sett mer Welschkann blanze. Des is en guder Daag." [On the fifteenth of May one should plant corn. This is a good day.] *Egypt*

1478.
"Seeweiwel"—mermaid. *Willoughby Troxell*

1479.
Riddle
"Wann en 3-Woche Seiche vier Daaler hollt, was hollt en aldi Loos?" [If a three-week-old piglet fetches $4, what will an old sow bring?] "En Kolwe Welschkann." [An ear of corn.] *Sidney Wotring*

1480.
"Zurickgeh is ken Glick." [To go back is no luck.] Going back after one has left home for a visit, a journey or on business brings bad luck.
Mrs. Sidney Wotring

1481.
Riddle
"So weiss wie Schnee,
So grie wie Graas,
So rot wie Blut?"—A cherry.

[As white as snow,
As green as grass,
As red as blood?] *Do*

1482.
"Laagerbier un Schweitzer Kees
Macht die alde Weiwer bees."

[Lager beer and Swiss cheese,
Makes the old women angry.]
Sidney Wotring

1483.
Riddle
"Grumm un graad, wu witt du naus?"
"Du Deckes-Chor, was frogscht du denno?"
"Ich bin net so deckes-chor as wie dei Loch zugefror."

[Crooked and straight, where do you want out?]
[You dope, what are you asking about?]
[I'm not as dopey as your hole is frozen shut.]
Hattie Schumacher, Treichler's

1484.
Riddle

"Grumm un graad, wu witt du naus?" [Cf. 1483]
"Du Decke-Schaar, was frogscht du denno?" [Cf. 1483]
"Ich bin doch net so katzgeschor as wie dei Loch zugefror." [I'm not as close-shaven as your hole is frozen shut.]

Ellen Levengood, Treichler's

1485.
"Hokemann" — the devil.

Indianland and other places

1486.
"Wie mer auschtaert uff Nei Yaahr, so dutt mer's Yaahr rum." [As one starts out on New Year's, so one does throughout the year.]   *"Sticks" Zerfass, Egypt*

1487.
"Wie mer darich der erscht Daag vum Yaahr rutscht, so rutscht mer darich's Yaahr." [As one slides through the first day of the year, so one slides through the entire year.]   *Egypt*

1488.
"Wann mer net bees watt uff Nei Yaahr, watt mer's ganz Yaahr net bees." [If one does not get angry on New Year's, one will not get angry the entire year.] *Do*

1489.
"Mer sett die Unnergleeder net wexle zwische Grischdaag un Nei Yaahr—weye Grankheede ufflese." [One should not change ones underclothes between Christmas and New Year's, to avoid disease.]
O. P. Leh, Egypt

1490.
"Fruchtbeem geblanzt uff Nei Yaahr lewe lang un draage gut Frucht." [Fruit trees planted on New Year's live long and bear good fruit.] (Note the use of "Frucht.")

"Till" Schlegel planted a cherry tree at "Drammhole" schoolhouse (near Egypt) on New Year's Day in the above belief.

1491.
Meat from butchering on "Gedember" [Ember day] will spoil. [cf. 1359]   *Egypt*

1492.
If there is no snow or ice on the trees between Christmas and New Year's Day, there will be little fruit.   *Do*

1493.
When I was young, shooting matches were still widely held—usually at hotels. Pharos Weidman, the crack shot in our neighborhood, had a heavy gun, seemingly made specially for match shooting. He had a long casing for loading, at least twice the length of the present 12-guage shell. This he loaded at the match.

I heard the elders speak of rifle matches, though I personally did not see one or know of one that took place.

The winner of a shooting match often spent all that he won in treating the other contestants and the spectators to drinks. This is termed "uffsetze" in the dialect.

1494.
In my youth the "bully" still reigned. The fights took place at the hotels, usually when picnics or fairs were held in town. "Pit" Ream was one of the local fighters. If he was fairly sober when he fought, he usually won. Otherwise not. The combatants would divest themselves of their coats and vests, roll up their sleeves and have at one another in the barroom or out in the stable yard. There was a bully "Ewerly" (Eberly) by name who came from Mt. Airy in Lancaster County. He and Ream often fought.

1495.
"Wann mer uff der erscht Daag vum Yaahr schafft, muss mer darich's ganz Yaahr schaffe." [If one works on the first day of the year, one must work the entire year.]   *Miller's Church, Laury's*

1496.
At Miller's Church the tradition is current that on New Year's Day, one should shoot into the bole of unfruitful trees to make them bear.

1497.
On "Aschermittwoch" [Ash Wednesday] wood ashes were sprinkled on cattle to prevent lice—also on the heads and eyebrows of human beings for the same purpose.

Alfred Peters, Laury's, sexton of Miller's Church

1498.
The fat in which "Faasnacht Kuche" [doughnuts] were fried was used as a "Waggeschmier." [wagon grease] Very good.   *Do*

1499.
Tar was used to grease the axles of the heavy wagons. In place of tar fat drained from fried sausages or ham was used.   *Leb*

1500.
"Bumbernickel Bill" tells me that his grandmother called coffee of a second or third heating "Maddlenbrieh." At first impression the name seems to go back to Magdalena. Is this a reference to penance? (I have also heard "Maddeleene Brieh.")

1501.
"Maddeleene" — Magdalena.   *Common*

1502.
"An Lichtmess sett der Bauer noch die Helft Hoi un Schtroh hawwe." [By February 2 the farmer should

still have half his hay and straw left.]
Mrs. Danner of Laury's

1503.
To make unfruitful trees bear drive nails into the roots. (The exposed roots at the foot of the tree.) *Do*

1504.
"Schlechder Aafang, gut End." [A bad beginning means a good end.] *Not infrequently heard*

1505.
"Guder Aafang, schlecht End." [Good beginning means a bad end.] *Do*

"Der Parre is gut ausschtaert un ich hab gmeent es geebt en sanderbare Breddich, awwer glei waar nix dazu." [The pastor began well and I thought it would be an especially good sermon, but soon there was nothing to it.]

1506.
"Wie mer die Woch aafangt, so dauert's die ganz Woch." [As one begins the week, so it will be all week.]

"dauere" [to last] is a common dialect word.

UFF NEI YAAHR SCHIESST MER IN DIE UNFRUCHTBAARE BEEM:
[On New Year's Day one shoots into the unfruitful trees:]

(All heard at Egypt)

1507.
"In die Giwwel." (Also pronounced "Gibbel") [Into the top of the tree]

1508.
"In der Schtamm graad am Boddem." [Into the trunk right at the bottom]

1509.
"Frieh maryets uhne en Watt schwetze." [Early in the morning without speaking a word]

1510.
"Eenziche Zeit vum Daag." [Any time of the day]

1511.
"Uff Nei Yaahr sett mer uffschteh un der Baam briggle an die Nescht. Wann mer die Nescht net reeche kann, graddelt mer der Baam." [On New Year's Day one should get up and beat the tree in the branches. If one cannot reach the branches, one climbs the tree.]
Egypt

1512.
"Uff en unfruchtbaarer Baam odder en Baam mehner fruchtbaar zu mache, henkt mer aldi Kedde, Hufeise, odder alt Eise an die Nescht." [On an unfruitful tree or in order to make a tree more fruitful, one hangs old chains, horseshoes or old iron on the branches.]

1513.
"Uff Nei Yaahr bind mer Schtroh Seele an die Fruchtbeem (am Schtamm wennich unnich em erschde Nascht), so as sie recht arig draage." [On New Year's Day one ties bands of straw around fruit trees (around the trunk just below the first branch) so that these trees bear more fruit.]

This was frequently done around Green Lane when I was pastor there.

1514.
Stones of considerable size are "planted," i.e. "geblanzt zwische em Hauptschtamm un der erscht Nascht fer Fruchtbaarkeit." [planted between the main trunk and the first branch for fruitfulness.] The size of the stone would influence the size of the fruit.

(There seems to be a "sympathy" between the stone and the stone of the fruit.) *More frequently seen in the past than now.*

1515.
The seed of the peach is "Paschingschtee."
Throughout

1516.
The seed of the plum is "Blaumeschtee." *Do*

1517.
The seed of the cherry is "Kascheschtee." *Do*

1518.
The seeds of an apple, a strawberry, a huckleberry, a currant, are "Kanne." "Ebbelkanne" — apple seeds "Hockelbiereekanne" — huckleberry seeds.

EXPRESSIONS OF MRS. HARVEY ZIEGLER,
Egypt, Pennsylvania

1519.
"Mer lebt uff Hoffning." [One lives on hope.]

1520.
"Mer muss Mut fasse." [One has to have courage.]

1521.
"Die Sunn scheint immer." [The sun is always shining.]

1522.
Nr. 1519 is usually heard as "Mer lebt immer uff Hoffning." [One always lives on hope.]
Quite commonly heard

1523.
Nr. 1520 is usually heard as "Mer muss frischer Mut fasse." *Do*

1524.
Nr. 1521 is usually heard as "Die Sunn scheint immer wieder." *Not infrequently heard*

1525.
A rhyme made without thought in a conversation foretells the coming of visitors. *Leb*

1526.
When women gossip across the street or over the yard fences, there will be rain. *Egypt*

1527.a.
"Mer sett nix Neies draage uff Himmelferdaag." [One should wear nothing new on Ascension Day.]

1527.b.
A barn, whose walls were laid up on Ascension Day, was an unlucky structure. There was always something falling down or breaking. The mortar fell out; stones crumbled. Finally the barn was burned to the ground.
Clarence Laub, who never works on Ascension Day

1528.
"Mer sett net heiere uff Himmelferdaag." [One should not marry on Ascension Day.] *Egypt*

I do not see the line of thought back of this belief. Maybe it is associated with Nr. 1527 or with the belief that it is wrong to sew on Ascension Day and occasion might arise at a wedding which would necessitate sewing or the tying of a knot.

1529.
Charles Snyder died in December. His granddaughter Marie gave birth to a child the last day of the year. Much as she would like, she will not name her child after her grandfather, because "one is not to name a child after a close relative that died recently."

1530.
Manure should not be taken out of the stables on New Year's Day, "schunscht deed mer's Vieh's ganz Yaahr nausdraage." One would be taking dead animals out of the stable through the year.
Mrs. Sidney Wotring

1531.
"Net wesche die Unnergleeder zwische Grischdaag un Nei Yaahr— weye Gschweere." [Do not wash your underclothes between Christmas and New Year's Day to prevent boils.]
Mrs Sidney Wotring

Sidney Wotring did not go visiting on January 1, 1937, on account of his dirty underwear.

1532.
"Ken neie Unnergleeder aaduh uff Nei Yaahr." [Put no clean underwear on on New Year's Day.] *Do*

1533.
"Ken Ebbel esse uff Nei Yaahr weye Gschweere." [Eat no apples on New Year's Day to prevent boils.] *Do*

1534.
"Ken Eis uff die Beem zwische Grischdaag un Nei Yaahr, ken Frucht, ken Obscht." [If there's no ice on the trees between Christmas and New Year's Day, there will be no fruit.]

1535.
For unfruitful trees, strike nails into the tree any time of the year or of the day. *Do*

1536.a.
"Matteis, bricht Eis.
Wann's kein hot, bring's Eis."

[On St. Matthew's Day the ice
will break. If there is no ice, ice will form.] *Do*

1536.b.
1.
"Wann en Grott schlucke witt, guck sie net lang aa." [If you want to swallow a toad, don't look at it very long.] *Leslie Peters, Laury's*

2.
It was looked upon as unlucky to marry on ones birthday. Persons who would marry on ones birthday, would marry the day before. *Do*

3.
On New Year's Day N- N- hung old iron on fruit trees, saying: "Do gewwich dir en Bresent; nau geb du mir aa en Bresent!" [Here I give you a present; now you give me a present also.] *Do*

4.
"So oft as die Fresch die Meiler uff hen in Abbril, misse sie sie zuhawwe in Moi." [As often as the spring peepers have their mouths open in April, they have to keep them closed in May.] *Do*

1537.
"Lichtmess, halb Fuder fress." Half of the feed, hay and straw still to remain. *Mrs. Sidney Wotring*

1538.
"Die Hunsdaage hees, die annre danach noch heeser." [The dog days will be hot; those that follow will be hotter.] *Do*

1539.
"Die Hunsdaage sin hees un noch der Hunsdaage kumme die Bitsch Daage. Selli sin noch heeser." [The dog days are hot and after the dog days come the bitch days. Those are even hotter.] *Harold Kuhns, Egypt*

This was only time I heard the name "Bitsch Daage." The name was current at one time around Egypt, according to Kuhns.

1540.
"Wann's uff Karfreidaag regert, watt's arig windich darich der Summer un die Rege badde nix." [When it rains on Good Friday, it will be very windy during the summer and the rains will be of no avail.] A dry summer. *Mrs. Sidney Wotring*

1541.
"Uff Himmelferdaag sett mer net nehe, schunscht

deed mer die Hinkel die Hinnerdeeler zunehe." [One should not sew on Ascension Day, otherwise one would sew shut the hind ends of the chickens.] They will lay no eggs. *Do*

1542.
"Fer viel Bieblicher, setz die Hinkeloier vammidaags vor 12 Uhr." [In order to have many chicks, set the chicken eggs in the forenoon before noon.] *Do*

The number of eggs was usually 13. Was there a connection between 12 and 13?

1543.
"Setz ken Oier uff Mittwochs." [Set no eggs on Wednesday.] *Do*

1544.
"Oier gelegt uff Karfreidaag gebt scheckiche Hinkel." [Eggs laid on Good Friday will hatch into variegated chickens.] *Do*

1545.
"Mer sett hattgekochde Oier esse uff Karfreidaag Owed un uff Oschder Marye." [One should eat hard-boiled eggs on Good Friday evening and on Easter morning. *Do*

1546.
"Ken Arwet uff Sunndaag—yuscht an's Esse schaffe." [No work on Sunday—just work at eating.] *Do*

1547.
"Uff Freidaags heire die Schwatze." [Blacks marry on Fridays.] *Do*

1548.
"Mer sett net schaffe uff der Daag as mer heiert." [One should not work on the day one marries.] Or else one will work all the days of his (her) married life. *Do*

1549.
"Rege uff der Hochzichdag meent en driebe Hochzich." [Rain on the wedding day means a cloudy marriage.] *Do*

1550.
"Am Nei Licht un an Voll Licht geb's en Wexel im Wedder." [At the time of a new moon or at full moon there will be a change in the weather.] "Geb's Rege odder Schtarm." [There will be rain or storm.] *Do*

1551.
"Mer sett schlofe mit der Fiess geye Sunnuff—schunscht leit mer unnersewwerscht." [One should sleep with the feet toward sunrise (east)—otherwise one lies upside-down.] *Do*

1552.
"Wammer en Kuh kaaft, sett mer Brot un en Ax am Kiehschtall Dier lege un die Kuh driwwer nemme. Noh grickt sie ken Heemweh." [When one buys a cow, one should place bread and an ax at the door of the cow stable and take the cow across them. Then she will not be homesick.] *Do*

1553.
Odder: Schaab wennich ab unne am Disch un geb's re zu esse." [Or: Scrape a bit from beneath the table or at the legs of the table) and give that to her.] *Do*

1554.
"Wann mer en Hammel verkaaft, sett mer's hinnerschich aus em Schtall nemme. Noh blatt die Kuh net." [When one sells a calf, one should take if from the stable backwards. Then the cow will not low.] *Do*

1555.
"Am Aller Heil un Seel Daag sett der Gaarde sauwer sei." [By All Saints' and All Souls' Days, November 1 and 2, the garden should be clean.] *Do*

1556.a.
"Nachts dutt's net schloose." No hailstones at night. *Do*

1556.b.
N- N- raised strawberries. He would hawk them in Northampton, calling: "Strawberries, acht Sent die Bax. Drei Baxe fer en Vaddel," and sold all of them at three boxes for a quarter.

1557.
"In alli Yaahr geb's zwee—un yuscht zwee—Samschdaage, wu die Sunn gaar net scheint." [In every year there are two—and only two—Saturdays when the sun does not shine at all.] On all other Saturdays the sun shines, if only a minute. *Do*

1558.
"Grischdaagnacht am zwelf Uhr dutt's Vieh zamme schwetze." [On Christmas night at twelve o'clock the cattle talk to each other.] *Do*

1559.
"En Fraa sett ken Pederli blanze, schunscht schtarbt ihre Mann." [A wife should plant no parsley, otherwise her husband will die.]
Planting of a stalk of parsley, "Pederli," erotic?

1560.
"Wann mer en Kaschebaam ausblanzt, sett mer ihn schtelle wie er gschtanne hot, schunscht draagt er ken Kasche. En Kaschebaam schtellt sich geye die Sunn." [When one transplants a cherry tree, one should set it as it stood before, otherwise it will bear no cherries. A cherry tree turns toward the sun.] *Do*

1561.
"Grummbiere sett mer blanze im zunemmende Leeb—fer grosse." [Potatoes should be planted in the waxing sign of Leo—in order to have big potatoes.] *Do*

1562.
"Wann en Schtann fallt, geht eens aus der Welt."
[When a star falls, one goes from the world.] *Do*

"Aus der Welt" is an expression meaning "to die." "Aus der Welt in der Himmel." [Out of the world into heaven.]

1563.
"Fer die Peils, reib mit me Schtick Schpeckschwaart un graab's unnich der Dachdrapp." [To cure piles, rub with a piece of rind of bacon and bury it beneath the eaves.] *Do*

1564.
Game
London Bridge is falling down, falling down, falling down.
London Bridge is falling down,
Will you marry me?

Now we build it up again, up again, up again.
Now we build it up again,
Will you marry me?

Take the chopper and chop off their heads, chop off their heads, chop off their heads.
Take the chopper and chop off their heads,
Will you marry me?

Take the key and lock her in, lock her in, lock her in.
Take the key and lock her in,
Will you marry me?

After all have taken sides, there was the pulling to see who was the "rotten egg."
Mrs. Lottie Strauss, Treichler's

1565.
"Mammi, Mammi, Budderbrot,
Schlack die Katz im Keller dod.
Heng sie uff un zieg sie ab,
Un mach en guder Schtribberkapp."

[Mommy, mommy, butter-bread,
Strike dead the cat in the cellar.
Hang her up and skin her,
And make a good stripper cap.] *Do*

SONGS SPOKEN OF BUT NOT COLLECTED:

1566.
"Es glee groh Mennli." [The little grey man.]
Spoken of by John Algard

1567.
"Werkelholz will nimmi rolle." [The rolling pin no longer wants to roll.] *Spoken of by N- Andrews*

1568.
"Sei Lewe wie die Schwowe." [Always like the Suabians.] *Mentioned by R.D. Schaeffer, Northampton*

1569.
"Vier Deitsche Limmel,
Yedre uff en Schimmel."

[Four German good-for-nothings,
Each on a white horse.] *Do*

1570.
"Es hockt en aldi Grabb
Un greischt haa, haa!"

[There sits an old crow
And cries: Haw, haw!] *Do*

1572.[sic]
"Geld hawwich kens,
Leis awwer doch."

[Money I have none,
Lice however aplenty.] *Do*

1573.
"Datt driwwe, datt drowwe an der Grick,
Datt leit en Riggel driwwe."

[Over there, up there at the creek, There lies a rail across.]

1574.
"Unser schwatzbrau Bellekuh."

[Our dark brown bell cow.] *Do*

1575.
"Fer Seidschteches, les en Schtee uff, schpau uff ihn un werf en iwwer die Axel." [For side "stitches," pick up a stone, spit on it and throw it over your shoulder.]
Mrs. Sidney Wotring

1576.
"Odder: leg ihn graad hie wie er gelege hot." [Or: put it back exactly as you found it.] (For Nr. 1575) *Do*

1577.
"Dunnere im Winder vor Grischdaag meent kalt; noch Grischdaag warem." [Thunder in winter before Christmas means cold weather; after Christmas means warm weather lies ahead.] *Do*

1578.
"Hollerbiere Bledder in der Hut lege fer Hitz." [Place elderberry leaves in your hat for protection against sunstroke.] *Do*

1579.
"Mer sett Tee robbe wann die Marie heemgeht." [One should pick tea when Mary goes home, i.e. August 15.] *Do*

1580.
"Wann die Rauwe lang hausbleiwe, geb's ken hadder Winder." [If the caterpillars remain outside longer than usual, there will be no hard winter.] *Do*

1581.
"Mer sett der Dreck net iwwer die Schwell nauskehre." [One should not sweep the dirt out over the doorsill.] *Do*

1582.
"Noch Sunnunnergang sett mer net auskehre." [One should not sweep dirt from the house after sunset.] *Do*

1583.
"Mittwochs die Kich hinnerschich auskehre fer Glick." [On Wednesday sweep out the kitchen backwards to insure good luck.] *Do*

1584.
"Die ausgschtreelde Haar sett mer verbrenne, as die Veggel sie net in ihre Neschder baue." [The combed out hairs should be burned, so that the birds do not use them in their nests.] *Do*

1585.
If a cow has lost "der Iedrich" [the cud], go to your neighbor and say: "Ich will der Kuh ihre Iedrich." [I want the cow's cud.] and they will give a piece of bread for the cow. Then go home and give the bread to the cow. *Do*

1586.
"So as die Hinkel lege, globb uff ihre Schwenz." [To make the chickens lay, beat on their tails.] (This was also done in Lebanon County, when I was a boy.) *Do*

1587.
"So as die Hinkel lege, geb ne die erschde Faasnachtkuche." [To make chickens lay, give them the first doughnuts.] *Do*

1588.
"Bleche Hannschaal, aldi Windmiehl,
   Blos es Schtroh naus, hol die Kieh heem,
   Yaag die Schof naus."

[Tin skull, old windmill,
   Blow out the straw, bring the
   cows home, Drive out the sheep.]

(Horace Witman?) Mont

1589.
Said by someone: "Bei Gusche Danyel in Lewegruwe un bei Gusche net verrisse warre." [By gosh Daniel in the lion's den and by gosh not torn to pieces.] *Do*

1590.a.
"Heit gehne mer der Rewwer nunner,
   Marye gehn mer nuff,
   Kumme in der Grog Shop,
   Kumme in der Suff.

[Today we go down the river,
   Tomorrow we go up,
   We come into the grog shop,
   And become intoxicated.]

Kumme heem, hackt der Daadi Holz,
   Die Mammi lees die Schpee,
   Der Gnecht hockt im Geilschtall
   Un butzt die Geil die Beh."

[We come home, daddy chops wood,
   Mommy picks up the chips,
   The hired man sits in the horse
   stable and cleans the legs of the horses.] *Do*

1590.b.
"Wann en grossi Schpinn ins Haus kummt, kummt glei en guder Freind ins Haus." [When a big spider comes into the house, a good friend will soom arrive.]
Mrs. Sidney Wotring

1591.
"En Grixlicher im Haus bedeit Glick." [A cricket in the house means good luck.] *Do*

1592.
"Wann die Haahne arig greeye, geb's glinck[sic] Wedder odder Regewedder." [When the roosters crow a great deal, there will be ? weather or rain.] "Der Rege kummt mit gelinck [sic] Wedder." [The rains comes with ? weather.] *Do*

1593.
"Maryerot, wann's geye die Sunn, geb's Rege." [When the morning red occurs toward the sun, there will be rain.] *Do*

1594.
"Maryerot, wann's weck geht vun der Sunn, meent schee Wedder." [When the morning red moves away from the sun, there will be good weather.] *Do*

1595.
"Owedrot, wann's fer odder geye die Sunn geht, meent Rege." [A red glow in the evening which goes before the sun or against the sun means rain.] *Do*

1596.
"Owedrot, wann's vun der Sunn herkummt, meent schee Wedder." [A red glow in the evening which comes from the sun, means good weather.] *Do*
(Numbers 1593-1596 are acute observations. The direction of the wind.)

1597.
"Wann die Sunn drieb unnergeht Dunnerschdaags, gebt's ken Rege iwwer Sunndaag." [When the sun goes down in an overcast sky, there will be no rain on the weekend.]

1598.
"Ganz gleene Hinkeloier sett mer hinnerschich

iwwer die Scheier schmiesse." [Quite small chicken eggs should be thrown backwards over the barn.] *Do*

1599.
"Grummbiereschaale in's Feier verbrenne fer der Rus." [Burn the potato peelings in the fire for the soot.] *Do*

1600.
"Salz uff der Feier fer's recht brenne mache." [Throw salt on the fire to make it burn faster.] *Do*

1601.
"Gwiddekanne gekocht in Wasser un's Haar mit gwesche macht grolliche Haar." [Wash your hair in water in which quince seeds have been cooked and your hair will become curly.] *Do*

1602.
"Wer's erscht im Bett is noch der Hochzich watt Baas." [The first into bed after the wedding will be the boss.] *Do*

1603.
Wrap a stinking stocking around the throat for a sore throat. *Do*

1604.
To spell Catasauqua: "C-A-T cat, Mei Sack dut weh." [My paunch hurts.] *Do*

1605.
Drop the child's old tooth into a mouse hole and say: "Meisel, Meisel, geb mer en annre Zaah fer den alde." [Mousey, mousey, give me another tooth for the old one.] *Do*

1606.
"Wann mer en Schpiggel verbrecht, verliert mer sei Glick fer siwwe Yaahr." [When you break a mirror, you lose your luck for seven years.] *Do*

1607.
"Wann en leddich Weibsmensch en Schpiggel verbrecht, grickt sie en Kind leddicherweis." [When an unmarried woman breaks a mirror, she will bear a child out of wedlock.] *Do*

1608.
"Wann die Grabbe greische fer 8 Uhr, geb's noch viel Rege seller Daag." [When the crows call before eight o'clock, there will be much rain that day.] *Do*

1609.
"Wann's regert as der Regeboge schteht, geb's noch drei Daag Rege." [When it rains and a rainbow is formed, for the following three days there will be rain.] *Do*

1610.
Rainbows are caused by the sun shining "geye die Eisbarye." [against the icebergs] The icebergs are where "der Schnee un's Eis sin." [where the snow and ice are] *Do*

1611.
"Die erscht verpissde Windel iwwer's Gsicht reiwe fer scheene rode Backe." [Rub the first diaper into which the child has urinated into the child's face to produce beautiful red cheeks.] This was done by the maid in the home of Sydney Wotring. *Do*

1612.
"Der erscht Moi uffgschtanne un unne gschwetzt sich wesche mit Dau fer die Summerflecke." [Get up on the first day in May and wash yourself in the dew without speaking to anyone. This will rid one of freckles.] *Do*

1613.
"Fer schtaryer Esich mache, die Naame vun die drei beeschde Weibsleit ins Fass saage." [To make strong vinegar speak the names of the three most evil women into the barrel.] *Do*

1614.
"Odder: en Babier gschmiert mit Molassich ins Fass duh." [Or: put a piece of paper smeared with molasses into the barrel.] *Do*

1615.
"Die Mannsleit hen als Ohrering gedraage un ihre Haar gflochde." [Men used to wear earrings and plait their hair.] *Mrs. Charles Snyder, the mother of Mrs. Wotring*

1616.
"Wann eens schtarbt, sett mer der Schpiggel schwatz zuhenke un die Uhr schtoppe." [When someone dies, one should cover the mirror with black (cloth) and stop the clock.] *Do*

(The Wotring family group, Mrs. Sydney Wotring, his wife, his mother-in-law, Mrs. Charles Snyder and his father-in-law, when living, were a most fertile soil for the unearthing of folklore. The lore attributed to them, immediately above, was collected on January 8, 1937.)

1617.
A reddish glow to storm clouds when seen at a distance shows that hail fell. *Leh*

1618.
When hail falls, it is commonly said: "Nau watt's kelder." [Now it's getting colder.]

1619.a.
Mrs. Mary Koch, my neighbor at Egypt, when the warm weather of spring comes along, customarily says: "Gewwacht, der Lenz grickt dich." [Watch out, you'll get spring fever(?).]

1619.b.
If during a thunderstorm there is a very noticeable drop in temperature, we usually say: "Do hot's ammenens gschloost." [It hailed somewhere.] ("Ammenens" is a Lebanon County form.)

1620.
"Halsbrechendi Arwett" [neck-breaking work] refers not only to dangerous work like repairing a barn roof without adequate protection against falling, but more particularly and more commonly for heavy burdensome work, as of lifting and carrying heavy weights. "Des is halsbrechendi Arwett, Arewett."

1621.a.
"Wann en Bauer verhungert, is es sei eegni Schuld." [If a farmer starves, it's his own fault.]   *Often heard*

1621.b.
"Wann die Koch hungrich geht, is es ihre eegni Schuld." [If the cook goes hungry, it's her own fault.] "Sis noch ken Koch verhungert." [No cook has ever gone hungry.]

1622.
From January 1 to January 9, 1937 the weather was warm. I heard it said: "Des is hatt Wedder fer die Granke." [This is trying weather for those who are sick.]

1623.
A falling star seen by you means "as ebber in der neegschde Freindschaft gschtarwe is." [that someone in the immediate family has died]   *"Sticks" Zerfass*

1624.
There is a prevalent belief that a damp open winter is dangerous to the health. Such weather causes illness and death.

1625.
Rev. Smith of Northampton tells me that one of his former parishioners planted grapevines upon old hollow shoes and filled the hole with stones and ground.

1626.
When I was a child, if anything was lost, we would drop spittle into the palm of the left hand and strike it smartly with the index finger of the right hand. The direction in which the spittle flew was the direction in which the lost article was to be sought.

1627.
Something lost cannot be found by searching for it. That is, something lost accidentally must be found accidentally.

1628.
Edible mushrooms are known as "mushrooms." This is usually confined to the Morchellae variety. Inedible mushrooms, and commonly all except the Morchellae are regarded as inedible, are called "toadstools," "Groddeschtiel."

1629.
Toadstools are made by toads.   *Children, Leb*

1630.
If cork is swallowed, it will swell up and close the bowels.

1631.
Pennypacker, the miller at Schwencksville, when Washington's army lay encamped at the Perkiomen Creek, ground glass in the flour. This he did because he was a Tory.   *Heard at Schwencksville, when I was a pastor at Old Goshenhoppen*

1632.
Children ate the white locust flowers.

1633.
Children ate the leaves of the yellow wood sorrel.

1634.
Children ate the gall apples on Rhododendron nudiflorum.

1635.
Children ate the ears of calamus, "Kalmuss Kolwe."

1636.
Children ate the white moist lower ends of the inner calamus leaves.

1637.
One should not point at flowers or at young fruit on fruit trees. As a consequence of so doing, they will fall off prematurely.   *Leb*

1638.
Wheat on poor land will turn into chess or cheat.   *Mont*

1639.
Swallowing chewing gum will cause death. It will close the bowels.   *Heard when a child*

1640.
Swallowing cherry stones will cause death.   *Do*

1641.a.
If you swallow a cherry stone, peach stone, or plum stone, it will sprout and grow in your stomach.   *Do*

1641.b.
"Sack" — bag.
"Weezesack" — wheat bag, a tightly woven bag for wheat, size two bushels. An unusual size was three bushels, hence "Zweebuschel Sack" [two-bushel bag], "Dreibuschel Sack" [three-bushel bag]
"Gleiesack" — bran sack; gunny sack.

"Geldsack" — money bag.
"Mehlsack" — a very tightly woven tag for fetching flour from the mill.
"Salzsack" — a bag for salt, big or little.
"Rocksack" — coat pocket.
"Saddelsack" — saddlebags.

1642.
"Wann en Pasching Schtee odder en anner Schtee schluckscht, grickscht en Schtee in der Maage un noh verlierscht die Gsundheet." [If you swallow a peach stone or some other stone, you will have a stone in the stomach and you will lose your good health.]
Sumneytown

(I wonder when these beliefs arose. When I was young, children and even adults would crack hickory nuts with their teeth; always chestnuts.)

1643.
Cracking hard objects with the teeth will crack the teeth and cause them to rot. This used to be a common admonition of parents who cared.

1644.
Swallowing cherry stones will cause bad luck. *Leh*

1645.
Eating too many calamus ears, "Kalmoss Kolwe," will cause sleepiness. There was a young man who ate plentifully of calamus ears. He fell asleep and would not waken. He slept and slept. Finally they stuck needles into his body and in this way succeeded in wakening him. This story I often heard as a warning against eating too many calamus ears. It was supposed to have happened in Lancaster County.

1646.
Seeds of raspberries, strawberries, grapes, etc. lodge in the appendix and cause appendicitis.
At one time quite commonly believed

1647.
A boy attending a country school brought to the teacher the cherry stones of dried cherries. (It was customary to dry cherries, unpitted. These were used in pies.) The teacher was very fond of the kernels and always gladly received the handfuls of stones. The time came when the boy no longer brought cherry stones. The teacher asked him: "Why do you no longer bring cherry stones?" The answer: "The boys have changed their shitting place." One may compare this story, which has actuality in it as far as the conduct of the boys goes. There were preferred places along fence rows, at some trees, etc. And it was not unusual to eat cherries, stone and all in a pie. (Cf. Nr. 1641.a.)

1648.
Horsehair will turn into eels if placed in a rain barrel. *Leb*

1649.
Dragon flies sting and are poisonous.
Quite commonly believed

1650.
Do not count the eggs under a setting hen. *Leb*

The reference is here not to the eggs before setting, but while the hen is sitting on them. (There are eggs which are broken or which fall out of the nest.)

1651.
Newly born kittens and puppies are blind for nine days. *Leb*

1652.
Greasing a horse's hoofs prevents them from becoming brittle. *Leb*

1653.
Eggs given to a sitting hen are "reeded," that is marked.
The reasons given: So as to be distinguished from any eggs which the hens may lay in the nest.

1654.
Horsehair is used to clean the throats of chickens having "gaps." *At one time common*

1655.
When you have seen 100 white horses, make a wish and the wish will come true. *Childhood*

1656.
As children in going to school passed excrementa, they would spit. The last one to spit ate "it" or the one who didn't spit ate "it." *Childhood*

1657.
Spitting into the palms of the hands (and then rubbing the hands) to gain a better grip on an object, axe, plow, heavy weight—or to give a better blow—was a common custom.
I knew a boy at Green Lane who in playing ball always spat into his hands when he rounded second base on a home run.

1658.
Rolling up the shirt sleeves was supposed to give added strength. This was usually done in tavern brawls or in rough and tumble fights.

1659.
When I taught Buck's School near Green Lane, some of the boys (the Brey boys) would catch flies, tie strings to their legs and let them fly.

1660.
There was a farmer who fed his horse a little less each day with the purpose of training him to eat less. Finally, he fed him only an ear of corn a day. Then the horse died. The farmer said: "Wann er noch paar Daag glebt hett, hett ich ihm's Esse abgwehnt." [If he had lived a few days longer, I would have cured him of eating.]

1661.
"Der letscht bezaahlt alles." [The last one pays all.] Used when the last one winds up the work, etc.
At one time commonly heard

1662.
"Der letscht im Bett bezaahlt alles." [The last one in bed pays all.]
"Der letscht im Bett muss es Licht ausblose." [The last one in bed must blow out the light.] *Do*

1663.
Persons who sleep on feather beds are liable to contract rheumatism. *Leb*

1664.
"Er hot sei Bett gut gfeddert." [He feathered his bed well.] He married a wealthy person.

1665.
Proverb
"Was mer net wees, macht em net bees." [What one does not know does not make one angry.]

1666.
"Was em net brennt, brauch mer net blose." [One need not blow that which does not burn.]

1667.
"Was is dewert as mer der Schtall schliesst, wann der Gaul gschtohle is?" [What is the value of locking the stable when the horse has been stolen?]
Leb, Sydney Wotring

1668.
Counting-out rhyme:
"Edelmann, Beddelmann, Bauer, Soldaat,
Keenich, Kaiser, Hossescheisser."

[Nobleman, beggar, farmer, soldier,
king, Kaiser, one who defecates in his pants.]
Sydney Wotring

1669.
"En Bassemhaut is gut fer Gedrickdes." [The skin of a possum is good for "pressing" of horses.] *Do*

1670.
"Wann mer so weisse Dubbe uff die Fingerneggel hot, no deed em sei Laad (Laadeholz) noch bliehe." [If one has white spots on the fingernails, ones coffin (coffin wood) is still blooming.] *Do*

1671.
In the song, "Yulla," the words are:
"Sundaags—Ruherei,
Mundaags—Wescherei,
Dienschdaags—Dricklerei,
Mittwochs—Flickerei."

[Sunday—day of rest,
Monday—wash day,
Tuesday—dry the wash,
Wednesday—mending day.] *Do*

1672.
Swallows bring bedbugs. *Do*

1673.
Chimney swifts bring bedbugs. So said the old people. *Do*

1674.
Bats bring moths, "Schaawe." *Do*

1675.
Of a cold place it was said: "En Blatz wu die Sunn un der Mund net hiekummt." [A place never reached by the sun and the moon.] *Do*

1676.
To cause a tree to become fruitful, plant it close to another tree that is very fruitful, even though the second tree is of another variety. *Do*

1677.
"Ich schteh uff die Kanzel
Un breddich wie en Amschel.
Do kummt en Maus
Un schpott mich aus.
Noh is die Karich aus."

[I stand in the chancel
And preach like a robin.
Here comes a mouse
And makes fun of me.
Now the service is over.] *Do*

1678.
"Wann die Sunn mariyets glaar uffgeht un noh wennich schpeeder darich die Wolke lacht, no gebt's wiescht Wedder." [When the sun comes up in a clear sky and then later laughs though the clouds, there will be bad weather.] *Do*

1679.
For a child:

"Knock at the door,
Peep in,
Turn the latch,
Walk in.
'Howd'y do?'"

Tap on the forehead.
Lift up an eyelid.
Twitch the nose.
Open the mouth.
Tickle the chin. *Hilda Wotring*

1680.
When Rev. Yaeger wanted to take the train at Copley, it pulled out before he could board it. He cried out: "Waard, ich bin der Parre Yaeger!" [Wait, I'm Pastor Yaeger.] *Do*

1681.
When Rev. Dieder examined the block of wood at which he shot in a shooting match—and having wholly missed—he cried out: "Ich hab's in die Hell nei verfehlt!" [I missed it all to hell!] *Do*

1682.
Eating horseradish will sharpen the wits. The horseradish is "scharef" [sharp] and will "scharefe" [sharpen] the wits. *Common*

1683.
Vinegar when sharp, "scharef," has the same results as horseradish. *Common*

1684.
Eating the brains of an animal (of a hog) will strengthen the mind. (Curious that this is said of the brains of a pig, for "Sau" [pig] and "seiyisch" [piggish] are words of contempt when applied to man and his actions.)

1685.
Game
Children sit in a circle, scratching the ground with sticks. One on the outside comes and says: "Woi, woi, was graabscht du?" [Hawk, hawk, what are you digging?] Answer: "Die Mammi ihre Schtocknodel." [Mother's darning needle.] Question, as one throws something into the ring: "Is des es?" [Is this it?] Answer: "Nee!" [No!] And so on until someone throws in something which is "es." [It.] Thereupon that one becomes the inquirer. *Do*

1686.
"Drink ich, so schtink ich
Drink ich net, so schtink ich doch.
Besser gedrunke un gschtunke,
Wie net gedrunke un doch gschtunke."

[If I drink, I stink;
If I don't drink, I'll stink anyway.
Better to have drunk and to have stunk,
Than not to have drunk and have stunk anyway.]
*Mrs. Orville Gruver, Cementon
Collected also from Center County
per Rev. J.L. Roush*

1687.
The ends of the toes and of the fingers are nearest to the heart. *Mrs. Charles Johnson, Egypt*

1688.
Tie woolen thread around the toes for cracked skin at the toes. *Do*

1689.
"Wie mer in der Wald greischt, so schallt's zurick." [As one calls into the woods, so it resounds.]
Mrs. Morris Lindenmuth

1690.
For whooping cough get some food from the "Geddel," godmother, of the one afflicted.
Mrs. Charles Johnson

1691.
Riddle
"Was halt der Bluger im Feld?" [What keeps the plowman in the field?]—"Es Rumdrehe." [Turning around.]
Will Koch, Egypt

1692.
"Wer hett's gedenkt,
 as en aldi Fraa en Mensch sei kennt?"

[Who would have thought
 that an old woman could be a human being?]
Mrs. Raymond Remaley

1693.
"Peeder, wu schteht er?
 Hinnich die Leeder.
 Was dutt er datt?
 Macht die Geil's Fuder aa.
 Was noch?
 Butzt die Geil die Zeh.
 Was noch?
 Butzt die Geil des Loch."

[Peter, where is he?
 Behind the ladder.
 What's he doing there?
 Preparing the horses' food.
 What else?
 Cleaning the horses' teeth.
 What else?
 Cleaning the horses' hole.]
(Cf. Lothring. Woerterbuch, page 495.)
Richard Peters

1694.
"En Braucher hot en hadder Dod." [A powwower has a hard death.] (Er is dem Deiwel ergewwe.)[He has given himself over to the devil.] *Mrs. Will Koch*

1695.
"Fer ebber loslese muss mer hinnerschich lese." [To free someone who has been bewitched by a text, the text must be read backwards.] *Do*

1696.
"Rode Kolwe sin so schee,
 Geb re en Boss un loss sie geh.
 O, was waar sell so schee."

[Red ears (of corn) are so
 beautiful, Give her a kiss and
 let her go. Oh, that was so lovely.]
Willoughby Troxell

1697.
"Wann bese Weibsleit in's Feier gucke, no brenn's." [When evil women look into a fire, then it burns brightly.]
Mrs. Remaley

1698.
Song
"Susi Enderlein, Mary Enderlein,
  Hascht du nicht en Vogelsnescht?
  Ya, das Vogelnescht, das ist deine,
  Un der Vogel drin ist meine.
  Ya, so liewere mir die ganze Nacht,
  Bis die Susi Enderlein erwacht."

[Susi Enderlein, Mary Enderlein,
  Don't you have a bird's nest?
  Yes, the birds's nest is yours,
  And the bird therein is mine.
  Yes, so we will spend the night,
  Until Susi Enderlein awakens.]

(Lines three and four of the succeeding stanzas:)

"Ya, die gladde Schtirn ist deine,
  Un das Kissen drauf ist mein."

"Ya, die runde Naas ist deine,
  Un des Schnuffle draa ist meine."

"Ya, die zarde Bruscht ist deine,
  Un des Dringen drauf ist meine."

"Ya, das siesse Maul ist deine,
  Un das Schlecken draa ist meine."

"Ya, das lang Hals ist deine,
  An das Sucklen draa is meine."

"Ya, das runde Bauch ist deine,
  Un das Rutschen drauf ist meine."

[Yes, the smooth forehead is yours,
  And the pillow on it is mine.]

[Yes, the round nose is yours,
  And the sniffing there is mine.]

[Yes, the tender breast is yours,
  And the pressing there is mine.]

[Yes, the sweet mouth is yours,
  And the licking there is mine.]

[Yes, the long neck is yours,
  And the suckling there is mine.]

[Yes, the round belly is yours,
  And the sliding there is mine.]

Adam Hiester, Strausstown

This is a very interesting item. Note the use of terms.

1699.
June 9 is a good day for planting pole beans. *Egypt*

1700.
"Alles is gemacht fer ebbes." [Everything is made for something.]
Common

1701.
"Alles hot sei Zweck." [Everything has its purpose.]
Common

1702.
"Alles is gut fer ebbes." [Everything is good for something.]
Common

1703.
"Alles is gut in seim Blatz." [Everything is good in its place.]
Common

1704.
"Alli-ebber hot sei gudi Seit." [Everyone has a good side.]
Common
Our people cannot conceive that anything or person is absolutely worthless, not even a Canada Thistle.

1705.
"Mit Waarde verrecke die Hund." [Too much waiting kills the dogs.]
Common

1706.
"Ich waar iwwerich." I was not wanted. *Common*

1707.
July 5, 1937. Today I went down to the Stahl pottery. I saw the dish which Isaac Stahl is making for me. I went to Bally where Isaac Stahl lives. He has a notebook in which he has written the couplets which he has composed and which he has used or intends to use as decorative inscriptions for his ware. I have numbered them as in the original and also added the translations which he made. They illustrate the intellectuality and also the fact that while the German is understood and spoken, German phonetics are entirely forgotten.

3.
"Deisa Schussel ist von Orda gamacht
  Von sie zerbricht der Heffner lacht."

"This dish is made of clay,
  When it breaks the potter laughs."

1708.
4.
"Aus der Erde mit verstand
  Macht der Heffner allerhand."

"With brains and clay
  The potter can make anything."

1709.
5.
"GOTT GESEGNE DIESES HAUS
UND ALLES WAS DA GEHT EIN UND AUS.
GOTT GESEGNE ALLES SAMPT
UND DA-ZU DAS GANZE LAND."

[God bless this house
and all that go in and out.
God bless all together
and also the entire land.]

1710.
6.
"MENCH HAB FARSTOND GAY NICHT STUE WIDE, DRINK NICHT STUE FEAL UND BLIBE GASHITE."

"Man use manners, Drink not too much and stay in mind."

1711.
7.
"LIEBER FATTER IN DEM HIMMEL
WIE DU ARSHAFFEN HAST
SO BIN ICH."

"DEAR FATHER IN HEAVEN
THE WAY YOU MADE ME
SO I AM."

1712.
8.
LIEBER FATTER DAR DU HIMMEL UND EART ARSHAFFEN HAST, ALLES WAS DARINNEN IST GOTT SANE DARE GAKOMMEN HAT."

[Dear father, who has created heaven and earth,
All that is therein, God bless the one who has come.]

(While some of the above are not original, the following are definitely marked in the notebook as having been composed by I. S. Stahl.)

1713.
9.
"ALLY MANSHEN AUF DEASER WELD
Missen starben, Trutz al eram geld.
Und O due liber Augstine alles ist hean."

"All people throughout the whole
[world] have to die in spide
of all there money and wealth."

1714.
10.
"When the leaves bit the trees goodby,
The days of winter coming nigh."

1715.
11.
"Ine sthine fol Beer,
Macht Liebe mit mere."

[A stein full of beer,
Makes love with me.]

(I have noticed that in Montgomery County they say "mer" for "mir."

1716.
12.
"Gott gip mear wishite und farstond,
Dos ich mach laben we dus farlongs."

"God give me wisdom, So I may
live according to your coment." (command)

1717.
13.
"Dar Heffner hat mich arshaffen,
Far ine Sponch in mare stu backen."

"The potter made me, the sponch
[sponge] dish for a sponch cake in me to bake."

1718.
14.
"Ine Haffa bin ich arshaffen,
Now fill mich mit guda Sosah."

"The potter made me,
Now fill me with good things."

1719.
15.
"Dar Heffner hot mich arshaffen,
Warum sult ich nat gude machen."

[The potter created me,
Why should I not make good.]

1720.
16.
"Oh Blumie du so leab und shane
Warum must du so snel fargane."

"Oh flower so bright and gay,
Why is it you fade so fast away."

1721.
17.
"Dar Manchie danged
Awer Gott langed."

"Man thinks a lot to do,
But God might call before you are through."

1722.
18.
"Gott sagne Unser Hause
Und alles wass gayed ine und aus."

"God bless mine house, and Mines
everything that goes in and out."

1723.
19.
"Woe Menchen Hilfie ally ist
Gott du uns doch so naie bist."

"Where the help of men is all
God you us so near."

1724.
20.
"Trust in God with sole heart and thought."

1725.
21.
"GOTT du hast mich arshaffen,
Far wass aus mere stu machen."

"God you made me
to be of some use."

1726.
22.
"Dar Heffner hat mich arshaffen,
Fil mich mit Butter oder undri Sasa."

"The potter made me to fill
with butter and other things."

1727.
23.
"Ware nicht leab Gott un wipe,
Dar hat kine rue in Eavich kite."

"If you do not love your God and wife,
Have not rest in all his life."

1728.
24.
"My country I sing of Thee,
Sweet Land of Liberty."

1729.
25.
"Is das nicht ine irie weld,
Iner hat dar Bitel und dar ondry
hat das Geld."

"This is a wonderful world,
One has the pocket book and
the other has the money."

1730.
26.
"Mench Oh Mench so stulch du bist sitcht,
Wie inie Blumie du nemmer bist."

"Man oh man so proud you are,
Like a flower you fade away."

1731.
27.
"Groser Gott im Himmel Rich,
Far Dier sint ally Menchen kilch(!)."

"Almighty God in Heaven above,
Before Thee all men are alike."

1732.
28.
"Allie Menchen auf dease Weld,
Sint um Lamma Dearer far das Geld."

"All people on this world,
are going after the money."

1733.
29.
"Ach Gott wee gline bin ich fer dere
Duch blights arrab und hilfsts mare."
(blickst herab)

"Oh God so low I am before Thee,
But you have allways mercy and
helpest me."

1734.
30.
"Allie Menchen blose grose und kline,
Sint fol Uneru ally Szhite.
Allie Menchen Grose und Kline
Sint Fol Urune ere Gonsi Labens Szide."

"All people great and small,
Have no rest the whole time."

1735.
31.
"Rose O Rose so shane du bist
Honich und Garuch dine Laben ists."

"Rose O Rose so beautiful you are
Honey and flavor in your life."

1736.
32.
"Beer und Wine hatt Gasong allerline."
"Beer and wine is full of song of all kinds."

1737.
33.
"All Menchen auf deser Weld
Sint farricked ebers Gelg."[sic]

"All people of this world
are grazy for money."

1738.
34.
"Souffen und Drinken sint Szhy R LY (zweierlei)
Arber Drinken und Souffen macht Si-R-I." (Seierei)

[Drinking to excess and just drinking are two different matters,
But ordinary drinking and excessive drinking make a debauch.]

103

1739.
35.
"Alley Menchen auf deaser Weld
Missen starben Have-se feal oder Wanich Geld."

[All men in this world
must die, have they much or little money.]

1740.
36.
"Wen ich stu feal gadrunken haven
Don feal ich reich
un hap feel stu saugen."

"When I drink to much,
I feel rich
and have much to say."

1741.
When Isaac Stahl was young and working for his father, his work was pronounced unsatisfactory by the father. Thereupon he said: "Ich bin ein Topfer Sohn, Was ich do mach des hot ken Dron." The meaning is: "What I make has no place of honor, no throne." He said "Dron" meant "Ehr." [honor]

July 5, 1937. I was down to see Hommel today. I took lunch with him. He gave me a collection of rhymes which he made around th year 1912, when he came over. He tells me that he noted them down in High German instead of in the dialect. That those unnoted as to informant come from the Pennsylvania Germans. The others come from a woman who did housework. I have copied them from his notes.

[Rudolf Hommel was born on May 3, 1887, in Munich, Germany. He spent two years in the theological seminary at Neuen Dettelsau in Germany and later studied at Harvard and Lehigh universities. His two loves were the Pennsylvania Dutch country and the Orient. Between 1921 and 1937 he was the director of the Mercer expedition for historical research in the Far East. He died on March 18, 1950, of injuries received in an automobile accident. Cf. The Pennsylvania Dutchman, Vol. 1, No. 12, page 1.]

CHILDREN'S RHYMES

1742.
1.
"Da kommt e' Maus und baut e' Haus';
Da kommt e' Mueck und baut e' Brueck;
Da kommt e' Spinn, hat was im Sinn;
Da kommt e' Floh, macht so, so, so."

[Here comes a mouse and builds a house;
Here comes a fly and builds a bridge;
Here comes a spider, has something in mind;
Here comes a flea and makes so, so, so.]

1743.
2.
"Es war einmal ein Mann,
Der hatte einen Kahn.
Der Kahn war ihm zu nass,
Da ging er auf die Gass'.
Die Gass, war ihm zu kalt,
Da ging er in den Wald.
Der Wald war ihm zu gruen,
Da ging er nach Berlin.
Berlin war ihm zu gross,
Da ging es in die Hos'.
Die Hos' war ihm zu klein,
Da ging er wieder heim."

[There once was a man,
Who had a canoe.
The canoe was too wet,
So he went on the street.
The street was too cold,
So I went into the forest.
The forest was too green,
So he went to Berlin.
Berlin was too big,
So he messed his pants.
The pants were too small,
So he went home again.]

1744.
3.
"Eia Popeia, machs Gickerl tod
Es legt mer kei Eier
und frisst all mei Brod.
bringt mer viel Not."

[Eia Popeia, kill the rooster.
It lays no eggs
and eats all my bread.
brings me much trouble.

1745.
4.
"Schlof, Kindlein, schlof![sic]
Der Vater huet' die Schaf.
Die Mutter schuettelt 's Baeumelein,
Da faellt herab ein Traeumelein.
Schlaf, Kindlein, schlaf!"[sic]

[Sleep, baby, sleep!
Father tends the sheep.
Mother shakes the little trees,
And a dreamlet falls down.
Sleep, baby, sleep!]

1746.
5.
"Maikaefer, flieg!
Der Vater is' im Krieg.
Die Mutter is' im Pommerland:
Pommerland is' abgebrannt.
Maikaefer, flieg!"

[Cockchafer, fly!
Father is in the war.
Mother is in Pomerania:
Pomerania is scorched.
Cockchafer, fly!]

1747.
6.
"Der Schwed' is' komme,
Hat alle mitgnomme, etc."

[The Swede came,
Took all along, etc.]

1748.
7.
"Wenn Wir Wester-Waelder Wasch-Weiber
Wuessten Wo Warmes Wasser Waere,
Wuerden Wir Weisse Waesche Waschen."

[If we washwomen from the
Westerwald knew where warm
water was, we would wash the white clothes.]

1749.
8.
"Kleine Kinder Koennen Keine Kirschen Kochen."

[Little children cannot boil cherries.]

1750.
9.
"Pitsche, patsche, Kuchen,
Der Becker hat gerufen.
Wer will gute Kuchen backen,
Der muss haben sieben Sachen:
Eier und Schmalz,
Butter und Salz,
Milch und Mehl.
Safran macht den Kuchen gehl."

[Patty, patty, cake,
The baker has called.
He who wants to bake well,
Must have seven ingredients:
Eggs and lard,
Butter and salt,
Milk and flour.
Saffron makes the cake yellow.]

1751.
10.
"Sreiten drei Reiter ums Rathaus rum;
Sie tragen e' Schuessel voll Reisbrei rum."

[Three riders ride around the city hall;
They're carrying a dish
full of rice boiled in milk.]

1752.
11.
"Mit der Bassgeigen und dem Fiddelbogen an der
Wand, Kegelscheiben [sic]
Da ist gut, da schiebts sichs von selbst."

[With the bass viol and the fiddle bow in your hand,
bowling
It is good; all goes automatically.]

1753.
12.
"Ringe, Ringe, Rei'e.
'S Kaetzle geht auf zweie.
Holt dem Papa Schnupftabak,
Scheien alle: Quack! Quack! Quack!"

[Ring around a rosie.
The kitten goes on two.
Fetch father some snuff,
All cry out: Quack! Quack! Quack!]

1754.
13.
"Auf dem Berge Sinai,
Sitzt der Schneider Kikeriki,
Putzt seine gruenen Hosen aus,
Eins, zwei, drei und du bist draus."

[On Mt. Sinai,
Sits taylor cock-a-doodle-doo,
Cleaning his green pants,
1, 2, 3 and you are out.]

1755.
14.
"Ich bin e klins Bingel,
Stell mich ins Winkel.
Wenn ich nicht ka
Fang ich nicht a."

[I am a little fellow,
Stand in a corner.
If I can't do it,
I won't attempt it.]

1756.
15.
"1, 2, 3, 4, 5, 6, 7,
Wo frist dein Scheffe hin?
Wo denn hin nach Berlin,
Wo die schoenen Madeln sin."

[1, 2, 3, 4, 5, 6, 7,
Where's your lamb eating its
way to? [?]
Where to but to Berlin,
Where all the lovely girls are.]

1757.
16.
"Hotte, hotte, hoere!
So reitet Froere.
So reitet kleine Kinder,
Die noch nicht geritten sind,
Wenn sie groesser wachse,
No reiten sie nach Sachse.
Wenn der Bauer ins Wasser faellt,
Na schrecke alle Pflumrsack."

[Gee, gee, listen!
Thus Froere rides.
Thus ride the small children,

Who haven't ridden as yet.
When they are bigger,
They'll ride to Saxony.
If the farmer falls into the water,
All the ? will be frightened.]

Metzingen, Wuerrtenberg

1758.
17.
"Ringe, Ringe, Rose,
Zucker muss mer stosse.
Schopfche Wein,
Bretzel drein.
Komm, wir wollen lustig sein,
Lustig wie die Voegelein."

[Ring around the rose,
Sugar must be avoided.
Small glass of wine,
With a pretzel in it.
Come, we want to be merry,
Happy as the birds."

Wirtenberg

1759.
18.
"Schlaf, Kindlein, schlaf!
Dein Vater ist ein Graf.
Dei Mutter is e' arme Dirn',
Sie muss dem Graf sei' Kindlein wirn."

[Sleep, baby, sleep!
Your father is a count.
Your mother is a poor girl,
She must care for the count's child.]

Comitat Raab, Ungarn

1760.
19.
"Hott, Rosserl, hott!
Wir fahren in die Stadt,
Um ein Seidel Wein,
Un ein Semmel drein.
Wenn der Schimmel nicht mehr will,
Dann zeign mer ihm den Peitschenstiel."

[Gee, horsey, gee!
We're driving into town,
For a glass of wine,
And a roll (bun) in it.
If the white horse doesn't want to any more,
Then we'll show him the whip-handle.]

Comitat Raab, Ungarn

1761.
20.
"Mei Schatz is a Schreiner.
E Schreiner muss sein,
Der macht mir en Wiegel
Unds Kindle drin nei."

[My lover is a carpenter.
A carpenter he must be,
To make a cradle for me
And an infant to go in it.]

Metzingen, Wuerrtenberg

1762.
21.
"Schustermeister, mach mir Schuh'.
Gieb ein Leder auch dazu.
Ist kein Schuster in der Stadt,
Der ein so ein Leder hat.
Frau Schuster Ertlerin
Weiss nicht wem das Leder ghoert.
Es gehoert nicht mein und gehoert nicht dein,
Sollen ja 32 sein."

[Shoemaker, make me shoes.
And provide the leather.
There's no shoemaker in the city,
Who has such leather.
Shoemaker Ertler's wife
Doesn't know who owns the leather.
It isn't mine and not yours,
It's supposed to be 32.]

1763.
22.
"Der alte Posthalter von siebenzig Jahren,
Der wollte mit Schimmel nach Stuttgart fahren.
Die Schimmel, die Schimmel, die fahren im Trab
Und werfen den alten Posthalter hinab."

Metzingen, Wuertenberg

[The old postmaster of seventy years,
He wanted to travel to Stuttgart with white horses.
The horses, the horses, they trot along
And thow off the old postmaster.]

1764.
23.
"Ringe, Ringe, Rosen,
Die Buben tragen Hosen.
Die Maedeln tragen Roeck
Un fallen dann in Dreck."

[Ring around a rosey,
The boys wear pants.
The girls wear skirts
And fall in the dirt.]

Do

1765.
24.
"Weist du nicht wo Stuttgart liegt?
Stuttgart liegt im Tale,
Wo's so schoene Maedchen gibt,
Aber so brutale.
Die waeschen sich mit Eiergelb,
Dass sie besser glaenzen.
Bauermaedeln sind mir lieber
Als so Kaffeediardle."

[Do you know where Stuttgart lies?
Stuttgart lies in the valley,
Where there are lovely girls,
But such brutal ones.
They wash themselves with egg
yolks, so they shine more.
I prefer farm girls
To the coffee maidens.] *Do*

1766.
The blossoms of "Butter and Eggs" were in large quantity fried in lard and the salve was used to draw boils to a head. *Helen Summers*
(When a boil comes to a head, it becomes yellow.)

1767.
"Maulwarfgraut" — [cypress spurge] (Euphorbia Lathyrus L.) A succulent plant with four berries planted in gardens to protect against moles in Lancaster County. *Mrs. Hommel*

1768.
To transplant parsley successfully, steal it. *Egypt*

1769.
The genus Gallium in fruit were called "Schpelder." *Leh*

1770.
"Bordelmae.
Wer Graas hot, der meh,
Un wer Korn hot, seh."

[St. Bartholomew's Day, Aug. 24.
He who has grass, should mow,
And he who has rye, sow.]

*Told to me by J.B.Stoudt from Berks County
I have never heard this otherwise*

1171.
Fruit trees given with leaves when blossoming will bear little fruit. *Common*

1772.
What is planted on June 22 will grow long, big or thick. *Not infrequently heard*

1773.
Potatoes planted on June 21 will keep well over winter.
"Sie halde lang." [They will last long.] *Do*

1774.
A marriage on the longest day will last long. The couple will remain married long; will be potent long. *Do*

A SERIES FROM MRS. ELIZABETH MOYER AND HER DAUGHTER, ANNA,

Easton, Pennsylvania.
(Ultimate source, Frederick Township,
Montgomery County)
(Numbers 1775-1786)

1775.
"Der Hund, der blafft; es kommt Besuch.
Es kommt ein Mann mit einem Buch.
Nau Betz, nau schleicht mir net so faul
Und wescht dem Kind sei dreckich Maul."

[The dog barks; visitors come.
A man with a book is coming.
Now Betz, don't drag about
And wash the child's dirty mouth.]

1776.
"Die dreckich Wesch duh in die Schteeg."
"Die dreckich Wesch duh unnich die Schteeg."

[Put the dirty wash on the steps.]
[Put the dirty wash under the steps.]

1777.
"Donnert's in dem hohlen Wald,
Schterben viele yung und alt."

[When it thunders in the empty
woods, Many will die young and old.]

1778.
"Morye, Morye, nummer net heit,
Saage all die faule Leit."

[Tomorrow, tomorrow, but not today,
Say all the lazy folk.]

1779.a.
"Reide, reide, Geile!
Alle Schtunn e Meile.
Schtolber nur net iwwer der Graawe,
Fallscht du nei, so muscht es hawwe.
Blumps, datt leischt du!"

[Ride, ride, little horse!
Every hour a mile.
Don't stumble over the ditch,
If you fall in, you'll get it.
Bump! There you lie!]

1779.b.
"Reide, reide, Geile!
Alle Schtunn e Meile.
Marye woll mir Hawwer dresche,
Will es Buwli net vergesse.
Blumps, datt leischt du!"

[Ride, ride, little horse!
Every hour a mile.
Tomorrow we want to thrash oats,
Don't want to forget the little
boy. Bump! There you lie!]

1779.c.
"Der alt Jim Groff
Hockt uff em Baam.
Ich guck nuff
Un er guckt runner.
Ich grick en Schtee
Un schmeiss ihm ans Beh.
Ach, geh aweck
Un loss mich geh!"

[Old Jim Groff
Sits in a tree.
I look up
And he looks down.
I get a stone
And throw it at his legs.
Oh, go away
And let me be!]

1780.
"Bohne, Bohne sind mein Lebensgrone.
Riewe, Riewe hen mich vertriewe.
Hett meine Mutter Schpeck gekocht,
Waer ich lenger gebliewe."

[Beans, beans are life's crown.
Turnips, turnips drove me off.
Had my mother made bacon,
I would have remained longer.]

1781.
"Was mir net wees,
macht mir net hees."

[What one doesn't know,
doesn't bother me.]

1782.
"Der Ewer beisst....."

[The boar bites...]

1783.
"Vor em Esse hengt sie's Maul,
Noch em Esse is sie faul."

[Before the meal she pouts,
After the meal she's lazy.]

1784.
"Anna Marieli, Anna Maratz,
Melk die Kuh un fieder die Katz."

[Anna Marieli, Anna Maratz,
Milk the cow and feed the cat.]

1785.
The people of Frederick Township, Montgomery County, were fond of telling about an "aarmer Dropp" [poor fellow] who lived in the "Schtee Barig." [Stone Hill] He was quoted as having given the following account of the time that he was almost late for work:

"Ich bin wacker warre. No waar's hell, ball Daag un no hawwich die Schteg aagerisse un bin die Hosse nunner schprunge un hab ich die Meh genumme un bin Sense gange."

[I got awake. It was light, almost day and I pulled on the steps and ran down the pants and took the mow and sent scything.]

1786.
"Was?
Der alt Fass!
Duh en neier Boddem nei!"

[What?
And old barrel!
Put a new bottom in!]

1787.
I.
"Was hilft den alle Welt
Mit ihrem Gut und Gelt?
Alles, alles vergeht geschwindt
Gleich wie der Rauch von Wind.

Was hilft der hohe Tron
Der Sceptre und der Kron?
Sceptre, Sceptre und Regierment
Hat alles bald ein End.

Was hilft den Huebsch und Fein
Schoen wie die Engel sein?
Schoenheit, Schoenheit vergeht im Grab;
Diese Rosen fallen ab."

[Of what help the whole world
With its property and money?
All, all vanishes quickly
Just like the a puff of wind.

Of what help the high throne
The scepter and the crown?
Scepter, scepter and government
Soon have an end.

Of help handsome and fine
Lovely as the angels?
Beauty, beauty vanishes in the
grave; These roses fall off.]

1788.
II.

"Liebe Kinder, gieb nur Acht
  Das ihr mir das A, B, C recht macht.
  Immer musz ich Tinte riera
  Fettera schneida und vorschreiben
  Liebe Kinder, gieb nur Acht
  Das ich mir das A, B, C recht macht

  Schlag ich einen Kindlein
  auf sein dummen, duecken Kopf
  Kommt sogleich der Vater herein
  und schreidlt [sic] den armen Tropf.
  'Wer hat mir mein Kind geschlagen?
  Den will ich beim Haupt verklagen.'
  Liebe Kinder, gieb nur Acht
  Das ihr mir das A, B, C recht macht."

[Dear children, be careful
  That you make your A B C's
  correctly.
  Cut your quills and write your
  copy.
  Dear children, etc.]

[If I strike a child
  on his stupid, thick head,
  The father soon comes in
  and ? the poor fellow.
  'Who has struck my child?
  I'll take care of him.'
  Dear children, etc.]

1789.
III.

"Und wenn wir kommen zu Baltimore
  Da schtrecken wir die Haende vor
  Und rufen laut, 'Victoria,
  yetzt sind wir in America.'"

[And when we come to Baltimore,
  We stretch our our hands
  And call out: "Victoria,
  now we are in America."]

1790.
IV.

"O Strassburg, o Strassburg,
  du wunderschoene Stadt,
  Darinnen liegt begraben
  so mancher Soldat.
  So mancher und schoener,
  auch tafperer Soldat.
  Verlassen, verlassen,
  es kann nicht anders sein!
  Der Vater, die Mutter,
  die ging'n vors Hauptmanns Haus:
  'Ach Hauptmann, lieber Herr Hauptmann,
  gebt mir mein Sohn heraus.'
  'Eure Sohn, und der musz sterben
  im weit und breiten Feld.'
  Im Felde, im Felde, im Felde
  vor dem Feind
  Zu Strassburg, ja zu Strassburg
  Soldaten muessen sein."

[Oh Strassburg, oh Strassburg,
  you city of beauty,
  Therein lie interred
  many a soldier.
  Many a handsome
  and also brave soldier.
  Lost, lost,
  it cannot be otherwise!
  Father, mother, went
  before the captains's house:
  'Oh, captain, dear captain,
  return our son to us.'
  'Your son, and he must die
  in the far and broad field.'
  In the field, etc.
  before the enemy.
  In Strassburg, yes, in Strassburg,
  there must be soldiers.]

1791.
V.
(1)

"O, du lieber Augustin,
  Augustin, Augustin.
  O, du lieber August,
  was machen wir now?
  Das Haus ist verluffen;[sic]
  das Gelt is versuffen.
  O, du lieber August,
  was machen wir now?"

[Oh, dear Augustin,
  Augustin, Augustin.
  Oh, dear August,
  what shall we do now?
  The house is deserted
  the money has been drunk up.
  Oh, dear August,
  what shall we do now?]

(2)

"Wann ich gelt hab, bin ich lustig
  wann ich keins hab, bin ich durstig."

[When I have money, I am merry
  when I have none, I am thirsty.]

1792.
VI.

"Freund ich bin zufrieden,
  Geh es wie es will!
  Unter meinem Dache
  Leb ich froh und still.
  Mancher Thor hat alles,
  Was sein Herz begehrt.
  Doch bin ich zufrieden,
  Das ist auch Gold werth."

"Leuchten keine Kertzen
 Mir beim Abendmahl
 Blinken keine Weine
 Mir in dem Pokal.
 Hab ich was ich brauche,
 Mir in Zeit der Noth.
 Sueszer schmeckt im Schweitze [sic]
 Mir mein Stueckchen Brod."

[Friend, I am satisfied,
 No matter what happens!
 Beneath my roof
 I live in contentment.
 Many a fool has all
 That his heart desires.
 Yet I am satisfied,
 And that has the value of gold.]

[Even though no candles burn
 At my Holy Communion
 Or no wines shine
 In my chalice
 If I have what I need
 In time of necessity;
 All the sweeter will my bread
 Taste in my troubles.]

1793.
VII.

"Herz, mein Herz, warum so traurig?
 Und was soll das Ach und Weh?
 'S ist so schoen im fremden Lande!
 Herz, mein Herz, was fehlt dir mehr?
 Herz, mein Herz, was fehlt dir mehr?"

"Was mir fehlt? Es fehlt mir alles,
 Bin so ganz verlassen hier.
 Sey's auch schoen im fremden Lande,
 Dennoch wird's zur Heimath nie,
 Dennoch wird's zur Heimath nie."

[Heart, my heart, why so sad?
 And why this oh! and woe?
 It's lovely in a foreign land!
 Heart, my heart, what more do
 you need?, etc.]

[What do I need? I need all,
 I'm so desolate here.
 Even if it's lovely in the
 foreign land, it will never
 be my home.]

1794.
IX.[sic]

"Dat draus, dat draus,
 do kommt mohl einer rei.
 Ja lass en niwwer[?] komme;
 es wert woll meimer sei.
 Ja meiner, schuntst[sic] keiner!
 was geht mein Hertz so frish!
 Wie huebscher, wie feiner,
 wie liever dass 'r mir ist."

[Out there, out there,
 someone's coming in.
 Yes, let him come over;
 it's probably mine.
 Yes, he belongs to me alone!
 how my heart pounds!
 How handsome, how fine,
 how agreeable he is!]

"Zwisch Ostern und Pfingsten
 da ist die froehlichst Zeit
 Da paaren sich die Voegelein
 und alle jungen Leut'.
 Holzapfel suess,
 wie bitter ist die Koern
 Du schwartz-kofpiges Buebelein
 was haette ich dich so gern."

[Between Easter and Whitsuntide
 is the happiest time
 The birds form pairs
 and all the young folk.
 Crab apple sweet,
 how bitter are the seeds.
 You black-haired boy,
 how I'd like to have you.]

"Und wenn ich dich ja nehmen daeht
 do haettest du ja kein Haus.
 Da steck ich dich in den Hosensack
 Da gukst du oben daraus.
 Heute und Morgen
 so bin ich doch bei dir
 Aber wenn die naechste Woche kommt
 So reis ich weit von hier."

[And if indeed I took you,
 you'd have no house.
 I'll stick you in my pocket
 and you'll look out the top.
 Today and tomorrow
 I'll be with you indeed.
 But when next week comes,
 I'll travel far from here.]

1795.
X.

"Dort oben auf dem Berg
 Dort steht ein schnee-weisz Haus
 Dort schauen alle Morgen, alle Abend
 Drei schoenen jungen Mädchen heraus.
 Die erste heist Susannah;
 Die zweit die Lizabet;
 Die dritte die mag ich net nenne.
 Sie nimmt ihren Buben ins Bett."

[Up there on the mountain
 There stands a snow-white house.
 There every morning, every
 Evening 3 girls peer out.
 The first is called Susanna;
 The second is Elizabeth;

The third I don't want to name;
She takes her boys to bed.]

1796.
XI.

"Spinn lieve Dochter spinn
Ich kaufe dir ein Ring.
Nay, Mutter, ich kann net spinne

[Spin, dear daughter, spin.
I'll buy you a ring.
Nay, mother, I can't spin;

Es schwellt mir mein Finger
Und thut mir so weh."

My finger swells so
And is so painful.]

"Spinn, lieve Dochter spinn,
ich kaufe dir eine Kuh.
Nay, Mutter, ich kann net spinne
Es schwellt mir mein Finger
Und thut mir so weh."

[Spin, dear daughter, spin,
I'll buy you a cow.
Nay, mother, I can't spin;
etc.]

"Spinn, lieve Dochter, spinn;
ich kaufe dir ein Mann
Ja, Mutter, ich kann spinne
Es schwellt mir nicht mein Finger
Und thut mir net weh."

[Spin, dear daughter, spin,
I'll buy you a husband.
Yes, mother, I can spin;
My finger is no longer swollen
And is no longer painful.]

1797.
XII.

"Es huckt ein Bullfrog uf der Fens
Willy, willy, will kom boom.
Litorio, litorio
Willy, willy will kom heirum sol
Litorio, litorio
Willy, willy, will kom boom."

[There sits a bullfrog on the fence.
Willy, willy, etc.]

"Es hockt ein Bullfrog uff der Schteg etc.
Er schwert bei-gum er geht zu die Maid, etc."

[There sits a bullfrog on the stairs. etc.
He swears by gum he's already courting, etc.]

1798.
XIII.

"Ein alter Spann Ox und ein grumbuckliche Kuh
Das giebt mir mein Vater wenig [sic] Heirat do doo.
Fa de ra la la la, Fa de ra la la la
Spin Raetter, spin Raetter, spin Raeter, spin Rath."

[An old working ox and a humpbacked cow,
These I will be given by my father if I marry.
Fa de ra la la la, Fa de ra la la la.
Spinning wheels, spinning wheels,
spinning wheels, spinning wheel.]

1799.
XIV.

"Grasse gruene Grut im Haus
Grasse gruene Grut im Haus
Grasse gruene Grut im Haus
Geb ihr ein Kuech [sic] und jag sie naus"

[Grass green toad in the house, etc.
Give her a cake (?) and chase her out.]

1800.
XV.

"Es wollt drei Jaeger gehen jagen
Ein Stuendlein vor dem Tagen.
Wohl in das gruene Wald hinauf
Wohl in das gruene Wald."

[Three hunters wanted to go
ahunting an hour before daybreak.
Up into the forest green,
Into the forest so green.]

"Was wollten die Jaeger denn jagen
Ein Stuendlein vor dem Tagen?
Ein Hirschlein oder ein Roe, er e
Ein Hirschlein oder ein Roe."

[What were the hunters hunting,
an hour before dawn?
A deer or a roe, er e,
A deer or a roe.]

1801.
XVII.[sic]
1.

"Es war einmal drei Juden
Ju, Ju, den—den—den
Ju, Ju, den—den—den
Es war einmal drei Juden."

[Once there were three Jews
Jew, Jew, etc.]

2.

"Der erste, der heist Abram
A—a, A—a, bram, bram, bram
A—a, A—a, bram, bram, bram
Der erste, der heist Abram."

[The first is named Abram, etc.]

3.
"Der zweite, der heist Isaac."

[The second is named Isaac.]

4.
"Der dritte, der heist Jacob."

[The third is named Jacob.]

5.
"Nun sind sie alle gestorben."

[Now all have died.]

6.
"Jetzt sind sie in Jerusalem."

[Now all are in Jerusalem.]

1802.
XVIII.
"Reida, reida Geile
Alle Stund en Meili
Reida, rieda ivver der Grabe
Fallst du nei so musst du's havva
Blumps dort leisht du."

[Ride, ride, horsey,
Every hour a mile.
Ride, ride over the ditch;
If you fall in, you'll get it.
Bump! There you lie!]

"Reida, reida Geili
Alle Stund en Meili
Morje woll mer hovver dresha
Wull es Boovlie net vergessa
Blumps dot leisht du."

[Ride, ride, etc.
Tomorrow we want to thrash oats.
We don't want to forget baby boy,
Bump! There you lie!]

1803.
XIX.
1.
"Schlof Bave schlof
Der Dawdy huett die Schof.
Die Mammy huett die roda Kuh
Sie kummt net hame bis marje frueh
Schlof Bave schlof."

[Sleep, baby, sleep,
Daddy guards the sheep.
Momma guards the red cow;
She won't be home until early tomorrow morning.
Sleep, baby, sleep.]

2.
"Die Mammy schuttelst Baumelein
Es fallt herab ein Traumelein
Schlof Bave schlof."

[Momma shakes the little tree
A dream falls from the tree.
Sleep, baby, sleep.]

1804.
XX.
"Es regert, es schneet;
'sis kalt schtarmich Wetter.
Rei kommt en Bauer,
drinkt ein glaessli Cider.
Ich rech hovva;
wer soll es binna.
Hab amohl en schaetzel gehapt
und kann es nimme finna.

[It rains, it snows;
there's cold stormy weather.
In comes a farmer
and drinks a glass of cider.
I rake oats;
Who will bind it?
I once had a sweetheart
and can no longer find her.]

THE THOMAS R. BRENDLE COLLECTION OF PENNSYLVANIA GERMAN FOLKLORE

Volume I

Geographic Origins of the Lore
See the Appended Maps

Allentown
Anise, Montgomery County
Annville
Argus, near Tylersport
Avon
Babble Schpring, near the road from Cornwall to the Lebanon Pumping Station
Ballietsville
Bally
Bath
Berks County
Bernville, Berks County - Thomas R. Brendle served as a pastor here
Blecherschteddel = Blechersville, south of Myerstown
Blechersville = **Blechersteddel**
Boyertown
Brickerville
Buxloch
Carbon County
Catasauqua
Cementon
Cherryville, Northampton County
Coplay
Deep Creek
Dodder's Eck - located near Effort in Monroe County
Eagle Point
East Greenville
Easton
Efforts, above Kresgeville
Egypt
Falkner's Swamp
Feierschteeschteddel = Flintville, between Schaefferstown and Iona, Lebanon County
Finland
Fogelsville
Franconia, Montgomery County
Frederick (Keelor's Church)
Frederick Township, Montgomery County
Fredericksburg (Lebanon County)
Gehl Gaul = Yellow Horse, Berks County
Gettysburg

Gouglersville
Green Lane
Grewwelbarig, northeast of Schaefferstown
Groppeschteddel
Haahneschteddel = Hahnstown, Lancaster County
Hamburg
Hammergrick = Hammer Creek
Haschdaal, in South Mountain, west of Schaefferstown
Hinkelschteddel = Hinkeltown, Lancaster County
Indianfield Lutheran Church, near Telford
Indianland
Iona
Keelor's Church
Kleinfeltersville
Kresgeville
Lanark
Lancaster County
Laurys
Leather Cornerpost
Lebanon
Lebanon County
Leesport
Lehigh County
Lehigh Valley
Lehighton
Lititz
Long Run, near Weisport
Lowhill
Maryeland = Morgenland, Lehigh County
Mechanicsville
Mertztown
Middle Creek
Miller's Church, Laurys
Monroe County
Myerstown
Neffs (church)
Neffsville
New Goshenhoppen Church
Niantic
Northampton
Northumberland County
Obelisk
Old Goshenhoppen Church
Orefield
Ormrod - town near Egypt where Lehigh Portland Cement Company plants were located
Perkiomenville

Philadelphia
Promised Land, Pike County
Quakertown
Reading
Red Hill
Reistville
Robesonia
Rot Karich, near Orwigsburg
Ruchsville
Salfordville, Montgomery County
Sandbarig = Sand Hill in southern Lebanon County
Sassamensville
Schaefferstown
Scheidys, near Egypt
Schnitzgrick, the name of a creek
Schofbarig, southeast of Schaefferstown
Schtumpeschteddel = Fredicksburg, Lebanon County
Schwenksville
Saegloch, a hollow in the **Sandbarig**
Skippachville
Slatington
Snyder County
Society Barig = Sciota Barig, near Keelor's Church
Souderton
Spinnerstown
Strausstown
Sumneytown
Swamp Churches
Telford
Treichlers
Tulpehocken Lutheran Church, near Stouchsburg
Tulpehocken Reformed Church, east of Myerstown
Unami Creek, at Sumneytown
Unionville Cemetery
Vera Cruz
Walnut Springs, Lebanon County, west of Schaefferstown
Weisseecheland = White Oaks, Lancaster County
Weissenburg, Lehigh County
Wollewwerschteddel = Mt. Aetna, Lebanon County
Womelsdorf
Woxall

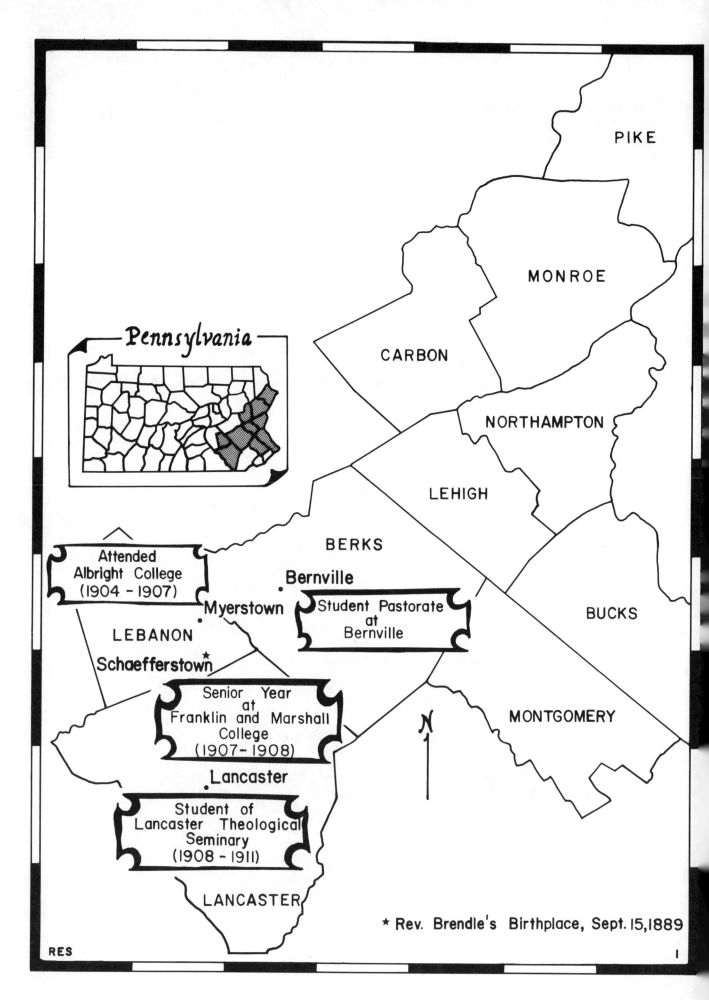

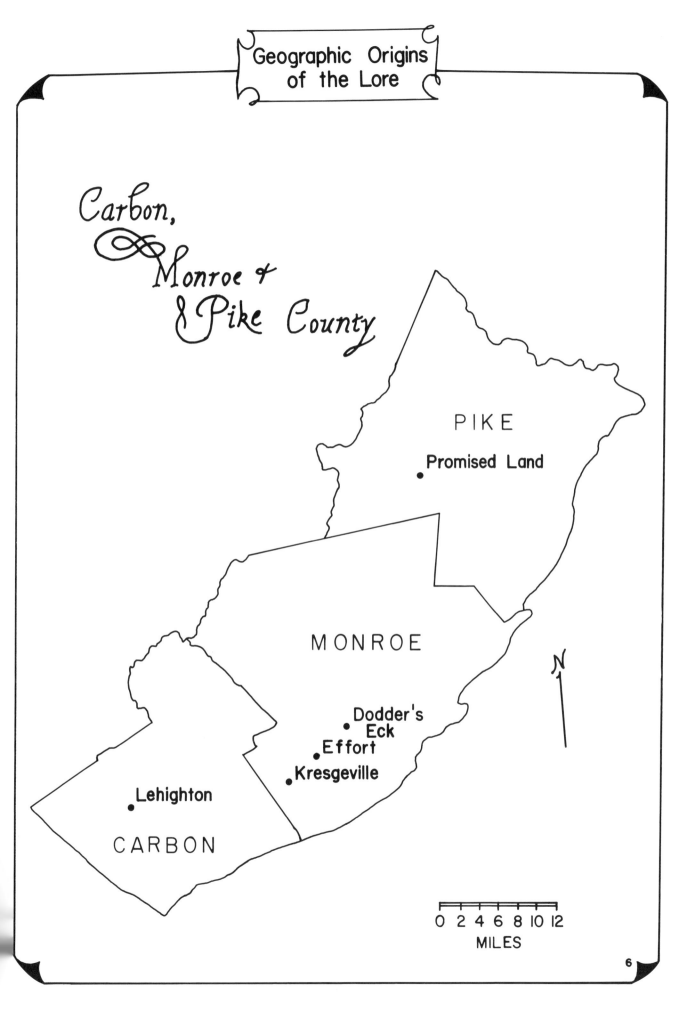

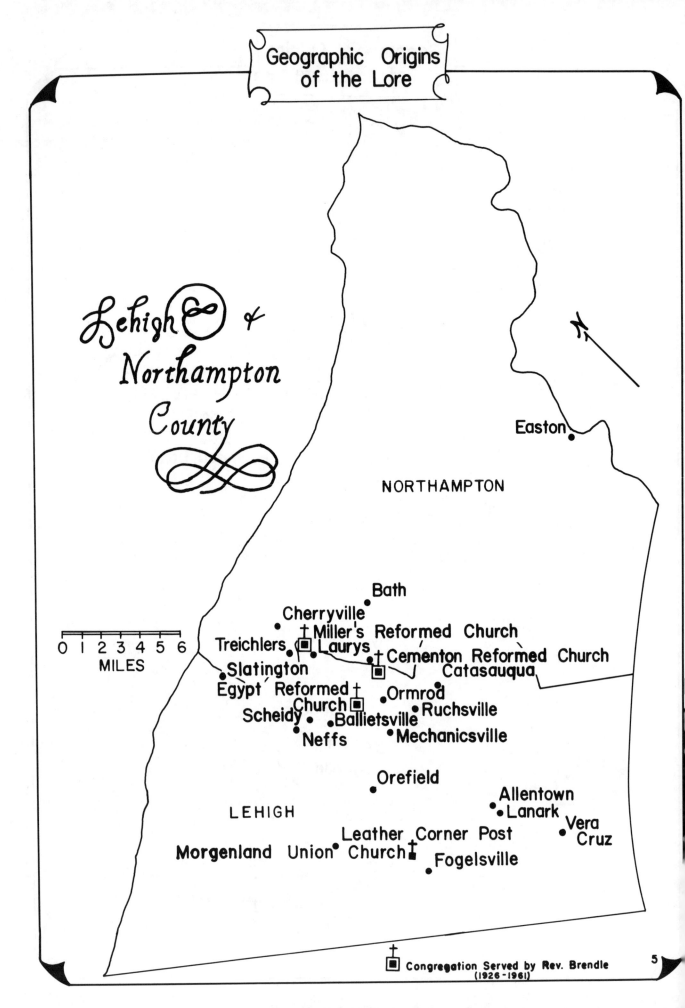

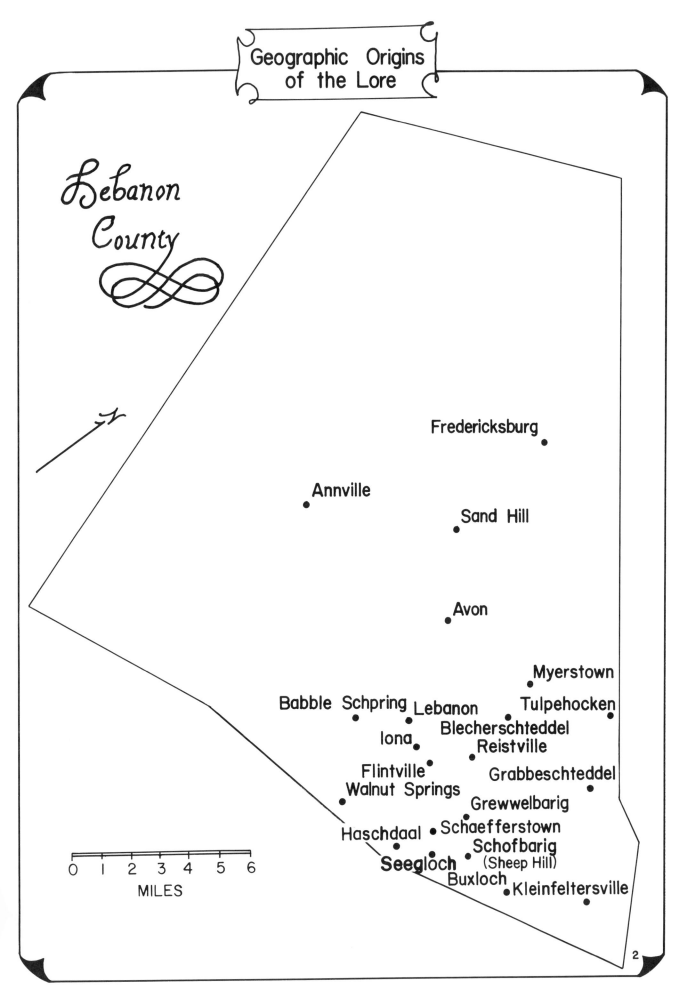

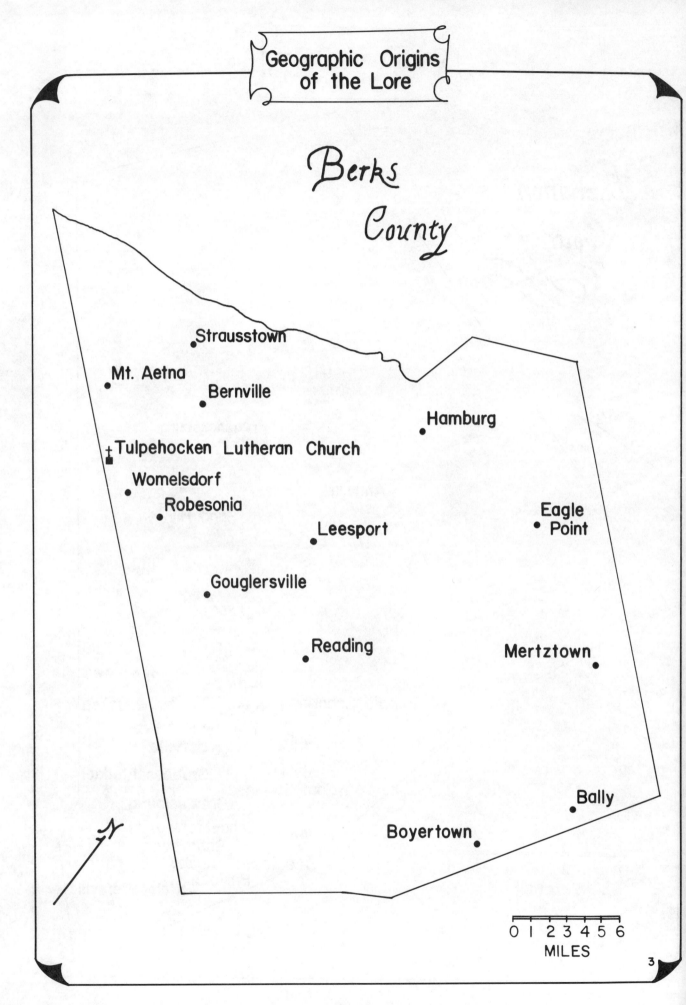

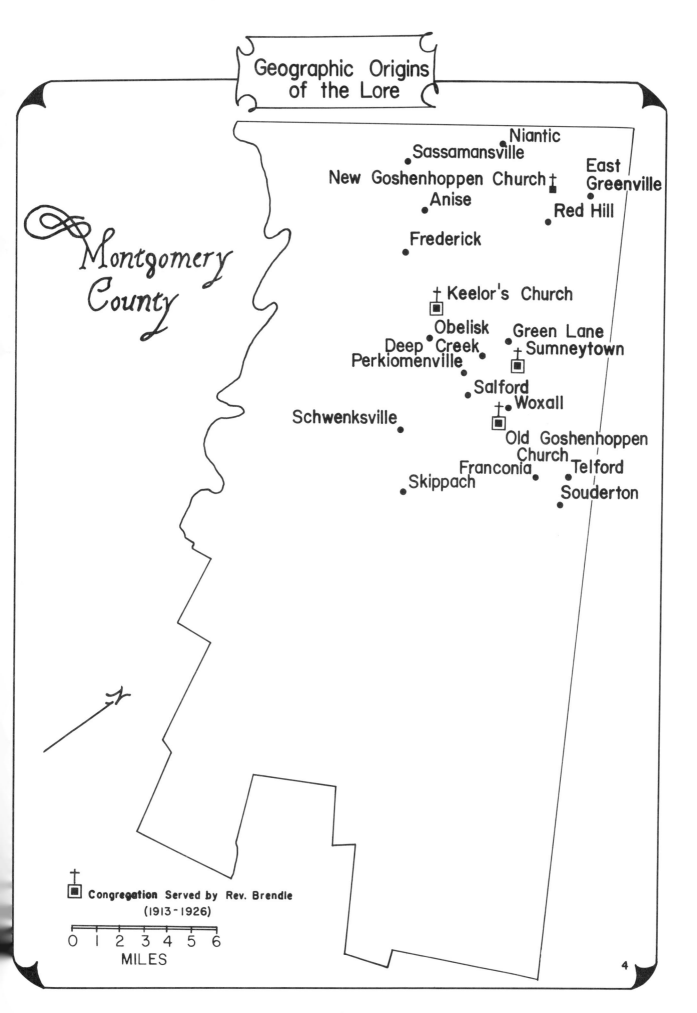

RENEE E. SPENCER, CARTOGRAPHER

Renee E. Spencer, born in Lancaster, PA on December 11, 1958, studied the Liberal Arts at Millersville University with majors in geography and psychology. Her main area of concentration was in cartography. She served as an undergraduate cartography laboratory assistant from September of 1986 to May of 1987. While an undergraduate, she completed cartographic work for the Lancaster County Department of Parks and Recreation. She was also employed by the Pennsylvania Power and Light Company. Miss Spencer graduated from Millersville University in December of 1987. She has served as a member of the Lancaster Forest Fire Crew. Her special interests are in farm preservation and aviation.

INDEX OF KEY PENNSYLVANIA GERMAN WORDS

The list below serves as an index to the numbered entries in which the word, name or concept is found. The number after each key word identifies the numbered entry.

A, B, C, 1788
Aa Beh Zeh, 89
Aage, die, 1050
aagebore, 582
aagewaxe, 37, 37.a
aahalde, 1004
Aahenger, 230
aamache, 1693
Aamet, der, 210
aarege, 821, 822
Aarm, 585
aarmer Dropp, 1785
aarmi Leit, 338
Aart, die, 517
Aawax, 866
Aazeeche, 897-912
Abendmahl, 904, 1792
abgebleecht, 446
abgekocht Seider, 1464
abgepumpt, 1015
abgwehne, 1063
Absatz, 445
abschtennich, 62
absolutt, 978
achde, 1190
Acht gewwe, 331
Adyee, 920
Aernappel, 479
Aerndefescht, 749
Aerndegemee, 910
Aernkarich, die, 749
Aff, 1012
Aftergscharre, pl, 216
Albrechtskarich, die, 723
alde Weiwerdenz, 1361
Alde, die, 19, 1117
Alder Mann, 156.a
aldi Kuh, en, 1466.b
Aldi Fraa, 156.a
alle Menschen, 1739
Allentaun Fair, die, 733
Aller Seel, 22.a.
Aller Heil, 22.a
Aller Seel un Heil, 22.a
Aller Heil un Seel Daag, 1555
alles, 1700-03
alli-epper, 1704

altfrenkisch, 439
altleinisch, 438
am Haus, 754
Amschel, 1677
Anfang, 341
Antwatt, 313
Appeditt, 607, 778
Appel, der, 51, 502
Aprille, 505
Aprillebliet, 1342
Aprillelaab, 1441
Aranchzwiwwel, 41
arrieyre, 1035
Aryelkarich, die, 667
Aschermittwoch, 1497
Auferschtehung, die, 1455
Augustin, O, du lieber, 1791
Ausgangs Moi, 952
ausgeschtreelde Haar, 1584
ausleine, 810
auslennisch, 1057
ausmischde, 794
ausringe, 812
ausschpodde, 741

Baas, 1462
babble, 492
Babble Schpring, 628, 629
Babier, 334
Backe, die, 1194
Backebuch, es, 308
Backerei, 1012.a
Backmoldgratz, 437
Baltimore, 1789
Balwiermesser, 449
Bandgraas, 40
banger Mensch, 127
Bank, die, 893, 1199
Barigkarich, die, 692, 693
Barigschtrooss, 616, 650
Barigschtroossschul, die, 724
Baschdert, 131
Bascht, 1199.r
Bassemhaut, 1669
Bassgeigen, 1752
Batsche, Batsche, Kichliche, 87
Bauch, 1081, 1698

123

Bauer, 1165
Bauer verhungere, 1621.a
Bauerei, 487, 1199.j
Bautz, der, 91, 1079
Bax, die, 1556.b
Becker, der, 1750
bedanke, sich, 27
Beddel, 461
Beddelmann, 1668
bede, 908
bedraage, sich, 1092
bees Feind, der, 230
beese Weibsleit, 130
beesi Zeide, 268
beglaage, sich, 20
begreeme, sich, 20
bei Lewe un Gsundheit, 398
bei Liewe, 399
bei Gott, 850.a.
Beidel, der, 1191, 1729
Bein, 894
Beint Schwamm, 659
beleidiche, 451
beleschdiche, 450, 451
beliege, 860
Bella, die, 1025
Bellebaam, 868
Bellekuh, 1574
Bellemanns Karich, die, 709
Belznickel, der, 573, 574, 575
Bense, die, 330
Berlin, 1743, 1756
Beschluss, 1035
Besemschtiel, 1024, 1122
besser mache, 571
Besuch, 1775
Betkapp, 906
Bett, 346
Bett mache, 110, 1175
Bettler, 335, 336
Bieblicher, 1542
biege, geboge, 1458, 1460
Bier, 1715
Bierebaem, 527
Biewel, 1168
Biggeleise, 36
Bigglerei, 1012.a
Bindel, 859
Bingel, 1755
Bisskatze, 1309
Bitschdaage, 1539
blaffe, 1775

Blankeweg, der, 653
Blaumeschtee, 1516
Blazier, 393
Blecherschteddel, 657
Bledder, die, 1465
blind, 1036
blindi Sau, en, 1457
Blohbarigkarich, die, 703
Blohbariyer, die, 1068
Blohhuschde, 932
Blohkarich, die, 701
Blug Karich, die, 708
Blug verrisse, 15.a
Bluger, der, 1691
Blummeschteck, 27
Blummezeeche, 1463
Blummi, 1720
Blut ziehe, 685
Blut schtille, 876, 943
Blut, das, 578
Blutschwamm, 435
Bock, der, 872
Bockdieb, 495
Bodde, 1025
Boddem, 1387, 1786
Boh [beau], 1254
Bohne, 1780
Boi, 1204
boose, 386, 828
Bordelmae, 1770
Bordfens, 53
Boss [kiss], 1425, 1696
Braeutigam, 1023
bralle, 918
Brand, der, 140
Braucher, 943, 1694
Breddich, 228, 1172
breddiche, 344
Breddicherschtand, 907
Breddicherschtul, 907
Breih, es, 1221
brenne, 318, 1666
Brennerei, 1199.j
Bresent, 1536.b.3
Bretzel, 1758
briggle, 1511
Brodfresser, 538
Brot, 1071
Brotschank, 1211
Brotwascht, 1172
Brunne, 1218
brunse, 1099

Bruscht, 1698
Bruschttee, 521
Buben, 1795
Buckel, der, 463
Buckelbautz, 1080
bucklich, 474
Bucklich Mennli, 1018
Budderbrot, 592
Buh, 729, 1191
Buhn, 235
Buhnedaag, der, 1469
Bullfragge, 1310
Bullfrog, 1797
Busch, der, 1025, 1169
Butzerei, 1012.a
Buwe, die, 296.a, 1027
Buwli, 1779.a
Buxloch, es, 636

Cent, 815, 818, 819
Chor, 754
Chrischtmonet, 1289

Daadi, der, 1025
Daag, 249
Daage, die, zunemme, 1411
Daage-un-Nacht Rege, 748
Daagshelling, die, 433
Dach, 1185
Dachfenschdre, 683
Dachlaade, 683
Dachs, der, 1337
Dachsdaag, 1420-1
Dachwerk, 452
daheem, 487
Damm, der, 328
Danke!, 915, 918, 1028
Dannpeik, 611
darbediene, 560
darich die Nacht, 1392
darre Wald, 1408
Darrenascht, 651
datt driwwe, 1573
datt draus, 1794
Dau, 1150, 1324
daue, 1306
dauere, 1506
Dausend Daaler, 1176
Dausich, 461
Dauwe, 271
deckere, 432
deitsch Waahret, 69, 69.a

Deitschland, 870
Deiwel, 33, 461, 463, 464
Deiwelsdreck, 160, 940
Deiwelslocherschtross, 617
Deiwelsschtreech, 561
denke, 325, 326
Dettlaus Daag, 1442
Diefgricker Schul, die, 726
Diereli, 1013
Dinschdaag, 1012.a
Dirn', 1759
Disch, 808, 1553
Dochder, 1199.b
dod mache, 761
Dod im Schpiegel, 153
Dod, der, 237, 238, 239, 241, 243
Dodder's Eck, 1025
Dode, 240, 242
Dodeheisel, 482
Dodeschtreech, 430
Dodewaage, der, 761
Dodsdaag, 483
donnere, 1408, 1777
Dor, es, 626
dort oben, 1795
draage, 1513
Drach, der, 52
Drammboddel, 19
Drammhole, 1490
Drauerhaus, 752
draus, 1258
Drawatz, 431
Drawutz, 431
Drechder, 939
Dreck, 790, 1188
dreckich Wesch, die, 1776
Dreckloch Schul, die, 727
Dreckschnee, 1451
Dreher, die, 763, 766
drei, 1190
drei Juden, 1801
Dreibuschelsack, 1641.b
dreischteckich, 929
Dreppe, 220.a
drepsle, 1325
Dricklerei, 1671
dridde, sich, 28
drieb unnergeh, 1368
Driebsaal, 1183
drink ich, 1686
drinke, gedrunke, 1740
dripple, 874

Drittmann, 1256
Drohtfens, 53
Dron, 1741
drucke Wedder, 1325
Druckeland Karich, 716
druckner Matz, en, 1341
drunne, 1251, 1253
Druwwel, 92, 93, 94, 95, 96, 156, 977
Dude, der, 1208
dufdich, 1114
dumm, 229
dummschde Mann, 1174
Dunker, 721
Dunkle, 999
dunnere, 1384
Dunnerschdaag, 1012.a
Dunnerwedder, 464, 469
Dunschloch, 1112
durstig, 1791(2)
Duwack, 815
Duwackkeefer, 403

Eck, 1217
Eckkarich, die, 702
Eckschank uff em Kopp, 35.a,b
Edelmann, 1668
Eechel, 254, 1457
Eechhaas, der, 830.C
Eechhaase, die, 1350
Eechhaasehund, 831.C
Eeg, 1199.k
Eegner, 350
eens, 1190
Eens, zwee, drei, 146, 858, 873, 1010
Eeyelob, 1045
ehner, 351
Ehr, 121, 214, 1741
Ehrenbreis, 862
Eia Popeia, 1744
Eiergelb, 1765
Eileschpiegel, 200
einander, 921
Eis, 321
Eisbarye, die, 1610
Eisbax, 909
Eise, 322
Eise im Feier, 107
Eishaus im Kalenner, 1366
Eisi [im Feier], 98, 98.a
Eldeschder Schtiel, 803
Elend, 429
elfe, 1190

elft Gebot, es, 211.a,b
End, 1012
enge Schuh, 1209
Engel, die, 267, 1071, 1787
Engle, 581
Eppel, 517, 1357
Eppelkanne, 1518
eppes Neies, 1173
er = ihr, 593
Erfaahring, 342
Ermaahning, 807
Ermunter euch, 1023
ernaehre, sich, 1264
erschde Disch, 10.a
erscht Schnee, der, 1351
erscht Aprill, der, 1448
Erzliegner, 441
Erzschisser, 442
Erzschwindler, 440
es regert, es schneet, 1804
Eschepuddeldaag, 1427
Esel, 33, 303, 1007-9
Esse, 1166
Esse, es, abgewehne, 1660
Essich, 198, 212, 1613
Ewich Yaeger, 56, 57
Ewichkeit, 854
Ewwer, der, 1782

Faahne, 775, 1272
faahre, 315, 316, 1020
Faasnachtkuche, 45, 1498
Faasnachtkuchefett, 45
Falckner Schwamm, 623
Falschgeld, 211
Famillye, die, 681
Famillyeumschtende, in, 156
Famillyeweg, im, 156
Farb, 392
farichderlich, 425, 426
Fashions, die, 327
Fass [voll], 100
Fass, 1232
Fatz, 770.b, 1219
Fauscht, 319
fechde, 105, 106, 1330
Fechteck, 534
Fedderdeck, 1081
feddere, 1664
Fehler, 295
feichder Moi, 1470
Feier, es, brummt, 1332

Feier, ins, gucke, 1697
Feier, ins, 17
Feier nemme, 596
Feierdaag, 529
feierich rot, 1323
Feierschteeschteddel, 644
Feil, 1199.q
Feischt, die, 476
Feldkatz = wildi Katz, 77
Feldschtee, 797
Fens, die, 1371
Fenschdre, 1067
Fense-eck, 55
Fenseschtreeme, 54, 55.a
fer Alders, 6.A, C
fer Lenger, 6.B
Ferd, 471.b
Fiddelbogen, 1752
Fiess, 314, 586
fimfe, 1190
Finger, der, 531
Fingerneggel, die, 1670
Fingerziehe, 1119
Fisch, der, 497, 776, 1083
Fittmann, 1256
Fix, 296, 297
Fleddermaus, 1050
Fleesch, 1033, 1260
Fleisch, 894
Flickerei, 1012.a, 1671
fliege un greische, 1380
Flint, die, 371, 595
Floh, 1742
fluche, 250
Fluggelnescht, 827
folye, 172
Fraa, en aldi, 1692
Fraa, 1181
Frack, der, 1027
Freidaag, 1012.a
Freiheit, 908
freilich, 423
Freind, die, 754, 758
Freindschaft, 758, 761
Fresch, die, 1437, 1536.b.4
Freschli, es, 1303.
Freschlocher Schul, die, 728
fresse, 263
Freund, 1792
Friede, der, 370, 570, 810
frisch geronne, 1072
froge, 304

frogeswert, 510, 511
Froscht, 1423
frosich, 422
fruchtbaar, 1512
Fruchtbaem, 1513
Fruchtbaem blanze, 1490
Fuder, 1537
furichbaar, 427, 428
Fuusszuwwer, 905
Fux, 204, 206

gaar ewich, 469
Gaarde, 253
Gaardebauer, 417
Gaardemauer, 53.a
Gaardezelaat, 280
Gadember, 1491
Gademberdaag, 1476
Gademberwoch, 1277
Gamber, 940
Gansdaag, 1116
garewe, 1115.a
Garwli, 896
Gass, die, 615, 1743
Gaul, 301, 302
Gebetbuch, 301
Gebethaupt, 906
Gebrauch, der, 1025
Geddel, 1690
Gedrickdes, 1669
Gegleed, 585
Gehaer, 420
gehe Mariye, 1321
gehe Owed, 1313
Gehle Wattshaus, 656
Gehlehaus, 656
Gehlgaul, 656
Geilche, 1020
Geilschtee = Gehlschtee, 39
Geilskeefer, 403
Geilsmicke, 973
Gelannder, 269, 270
Geld, 236, 298, 299, 300, 1082, 1791(2)
Geldsack, 1020, 1641.b
Gelegeheit, 908
Gens, die, 740, 1378
Gensedaag, 1107-8
Gensegnoche Mann, 1083
Gensgraut, 176
Gesang, 1736
geschder, 223

gesegne, 1709
Gesellche, 739
Gesundheit, 274, 1235
gewennt Hoi, 1367
Gewidderrutschtange, 215
gezoge, 371
Gickerigie, 870
Gickerl, 1744
gifdich, 1403
Gillerie, der, 1331
Ginni, 877
Gippel, 1115.a
Gippelwerk, 453
Giwwel, die, 1507
glaawe, 1139
Glabbordfens, 53
glatt Eis, es, 1357
Glee Schtrooss, die, 614
Glee, der, 1311
Gleeblaat, 13
Gleesume, 164
Gleiches, 925
Gleiesack, 1641.b
Glick, 1480, 609, 931
glitzere, 1381
Glockezieher, 415
Glofderholz, 1034
Gluck, 249.a, 672
Gnarr, 603
Gnecht, 571
Gnoche, die, 1033
Gnoddle, 790
Gott erbarmlich, 414
Gott im Himmel, 404.a
Gott, 465, 467, 577, 580, 1722, 1725, 1733
Gottes Hilf, 416
Gottes Naame, 461
Gottes Gesetz, 893
Gotts Dunner, 421
Graab, 485, 486
Graabadzi, 1011
Graabhof, 413
Graabschtee, 484
Graabshrift, 484
Graas, es, 1336
Graasich Leen, die, 618
Graassume, 164
Graawe, der, 1779.a
Graf, 1759
grank, 1238
Grankesbett, 26.A
Grapp, en aldi, 1570

Grappe, die, 504, 1286, 1380
Grappe fliege, 1400
Grappe greische, 1608
Grappeschteddel, 640
gratze, 463
Graut blanze, 1443
Graut, es, 730
Grautkopp, 202
Graewelpeik, 612
Grebs, der, 497, 1083, 1089
Grenk, die, 461
greppe, 530
Grewwelbarig, 631
griddlich, 1395
Griedunnerschdaag, 1454
Grienebaam, 652
Grippe, 866
Grischtdaag, 1345, 1577
Grischtdaagnacht, 1558
grischtlich, 225
Grixlicher, 1591
Groddeschtiel, 1628
Gross Schwamm, 622
Gross Schtrooss, die, 613
Grott, 1799
Grott schlucke, 1536.b
Grug, 1312
grummbehnich, 493
Grummbiere, 1561
Grummbierekeller, 352
Grummbiereschaale, 1599
Grummbierschtick, 306
grummbucklich, 1798
grummle, 1115.a
grumm un graad, 1222, 1483-4
Grund, 457, 458
grundaarm, 412
Grundachsedaag, 1419
Grundeechkekarich, die, 666
Grundeechle, 666
Grundkeller = Kiehlkeller, 133, 352
Grundsaudaag, 1376, 1421
Gruppeland, 645
Gruscht, 547, 1220
Gschiss un Wese, 411
gschosse, 1239
Gschweere, 1533
Gschwetz, 486
Gsicht, 86
gsuffe, 1389
Gsuffne, die, 602, 603
Gude [Ding], 102, 103

Gude Mariye!, 915
Guden Taach!, 916
Gudenowed!, 919
guder Aafang, 1505
Gut, 1787
Gut Blut!, 885
Gwidde, die, 951
Gwiddekanne, 1601
Gwidderrut, 215
Gwidderschtang, 215
Gwidderschtarm, 419
Gwidderschtee, der, 1291
Gwittre, 418, 419

Haahne, 548, 776, 1050, 1285
Haahne graehe, 1375, 1592
Haahnekamm, 38, 345
Haahneschteddel, 641
haarich Raawe, die, 1386
Haas, 75, 76
Haas, en alder, 73, 74
Haase, die, 71, 72, 296, 297
Hack, die, 344
hadder Winder, en, 1350
hadder Dod, 8, 1694
Hadyee, 920
Haffe, 1718
halde, 1773
hallich = uffgelebt, 137
Hals, 1698
halsbrechendi Arwett, 1620
Halskett, 448
halwer gewonne, 1072, 1074
Hammel verkaafe, 1554
Hammergaarn, 639
Hammergrick, die, 632, 639
Hannschaal, 546, 1588
Hannzaah, Hannzaeh, 933, 935
hariche, 171
Harr [Herr], 468, 853, 867
Harre Daage, 952
Harschel, 1006
Haschdaal, 624
Haschschtall, 625
hatt Wedder, 1622
hattgekochde Oier, 1545
Hatz, 202, 203
Hatzholz, 203
Hatzschparr, 866, 867
Hauptbreddich, die, 757
Hauptmann, 1790
Hauptschtamm, 1514

Haus, 205
Hauseck, 1284
Hausheldern, 309, 310, 519
Hausrot, 1298
Haut, die, 821
Hawwer, der, 911
Hawwer dresche, 1779, 1802
Hawwer reche, 1804
Hawweraern, 21
Hawwergees, 513
Hawwerschtroh, 262
hawweswert, 510
Heckefens, 53
Heckekaader, 77
Heedelbaryer, die, 1452
Heedelbaryer Karich, die, 711
heem geh, 232
heem kumme, 774
heeschde Daage, die, 1346
Heffel, 251
Heffner, 1707.3, 1708, 1717, 1719, 1726
Heh, in die, faahre, 1474
Heidelbaryer Karich, die, 710
heiere misse, 571
Heiland, 852
heile, 18, 684, 1071
heilige Kuss, der, 905
Heimat, 855, 1793
heit, 223
hell uffgeh, 1369
Hell, die, 17, 461, 463
Hell, in die, nei, 1681
Hellfeier, 17
Helling, die, 1067
Hemm, 1199.p
hendich, 582
henke, 1195
Herbscht, 1283
hernemme, 1044
Herr Jesu, 3
Herschel, 1365
Herz, 579, 1793
Hesse, die, 1058
Hex, die, 1076
hexe, 596
Hexe, die, 1190
Hexerei, 658
Hexeschteddel, 658
hiehalde, 554
hielenglich, 409
Hiesicht, 79
Himmel, 533, 1071, 1711, 1712

129

Himmelfaahrdaag, 1290
Himmelferdaag, 1472-4, 1527.a, 1528, 1541
Himmelreich!, 772, 823, 1731
Himmelswelt, 461, 823
Hinkel, 196, 1050, 1288, 1371, 1586-7
Hinkelbiebs, 345
Hinkeli, 870
Hinkeloier, 1598
Hinkelschtall, 348.a
Hinkelschteddel, 642
hinlenglich, 409
Hinnerdeeler zunaehe, 1541
Hinnergscharr, 216
hinnerschich auskehre, 1583
hinnerschich lese, 1695
Hinnerschitz Karich, die 717
hinnich, 356, 498, 1693
Hirschlein, 1800
Hitz, 410
Hitzwedderleeche, 1158
Hiwwelli up, 90
Hochzeit, die, 1023
Hochzich, 1602
Hochzichdaag, 1549
hocke, 1779.c
Hockelbiere-kanne, 1518
Hof, 1355
hohl, 815
Hoi, 210, 347, 1201
Hoischpritzer, 994
Hoischtock, 295
Hoisume, 408
Hokemann, 1485
Hollerbierebledder, 1578
Hollerschtock, 872
Holz, es, 1025
Holzapfel, 1794
Holzarwet, die, 1298
Holzax, 443
Holzfaare, 42
Horning, der, 1340
Hos', 1943
Hosensack, 1794
Hosse, die, 586, 892, 1199.m
Hossescheisser, 1668
hui, 277
Hummlernescht aushewe, 1135
Hund, 16, 25, 729, 1078
Hund sei Schwanz, 122, 123, 124
hungrich, 1621.b
Hunnich, der, 1064
Hunsdaage, die, 1538-9

Hunskett, 448
Huppe, 939
Hur, 335
hure, 125, 959
Hurer, 126
Hut, 1208
Hutzel, Hutzle, 524, 527
Huwerskarich, die, 669

Iedrich, der, 1585
Ieme, die, 1064
ihr = er, 593
im Feld, 1247
im Hof, 1246
im Schtier, 1362
imfindlich, 676
in der Bux fatze, 770.b
in Druwwel sei, 571
Inschingland Karich, die, 714
Inschinglenner Karich, die, 713
Inschingpeil, 777
iwwer acht Daag, 920
iwwerdemm, 920
iwwerich, 1706
iwwerschlucke, 406
iwwerzwarg, 1057

Jacket, der, 499, 813
Jaeger, 1800
Jammerthaal, 853
Jesu, 851
Jesus Christus, 578

kaaft, 1061
Kaanaa-aan, 857
Kahn, der, 1743
Kaiser, 1668
Kalb, 892, 1199.s
Kalmusskolwe, 1635, 1645
Kammer, die, 220.a, 1184, 1203
Kann, die, 1279
Kann [rye], 1449
Kannadaa [Schaefferstown], 35
Kanne, 1518
Kanzel, die, 1677
Karber, 141
Karbet macht Arwet, 1226
Karbetlumpefarbblumme, 177
Karfreidaag, 44, 528, 1343, 1540
Karich, die, 722, 957, 1067
Karicheroot, 541
Karichhofmauer, 53,a

Karwel, 1214.b
Karwersbarig, der, 663
Kaschebaam, 1560
Kascheschtee, 1517
katz un gut, 1177
katz un dick, 324, 1197
Katz, die, 1003, 1050, 1377, 1390
Katze, 16, 210, 609
Kautsch, die, 949, 1025
Keefer, 403
Keenich, 1668
Keller, 1140
Kelleresel, 1008
Kellerschtee schwitze, 134
ken Eis uff die Baem, 1534
Keschdebarig, der, 619
Keschdebaryer Karich, die, 712
Kesselgaarde, 1058
Kett, 448
Kichedrippel, 765
Kieh, 546
Kieh blarre, 1399
Kiehdreck, 255
Kiehfutz, 1230
Kiehkeller, 352
Kiehkett, 448
Kiehschwanz, 771
Kiehweg, 610
Kimmerlings Karich, die, 719
Kinder, 1788
Kinner, die, 497, 1083
Kinnergrankheede, 1439
Kinnerlehr, die, 528
kipperich, 1364
kleine Kinder, 1749
Kluppe, 402
Kolwe, die, 1349
Kopp, der, 314, 436
Kot, 880, 1188
Krickli, 1370
Kuddelfleckbarig, 665
Kuh, Kieh, 1022, 1025, 1040
Kuh kaafe, 1552
Kummet, 37.a
Kunschtschtick, 967

Laab, es, 1348, 1396
Laad, 1670
Laade, 1091
Laadeholz, 1670
laafe, 315, 492
laafender Brunne, en, 1370

Laagerbier, 1482
laahm, 981, 1012, 1036
lache, 474, 475, 476, 477, 478
Ladann, die, 892
lammediere, 1732
Landgschpiel, 1118-37
Landrege, 996, 1006
Lange Karich, die, 705
langsam un deitlich, 1178
langsam, 31.b
langsamer Bauer, 1438
Langschwamm, 621
Langschwammer Karich, die, 698
lanne, 265, 266
Lanning, 272
Laubfrosch, 1304
Laus im Graut, 114.a
Lebdaag, 460, 573
Lebensgrone, 1780
Lebenszeit, 1734
lecke, 463, 551
Leddereckposchde, 648
leddich, 1234
Leder, 1762
Leeb, der, 497, 1071, 1083
lege, sich, 1186
Leibschticker, 1046
leicht, 582
Leicht aabelle, 59
Leicht, 80, 761, 764
Leichtbreddich, die, 757
leiden, 856
Leinbach, Rev. Tom, 1109
Leinbachskarich, die, 704
Leinfens, 53
Leis, 339, 533
lengschde Daag, 226
Lenz, der, 400, 1619.a
letscht, der, 264
letscht Freidaag, der, 1358
letscht, der, im Bett, 1661-2
letscht lache, 29, 30, 115
lewe, 1019
Lewe, es, nemme, 374
lewendich Dod, 549
Lewesdaag, 434
Leweslauf, 754
Licht, es, 999, 1066, 1067
Lichtmess, 1337, 1416, 1042, 1502
Lieb, die, 255
Lieg, 118, 120
Liewesgruss, 922

Liewesmaal, 904, 905
Lieyebaschdel, 397
Limmel, 1569
Litorio!, 1797
Loch, Lecher, 1014
locke, 1287
Logessbeem, die, 1461
Loss es gut sei!, 920
lowe, 601, 1429
Luft, die, 996
Lufthutsche, die, 1374
Luftloch, 1110
lummerich, 498
Lump, Lumpe, 592, 1257
Lungeauszehring, 1094
luschdich, 1109
lustig, 1791(2)
Luttrisch, 536

Maad, 589, 1010, 1267
Maagedruwwel, 166
Maddeleene, 1501
Maddeleene Brieh, 1500
Maddlenbrieh, 1500
Maed, die, 296.a, 1027, 1036
Maedcher, 874
Maedel, 519, 873, 1140, 1196
Maehmaschien verisse, 15.a
Maikaefer, flieg!, 1746
Mammi, Mammi, Budderbrot, 1565
Mammi, 592, 859, 1199.a
Mann, 587
Mannem, 886
Mannheim, 886
marickwaddich, 1025
Marie, die, 1171, 1579
Marieye, die, 1344
Mariye-esse, 927
Mark, 894
Maryeland, 647
Maryerot, 880, 1188, 1593-4
Maryeschtund, 1257
masch, 526
Matheus brecht Eis, 1338
Matteis, 1536.a
Matteis macht Eis, 1431
Matzebliet, 1342
Matzeschtaab, 1441
Maul, 1036, 1698
Maul, es, henke, 1783
Maulwarfgraut, 1767
Maus, 1742

mause, 21, 22, 1391
Mausfall, 390
Meerreddich, 174
Mehl, 911, 1140
Mehlsack, 1641.b
mei Hand schteh (mache), 544, 545
Meili, 1802
meiner Seel, 459
meiner Sex, 456
Meisel, 1605
Mennli, 1018, 1566
Mensch, 1710, 1721, 1730
Menschehaut, 1082
Menschen, 1713
Menschen Hilfe, 1723
Mess, 396
Mick, 1742
Mickebabier, 787
Mickedier, 788
Mickegaarn, 789
Mickegift, 786
Mickegscharr, 789
Mickewehrer, 785
Midaag esse, 926, 927
Middelfens, 740
Middernacht, 1109
Mieh, die, 924
Miehl, 888
Minspei, 1038.a
mischde, 793
Mischt, 791, 891
Mischt schpraehe, 792
Mischtblanke, 792
Mischtbrieh, 792
Mischtgawwel, 792
Mischthaufe, der, 548, 793, 1308
Mischthof, 54, 792
Mischtpen, 792
Mischtschlidde, 792
Mischtschpraeher, 792
Mischtwagge, 792
mit der Karich, 753
mit Fridde, 239
Mittwoch, 1012.a
Moi, der erscht, 1612
Moi, 505, 952
Moibliet, 1342
Moivoggel, 913
Molassich, 1614
Mond, der, 1327, 1355
Moos, es, 1307
Morgen, 507

Morgenschtund, 506
morye, 1778
Mose, 998
Mudder, 198, 212
Mund, der, 472, 1675
Mundaag, 1012.a
mundaags, 1019
Muschgaatnuss, 262
Muss, 260, 261, 1182
Mut, 1520, 1523
Mutter, die, 1790
Muunschei, 514

Naame, 197
Naas, 259, 1179, 1698
Naas (Ohre) schpitze, 170
Nachtesse, 927
Nachtmol, es, 808
Naddschtann, die, 224
Narre, die, 602, 1448
naryets, 554
naus misse, 1105
neechtlich, 1285
Neeyerwissli, 628
negschtlich, 1367, 1370
Nei Yaahr, 1486, 1488, 1511
Neilicht, 1320, 1327, 1362
Nein Uhr Schtick, 927
neine, 1190
Neiyaahr, 1115.a
nemmeswert, 511
Neschder mache, 1372
Nescht, 348, 1115.a, 1512
Newesonn, 1356
Newwel im Yenner, 1335
newwelich, 1114
Nicodiemus Daag, 1108
Niss, 1350
nitzlich, 508
niwwer un riwwer, 407
nix, 258
noch emol, 471.a
Noochsummer, 21
nootsche, 687
nootschich, 687
Not, 256, 257, 1334
nuffgraddle, 463
numme, 1013

Offe, der, 1011, 1461
Ohre nunnerhenke, 1397
Ohrering, 1615

Oier, 207
Oier setze, 1543
Oierschlingel, 395
Orsch, der, 436, 463, 551
Oschderoier, die, 1453, 1456
Oschdre, 1345
Owedesse, 927
Owedrot, 1321, 1595-6
oweds, 581
Ox, Oxe, 1065, 1083, 1798
Oxekopp, 650

Paad, 1269
Paff, 1010
Paradeis, 533
parbes, 394
Parre Leinbach, 528
Parre, 908, 928, 1021, 1185, 1192
Paschingschtee, 1515
Paschingschtee schlucke, 1642
Pederli, 1559
Peil, der, 776, 777
Peils, die, 1563
Peitschenstiel, 1760
Pfingsten, 1794
Pieces, 966
Pilger, 857
pisse, 1098
pitsche, patsche, 1750
Pommerland, 1746
Poschdefens, 53
Posthalter, der, 1763
Potly, 193
Pracht, 1023
precies, 811
Prieschder, 1148
Priwwi, es, 1106
Psalder, 769
Pschie!, 552
pschimfe, 1190
Pump!, 1015
Pupp, 1102
puppe, 1102

Quack!, 1753
Quatember, 1359

Raad, 1202, 1267
Raddefall, 391
Rathaus, 1750
Raudebusch, 389
rausyaage, 1022

Rauwe, die, 1580
Rauwevoggel, 1302
Raziermesser, 449
recht, 495, 496
Redder, 914
Reef rolle, 849
Reetzel, 585-588
Reetzelche, 196-212
Reformiert, 537
Rege, 231, 733-738, 980-982, 991, 996, 1150, 1465
Regeboge, der, 1609
Regebrunne, 388
regere, 1383
regere vor 7 Uhr, 1360
regerisch, 1363
Regevoggel, 884, 965, 1292
Regewedder, 814
Regewerm, 1297
reide, 1007-9, 1013
reide, reide, Geile!, 1779.a,b, 1802
Reife, 1322
Reiter, 1751
Rewwer, 1590.a
rieche, 1200
Riewe, 166, 589
Riewesume, 165
Riggelfens, 54
Riggelhaufe, 54
Rind, 1199.n
Rindvieh, es, 1330
Ring mit Schtanne, 1354
Ring, 808, 812, 1013, 1301, 1353, 1385, 1796
ringe, 1753, 1758
Ringe, ringe, Rosen, 1764
ringle, 812
Rippe, 866, 867
Rippegraas = Bandgraas, 40
rischde, 764
Rischtloch, 1112-3
Rocksack, 1641,b
rode Kolwe, 1696
Rolldier, 387
rolle, 1240
rollich Moi, der, 1471
Ros, die, 255, 1425
Rose, 1735
Roseschteck, 27
Rosserl, 1760
Rot Brick, die, 632
Ruh, die, 83.a, 337
Ruherei, 1671
rumdrehe, 316

rumhocke, 1115.a
Rummadis, 980
rund im Grund, 1225
runzlich, 1086
rutsche, 1487

Saddelsack, 1641.b
Saegloch, es, 634
saehe, 245
Saenger am Graab, der, 754
Safran, 1750
Saft, 520.a
Salz uff der Feier, 1600
Salzsack, 1641.b
Samschdaag, 1012.a
Samschdaage, 1557
Sandbarig, 634, 637
sanderbaare Breddich, 1505
Sandloch, es, 635
Sandschtee, 797
Sarye, 883
Sau, 254, 310.a, 1039, 1684
Sauerambel, 516
Sauergraut, 747, 1409
Sauergraut un Schpeck, 1193
saufe, 329, 888, 1019, 1187
Saufen un Drinken, 1738
Schaale, 1456
Schaawe, 1674
Schadde, 199, 1337
schaele, 519
Schaetzel, 1804
schaffe, 1495, 1546, 1548
Schaffe, 1166-7
Schank, 1199.o, 1274
Schanschde, 1316
scharefe, 1682
Scharlatti, 874
Schatz, 1761
scheckiche Ende, 1473
scheckiche Hinkel, 1544
scheel, 1092
Scheener Daag!, 916
Scheffer, 1245
scheffiche Wolke, 82
Scheier, 1199.t, 1598
Scheissdreck, 1103
scheisse, 1103
Scheissmelde, 178
Schelmenlieder, 1047
schepp, 474, 475
Schibb, 1199.u

schiesse, 317
Schimmel, der, 533, 891, 1760, 1763
Schissel, der, 207
Schitz, der, 497, 1083, 1085
Schitze Karich, die, 707
Schkarpian, der, 1083
schlachde, 1063.A, 1422
Schlack, Ausschlack, 132
Schlack, 436
Schlaf, Kindlein, schlaf, 1758
schlagge, 436, 768
Schlang, 1305.a
schlechder Aafang, 1504
schlecht, 230
Schlof, 1271
Schlof, Bave, schlof, 1803
Schlof, Kindlein, schlof, 1745
schlofe, 1551
schloosse, 1556.a, 1619.b
schlucke, 74
schmaert, 385
Schmalzgass, die, 615
Schmatze, 462, 981
Schmidt, 1233
schmiere, 1278
Schmok, der, 201, 1316
Schmokkarich, die, 700
Schneck, 1241
Schneckehann, 773
Schnee, 991, 1142
Schneegens, die, 1163-4, 1388
Schneideise, 447
Schneider, der, 1754
Schneidmesser, 447
Schnitz, 252
Schnitz Grick, die, 638
Schnupftabak, 1753
Schnuppduch, 208
Schnutz, 525
Schof, 81, 82, 136, 157, 546
Schofbarig, der, 630
Schofrippetee, 182
Schoss, 856
Schpaltax, 444
Schpaltgscharr, 384
Schparkerei, 1012.a
Schpeck, 1217, 1467,, 1780
Schpeckzappe, 938
Schpeise, 577
Schpelder, 1769
Schpiese Karich, die, 718
Schpiggel verbreche, 1606-7

Schpiggel, der, zuhenke, 1616
Schpinn, die, 1379, 1590.b, 1742
schpinne, 1199, 1416
Schpitzeweddrich, 183
Schpottnaame, 660
Schprichwatt, 503
Schpuck, 381
schpucke, 382
Schpuckerei, 380
schpuckich, 383
Schreiner, 1761
Schtaabkiddel, 401
Schtaakefens, 1021
Schtaerm, 1333
schtaermich, 1330
Schtall, der, schliesse, 1667
Schtamm, 1508
Schtammgascht, 379
Schtammglied, 378
Schtandsbreddich, die, 757, 907
Schtang, die, 348, 1198, 1199.f
Schtann, en, falle, 1562
Schtarm, der, 419, 1161
schtarwe, 1623
Schtechmicke, 973
Schtee Barig, 1785
Schteebock, der, 497, 1083, 1087
Schteefens, 53, 53.a, 1092
Schteeg, die, 201, 892, 1776
Schteemauer, 53.a
Schteene Karich, 706
Schteetweg, der, 654
schtehle, 1436
schtelle, 455
schtelle die Schtanne, 1385
schtichdunkel, 1052
schtichle, 248
Schtiel, 1199.l
Schtier, der, 497
Schtirn, die, 1698
Schtocknodel, 1685
Schtoy, 1401
Schtraahle, 995
Schtreit, 9, 10
Schtroh, 347, 546
Schtroh draage, 1372
Schtrohseele, 1513
Schtrooselieder, 869
Schtrubbkatz ziehe, 1121
Schtul mache, 108, 109
Schtumpeschteddel, 643
Schuh, die, 958

Schuh, der, drickt, 156
Schuld, 1165
Schulhaus, 728
Schunke, 938
Schuster, 1762
Schustermeister, 1762
Schwaerl, 830.C
Schwalme, die, 1394
Schwalmelecher, 1043
Schwalmeloch, 1111
Schwamm, der, 623
Schwammer Kariche, die, 623
Schwammgrick, die, 664
Schwammgrickerschul, die, 725
Schwanz, 1078
Schwatze, die, 1547
Schwed', der, 1747
Schweezeland [Switzerland], 128
Schwefelhelzche, 1066
schwefle, 1064
schweige, 31, 377
Schwein, 894
Schweinche, 877
Schweitzer Kaes, 1482
Schwell, die, 1581
Schwemm, die, 1296
Schweschder, 546
Schwett, die, 376
schwetze, 325, 326, 1170
schwewe, 1315
Schwoger, 546
Schwowe, die, 1067, 1568
Sciota Barig, 665
seddle, 485
seeche, 1100
seelich, 500
Seeschaal, 773
Seeweiwel, 1478
Seiche, 1479
Seidel, 1760
Seider, 1215
Seidschteches, 1575
Seikopp, 469
Seil, 1199.q
Seiohrebledder, 175, 192
Seipenn, 968
Seischtall, 1068
seiyisch, 1684
selwer eppes duh, 70, 104
Semmel, 1760
sexe, 1190
Sexeckich Karich, die, 670

Siessgraut, 12
silwerich, 1318
Sinai, 1754
siwwe, 1190
siwwe Schtock, 473
Siwwe, der, 1382
Soldaat, 1668
sommere, 1424
Spinn, spinn, 1796
Stein, 894
Strassburg, 1790
Stuttgart, 1763, 1765
Summer, der, 599, 600
Summerflecke, die, 454, 1612
Sunn, die, 995, 1521, 1524, 1597, 1675, 1678
Sunndaag, 529, 1012.a, 1039-40, 1546
Sunndaags, 1022, 1041
Sunneblicker, 994
Sunnuff, 1186
Sunnunner, 1186
Sunnunnergang, 1582
Supperdisch, 1398

Tee roppe, 1579
Thuer, 1023
tintelliere, 1101
Tom Brendle, 735
Trostred, die, 754
Trump!, 850.a
Tschabb, en, schaffe, 1104
Tscheck, der glee, 1281

Ufer, 1136
uff Gott sich verlosse, 112.B
uff der Haffe, 1106
uff Mensche sich verlosse, 112
uff em Rick, 1327
uff Hoffning lewe, 1519, 1522
uffhelle, 1363, 1382
uffmundere, 1141
uffschtelle, 1109
uffwerme, 1409
Uhr, die, 205
Uhr, die, schtoppe, 1616
umbringe, sich, 373
ummechdich warre, 949
unerwaard, 372
Unflot, 236
unfruchtbaar, 1512
ungewehnlich, 1299
Ungeziffer, 1442
Unglicksdaag, 950, 1475

Ungraut, 1347
unheemlich, 218
unnerei, 1373
unnerewwerschich, 1071
unnergehnde Mund, 1464
Unnergleeder, die, 1531-2
Unnergleeder wexle, 1489
Unnerrock, 1199.h
Unnerschitt, der, 1021
Unnerschrief, 353
unnich em Wedder, 162
Unrecht, 550
Unreinichkeit, 914
Unruh, 1734

Vaader, Vadder, 320, 891, 1024
Vaddel, 820
Vanne hui, 97
Veddergscharr, 216
verbannt, 596, 597
verdamm sei, 471.a
verdiene, 246, 247
Verdruss, 1224
verhacke, 499
verkaaft, 1061
verleed, 1282
Vermaahning, die, 757
vernootscht, 687
verpissde Windel, 1611
verrecke, 1705
verrickt, 1737
verrissen, 1191
Versammling, die, 722
Versammlinghaus, 720
verschmisse (verschisse), 589
verschniert, 211.b
verschosse, 1199.m
verschpreche, 116, 117
Verschtand, 273, 274, 1716
verschtanne, 424
Victoria, 1789
Vieh, es, nausdraage, 1530
viel schwetze, 113, 114
Vier Uhr Schtick, 927
Vierde, 998
viere, 1190
Vogel, der, 1698
Vogelsnescht, 1698
voll Licht, 976, 1550
von Marye, 1373
Vorbereiding, die, 543
Vorschteher, 1109

Vorsinger, der, 754
vun Nadde, 1326

Waahret, die, 603
Waarde, 1705
Wadde, 233
Wagge, 1020
Waggeschmier, 1498
Wald, der, 1743, 1800
Walnissbrunne, 627
wann, 563
Waremfens = Schtaakefens, 53
Warfschaufel, 312
Warmet, der, 1347
Warrem, die, 1387
Waschweiber, 1748
Wasser, es, 1081
Wasser losse, 1097
Wasser ziehe, 1319
Wassergruck, 975
Wassermann, der, 497, 1083, 1086
Watt, 1509
waxe, 875, 955
Wedder, 419, 1004, 1049, 1143-7
Wedderfaahne, 775
Wedderglaawe, 1333
wedderleeche, 410
Wedderschprich, 1333
Wedderzeeche, 1356
Weezesack, 1641.b
Weg, aus em, schaffe, 375
Wei, 1010
Weib, 1727
Weibsleit, die, 1393
Weibsmensch, 197
weide Schuh, 1209
Weihnacht, 573
Wein, 1760
Weis, die, 1000-1002
Weisehaus, es, 736
Weiserkarich, die, 668
Weisheit, 1716
weisse Duppe, 1670
Weisseecheland, 646
Weissgraut, 12
Welf, 101
Welfe, die, 1190
Welschkann blanze, 1477
Welschkannbascht, es, 1349
Welt, aus der, geh, 1562
Welt, die, 234, 854, 1430
Werkelholz, 1567

wermich, 72
Wesch ausdrehe, 812
Wescherei, 1012.a, 1019, 1671
Weschesel, 591
Weschgaul, 591
Weschlein, 1379
Weschlumpedaag, 1428
Weschringer, 812
wessrich, 1086
Westerwaelder, 1748
Widder, der, 1263
Widderbock, der, 497, 1083
Wie geht's?, 323, 323.a
Wiegel, 1761
wiescht Wedder, 1395
wilde Gens, die, 1352
Wildvieh, 1051
will, 358, 369
willkumm, 219
Wind, der, 997, 1048, 1161
Winder, der, 599, 600
windich, 1329
Windmiehl, 546
Windschtarm, 1162
Windwerwel, 1317
Winkel, 1755
winnisch, 357
winsche, 508
wisse, 1665, 1781
Wisse, 1140
Wittmann, 1256
Woch, die, 1024, 1506
Wohlwinscher, 244
Woi, Woi, 1685
Wolke, die, 1678
Wolkebruch, 355
Woll, 584
Wollewwerschteddel, 649
Woog, die, 497, 1083, 1084
Wuh-hie, 35

Yaahr, es, aafange, 1404

Yacht, 1300
Yaeger, 1013
Yagowi, der, 734
Yammer, 404, 462, 1184, 1203
Yenner, 1336
Yenner, in, gebore, 1413
Yesus, 579, 866
Yesuwidders, 405
Yuchend, die, 275, 276
Yuddebiewel, 168
Yulla, 1019, 1671
Yungebarig, der, 662
Yungfraa, die, 497, 1083, 1088

Zaah, 1036
zammegebrochde Kinner, 213
Zeeche, die, 497, 1322-33
Zeh, 490, 491
zehe, 1190
Zeit, die, biede, 917
Ziegelskarich, die, 699
zimmlich, 918
zoppe, 1179
zu Owed esse, 926
zu Nacht esse, 926
zu Mariye esse, 926
zu die Maed geh, 571
zu Grund geh, 1237
zu Gnaade kumme, 680
Zuck, Zick, 354
zufridde, 1305.b
zurickgeh, zurickgange, 1027
zurickschalle, 1689
Zweck, 1701
zwedde Disch, 10.a
zwedde, sich, 28
zwee, 1190
Zweebuschelsack, 1641.b
zwelfe, 1190
zwinge, 1210
zwitzere, 874
Zwiwwleschnee, 1450

THE THOMAS R. BRENDLE COLLECTION OF PENNSYLVANIA GERMAN FOLKLORE

Volume I

Index of Key Concepts by Page Number

Aa Beh Zeh, 8
Adamstown, Lanc. Co., 52
Addressing the preacher, 48 (#802)
Afterbirth, 6
Air, 82
Alexander Schaeffer Farm, Schaefferstown, Lebanon Co., 47
Algae, 81
Allentown, 85
Allentown Fair, 42
All Saints, All Souls, 93
Angel, 17
Apples, 30-1
April 1 lore, 19, 88
Army of the Potomac, 28
Arrowhead (Indian), 47
Ascension Day, 80, 89, 92, 92-3
Ash Wednesday, 87, 90
Asking, 19
Badness, 16
Bag, 9
Barn, 84
Barn (air holes), 69
Barn decorations, 13, 86
Barns (dormer windows), 40
Barn signs, 57, 65, 66
Barrel, 8
Bath, Northampton Co., 84
Bats, 99
Batsche, Batsche, Kichliche, 8
Battle of Gettysburg, 28
Bean Day (May 3), 89
Beautiful Words, 16
Bed, 9, 22
Bedtime prayer, 1
Bedtime prayer (parody), 1
Bees, 51
Beginning, 91

Beheaded fowl, 2
Belznickel, 34
Bent tree, 88
Berks County, 66
Besemschtiel (game), 70
Bewitched gun, 36
Bible (family memoranda), 40
Billy Lyon (PG song), 54
Birth of first child, 28
Blind sow, 17, 88
Blood (purify), 18
Blue Mountain folks, 66
Body of a drowned person, 36
Boss, 88, 96
Bucklich Mennli (song), 63
Bullfrogs, 81
"Bully," 90
Burial, 11
Burial Service, 48 (#800)
Burn, 10
Butchering, 87
Butter and Eggs, 107
By-O-Baby (lullaby), 12
Calamus ears, 98
Calf, 93
Candlemas, 65, 86
Cat, 80, 82, 84, 85
Catasauqua, Northampton Co., 50
Cat, dog, 35
Catechetical class, 32
Caterpillars, 61, 85, 94
Cats, 7
Cats, dogs, 2
Cats (leave house), 36
Cattle, 82
Cementon, Lehigh Co., 43, 53, 57
Cemetery, 7
Chair, 9

139

Cherry stones, 97, 98
Cherry tree, 93
Chewing gum, 97
Chicken pox, 12
Chickens, 22, 80, 84, 85, 95
Childbirth, 6
Children, 85, 97
Children's games, 42-3
Children's rhymes, 104-7
Child's tooth, 96
Chimney, 80
Chimney swifts, 99
Christmas, 83
Christmas, New Year, 90
Christmas night, 93
Christmas tree, 88
Church council, 32
Church harvest festival, 56
Cider, 88
Clouds, 7, 84
Clover, 81
Common cold, 13, 18-19, 53
Common sense, 18
Communion Service, 6
Complaining, 3
Consumptives, 68
Cook, 97
Cooling board, 56
Coplay, Lehigh Co., 90
Corn, 39, 83
Corn (on foot), 89
Corpse, 6, 7, 7-8, 11, 32, 46, 56, 66
Counting out rhymes (PG), 54
Couplet (PG), 17, 20, 21, 28, 29, 30, 32, 35, 54, 65, 73-4, 76, 86, 107, 108
Courtship, 62, 64
Cow, 85
Cricket, 80, 85, 96, 96
Crows, 80, 85, 86, 96
Cud, 95
Dandelion, 55
Datt driwwe, datt drowwe (PG song), 53
Datt drunne in dem Wissegraas, 71
Day and night rain, 43
Day of death, 28
Death, 3, 5, 10-11, 16, 17 (#260, 261), 73

Deep Run, 53
Dettlaus Day (Mar. 31), 88
Devil, 4
Dew, 81
Diaper, 96
Diarrhea, 19
Dietz's Mill, 19
Dirt, 95
Divided front door, 47
Dog, 4, 9, 10, 80
Dog Days, 92
Double Sun (**Newesunn**), 83
Doughnuts, 90
Do waar ich emoll in Deitschland (PG song), 53
Drach (mythical creature), 5
Dragon flies, 98
Dreaming, 3
Drought, 42 (#738)
Duck eggs, 89
Ducks, 22
Earache, 53, 58
Earning, 16
Earring, 96
Earthworms, 80
Easter, 83
Easter eggs, 88 (#1453, 1456)
Easton, 107
Eating, 72
Eating brains, 100
Eating chicken, 59
Edelmann, Beddelmann, 99
Education, 18
Eels, 64
Eens, zwee, drei, 11, 53, 62
Eggs, 98
Egypt, Lehigh Co., 28, 43, 44, 45, 48, 66, 67, 69, 90. 91
Egypt Church, 46, 49
Eileschpiegel, 14
Elderberry flour (tea), 18
Elderberry leaves, 94
Eleventh Commandment, 14
Ember Day, 83, 89, 90
Ember Week, 79
Es war einmal drei Juden, 111-2

Evil woman, 101
Excessive demands, 3
Excrementa, 47-48, 98
Excuses, 21
Expletives (PG), 27, 46, 50
Expressing thanks, 3
Expressions for worthlessness, 50
Ewich Yaeger, 6
Falling knife, 54
Falling star, 94, 97
Family Bible, 39
Farmer, 72, 73, 97, 98
Farmer in the Dell (game), 11
February, 82, 86
Felon, 12
Fences, 5, 6
Fever, 13
Fighting, 9
Fire, 10
Fire in stove, 82
First day of the week, 86
First evening star, 2
Fish, 33
Fishing, 51
Flowers blooming out of season, 58
Flowing spring, 83
Fog, 87
Fog in January, 82
Follow the Leader (game), 11
Fools, drunks, 36
Forgetfulness, 20 (#314)
Fornication, 10
Four-leafed clover, 2, 88
Fox and Geese (game), 11
Freckles, 96
Frederick, Mont. Co., 46
Fredericksburg, 80
Frederick Township, Mont. Co., 107, 108
Fresh cow, 88
Friday, 93
Frost, 82
Fruit tree fails to bear, 69-70
Full moon, 60
Funeral, 7, 73
Games of the countryside, 70
Geese, 82, 83, 84, 85

Ghostly riders, 4, 5
Gleaning, 56
God, 9
Good Friday, 5, 31, 83, 92, 93
Good turn, 17
Goose Day, 69, 70
Grace before a meal, 56
Grass, 82
Grave, 28 (#485-6)
Green Lane, Mont. Co., 42, 48, 51
"Greens," 13, 14
Greetings, 57
Ground, 80
Groundhog, 82
Groundhog Day (Feb. 2), 82, 84, 86
Guinea hens, 22
Gun, 36, 39
Hail, 96
Hair, 95
Hair in stomach, 12
Harness, 15
Harre Daage, 59
Harvest Home Service, 43
Harvesting (grain), 56
Hatzschparr, 53
Hawk, hawk (game), 100
Herschel, 62, 84
Hide and Seek (game), 11, 63
Hill Church, 65
Hiwwelli up, Hiwwelli down, 8
Hommel, Rudolf, 104
Horror, 15
Hopscotch (game), 11
Horsehair, 98
Horseradish, 100
Horses, 2
Housekeeper, 20
Howling (dog), 15
Hunting, 33
Hydrophobia, 86
Ice, 59
"Icehouse," 84
Ich schteh uff die Kanzel, 99
Indian, 5
Infant walking, talking, 29
Injustice, 33

Innocent man hanged, 59
Invitation to eat, 1, 4
Irons in the fire, 8, 20
Ivy poisoning, 53
Jack be nimble (game), 70 (#1126, 1133)
"Jewish Bible," 12
June 9, 101
June 21, 107
June 22, 107
Keelor's Church, 45, 46, 49, 65
Kick the Wicket (game), 11
Kidneys (clean), 18
Killdeer, 82
Lanark, 73
Lancaster, 66
Laughing, 9, 15
Laughter, 3, 28 (#474-8)
Lamb, 5
Laxative, 18
Lazy horse, mule, 19
Learning, 17, 73
Leaves, 83, 85, 88
Lichtmess (Feb. 2), 90-1, 92
Lie (untruth), 9
Lining out hymns, 49 (#810)
Lititz, 50
Lititz Moravian Church, 50
Little children, puppies, 72
Liver, 18
Liver-grown, 4
Loaf of bread, 66
Local names (PG), 36-7
Local rhyme (PG), 42
Log houses, 47
London Bridge (game), 94
Longest day, 107 (#1772-4)
Long Town (game), 63
Loons, 84
Lord's Prayer, 55
Love, 17
Love Feast (Dunkard), 56
Making a wish, 98
Making the bed, 73
Man, 9
Manure, 92
Manure pile, 81

Maple sap, 51-2
Maple seedpods, 30
Mary goes over the mountain, 72, 83
Maundy Thursday, 88
May 1, 89, 96
May 15, 88
Measles, 12
Measure, 8
Miller's Church = Laurys, 43, 90
Mirror, 2, 11, 59, 66, 96
Mistakes, 19
Moon, 81, 82
Mose Dissinger, 4, 52
Mother-hen, 16-7
Moulding magic bullets, 5
Mt. Airy, Lanc. Co., 90
Muddy Creek, Lanc. Co., 67
Mules, 85
Mulberry Bush (game), 21
Multiple weddings, 59
Mushrooms, 80
Myerstown, Lebanon Co., 88
Names of churches (PG), 40-1
Names of schoolhouses (PG), 41-2
Need, 17
Needle, 15-6
Neffsville, Lanc. Co., 56
Nerves, 18
New moon, 84
New moon, full moon, 93
New Year, 90, 91, 92
Nipsi (game), 11
Noise, 81
Northampton, 62
Nose, 81
Nuts, apples, 83
Obeying, 13
O, du lieber Augustin, 109
Old cemeteries, 48
Old Goshenhoppen, 44, 48
Old Goshenhoppen Church, 43, 49
Old women's dances, 84
Omens of death, 56
One, two, button my shoe (game), 22
Onion snow, 88
Ormrod, Lehigh Co., 69

O Strassburg, 109
Our Father (parody), 55
Paper, 21
Parody on "Nearer, My God, to Thee."
Parsley, 93, 107
Partridge, 7
Passing two persons (in conversation), 13
"Peach hutzels," 31
Peach stone, 98
Peeling apples, 31
Perkiomenville, Mont. Co., 46
Phoebe Home, 43
Pig in the Parlor (game), 29-30
Pigs, 84
Piles, 94
Pin, 15-6
Pitcher (water), 81
Place names (PG), 37-9
Planting, 5, 15, 67, 68
Planting cabbage, 88
Plover, 80
Pointing (at someone), 97
Polecats, 81
Police (game), 77
Postponed wedding, 59
Potato peelings, 96
Potatoes, 93
Powwower, 100
Powwowing, 54
Prayerbook, 19
Prayers, 52-53
Prayers (at table), 1, 34
Prayers (bedtime), 1, 34-5
Preacher story, 68, 69
Pregnancy, 6
Preparatory Service, 32
Profanity, 17
Promises, 9
Quail, 80
Quince, 59
Quince seeds, 96
Rabbit, 2, 7
Ragweed, 83
Rainbow, 96
Rattlesnake, 36
Reading backward, 100

Recitations for Christmas, 34
Red glow in the morning, 81, 95
Red glow in the evening, 95
Reide, reide, Geili, 107, 108, 112
Resurrection, 88
Rheumatism, 18, 60, 99
Rhymed expressions, 73-79
Riddles, 14, 15, 29, 35, 42, 54, 55, 61, 62, 63, 67, 89, 90, 100
Ring around the sun, moon, 81, 83, 85
Robins, 59
Roof, 73
Rooster, 80, 84, 85, 95
Rounds, 65
Ruchsville, Lehigh Co., 65
Rusty gun, 40
Sadiron, 4
Salt (in fire), 96
Saturday, 93
Sauerkraut, 86
Schaefferstown, Lebanon Co., 28, 42, 45, 47, 48, 50, 66
Schaefferstown Reformed Church, 49
Scharlatti (Charlotte), 54
Schlof, Bawe, schlof, 112
Schpinn, schpinn mei liewe Dochda 74-76
Schtoy, healer, 86
Schtreech (tricks), 33
Seating in church, 49
Second Christmas, 34
Sermon, 73
Setting eggs, 93
Sharing washing, drinking water, 2
Sheep, 12
Shooting (cat), 39, 66
Shooting matches, 90
Short sermon, 72
Sickbed, 3
Side stitches, 94
Signs for lovely or dry weather, 82
Signs for windy weather, 82
Signs of derision, 33
Signs of the Zodiac, 29, 67
Silence, 3-4
Singing, 3, 15
Skipping stones (game), 52

Slowness, 4
Small game, 33
Small pox, 58
Smoke, 81
Snake, 81
Sneezing, 64
Songs of tavern and street, 65
Sore eyes, 12, 18, 59
Sores, 4
Sore throat, 13, 18, 59
Sowing, 3, 12
Sowing - harvesting, 16
Spacing of front teeth, 59
Spider, 85
Spilled salt, 55
Spinn, liewi Dochder, spinn, 111
Spittle, 97
Splinter, 12
Sprains, 13
Spring, 88
Spring peepers, 81, 97, 92
Squeaking shoes, 33
Squirrel calls, 51
Stahl pottery, 101-4
Stars, 85
Staunching the flow of blood, 10
St. Bartholomew's Day (Aug. 24), 107
St. Matthew's Day, 87, 92
Stomach, 18
Stomach cramps, 13
Stone wall, 5
Stop blood, 58
Stove, 88
St. Patrick's Day, 87
Straussdown, Berks Co., 65
Stumbling, 15
Stupidity, 16
Suabians, 66
Sumac poisoning, 13
Summer freckles, 26
Sumneytown, Mont. Co. 19, 42, 44, 45, 47, 48, 51
Sumneytown Church, 49
Sun, 81, 82, 84
Sunday, 15, 93
Sunday illness, 58

Sun, moon, 99
Sunrise, 99
Sunset, 95
Swallows, 59, 66, 81, 85, 99
Sweet fern (tea), 4
Sweeny, 55
Switzerland, 10
Tablecloth, 87
Table prayer, 1
Taking away luck, 58
Taking leave, 57
Talking, 9
Teething, 28 (#489-91), 58, 59
Thrift, 21
Thunder in winter, 94
"Thunder-stone," 80
Thunderstorm, rainstorm, 60
Toad, 92
Toadstools, 97
Tolling, 6, 12, 25 (#430)
Tombstone, 32 (#532, 540)
Tonic, 13
Toothache, 12
Tree toad, 81
Trouble, 8, 12
Turnips, 12
Twins, 6
Underclothes, 90, 92
Und wenn wir kommen zu Baltimore, 109
Unfruitful tree, 88, 91, 92
Union Army, 46
Unionville, 45, 48
Unlucky day, 59, 89
Urinating, 68
Vera Cruz, 73
Vinegar, 96, 100
Voiding the bowels, 68, 69
Waiting, 101
Warts, 4-5, 53
Washing dishes, 66
Washing hair, 58
Washrag Day, 87
Wasp sting, 13
Weather, 3, 6, 10, 12, 30, 36, 42, 54, 60, 61, 71, 72, 80-5, 88, 92
Weather vanes, 46-7

Wedding day, 93 (#1548, 1549)
Wednesday, 95
Wednesday birth, 58
Wednesday illness, 58
Whirlwinds, 81
Whistling, 2, 3, 15
Whitehalls, Lehigh Co., 88
White spots on fingernails, 99
Whooping cough, 58, 100
Wie gefallt dir dei Gesellche? (game), 42
Wife, 73
Wind, 73, 84
Wolves, 8
Womelsdorf orphanage, 42
Woodwork, 80
Woolen thread, 100
Working, 72
Worms, 85
Worthlessness, 16
Yarrow (tea), 13
Youth, 18
Yulla (song), 99
Zu Ulla (song), 62
Zu Yula (song), 63

THE THOMAS R. BRENDLE COLLECTION
OF PENNSYLVANIA GERMAN FOLKLORE

Volume I

Informants

All locations are in Pennsylvania unless otherwise indicated.
P.B. = Pumpernickle Bill, William S. Troxell

Acker, John R. - Allentown.

Algard, John.

Andrews, ---, - Laurys.

Anthony, ---, - Strausstown.

Aston, Frank - Green Lane - Nov. 9, 1870 - July 20, 1844. He was a farmer and attended Rev. Brendle's church.

Bachman, Rev. A. J. - Brendle's Reformed pastor in Schaefferstown.

Barndt, Mrs. Harvey - Sumneytown - Aug. 28, 1843 - Sept. 28, 1921 - member of Rev. Brendle's church.

Beidleman, Frank - Sumneytown.

Bernville, Berks County - Thomas R. Brendle served as a student pastor here.

Billig, ---, - Egypt, PA

Bittner, Amandus - Weissenberg, Lehigh County.

Bobscht, Mrs. ---, - Northampton.

Bolig, Ed - Sumneytown - 1882-1967 - a member of Rev. Brendle's Church and a merchant at the Sumneytown Store (known as Rahn and Bolig Store).

Bomberger, Henry H. - Lititz.

Brendle, A.S. - Rev. Brendle's uncle; a lawyer. He is the author of *A Brief History of Schaefferstown*, reprinted by Historic Schaefferstown in 1979.

Brendle, D. D. - Rev. Brendle's grandfather.

Brendel, John B. - Reinholds, Lancaster County. He was distantly related to Rev. Brendle. John Brendel was a founding director of Historic Schaefferstown. Between 1967 and February, 1971, the time of his death, John Brendel passed along to his radio listeners much of the folklore he had learned from his grandmother and others.

Brendle, Mrs. Thomas R. (Anna S.), 1886-1968 - Myerstown, her native town.

Brendle, Thomas R. - memories of childhood days at Schaefferstown.

Brendle, **Mrs. D. D.** - Rev. Brendle's grandmother.

Brendle, Thomas S. - Rev. Brendle's father, Schaefferstown.

Brown, Henry H. - Lititz.

Brown, Henry - Laurys.

Brown, Mrs. Henry - Laurys.

Brown, William - Klingerstown.

Buck's School - near Green Lane.

Danner, Mrs. Emily - Laurys.

Dasheimer, Mrs. Rosa - Effort, above Kresgeville.

Dechant, Rev. - Keelor's Church, Frederick, Mont. Co.

Diehl, Marcus, 1891-1951 - Egypt. Electrician.

Dietz's Mill.

Esterley, Charles - lived between Vera Cruz and Lanark. Via P.B.

Faust, Samuel - Obelisk, Mont. Co.

Fehnel, Elmer.

Fenstermaker, Mrs. Joe - Drumhole, Egypt; farmer's wife.

Fetter, Rev. F. C. - Lutheran pastor at Old Goshenhoppen church, Woxall, PA.

Frantz, Irwin J., 1896-1954. A dairy farmer who lived at Scheidys. He was a member of the original **Raad** of Groundhog Lodge Number 1, Lehigh County.

Frantz, Mrs. Tilghman - Mrs. Frantz' mother.

Gable, Jacob - Old Goshenhoppen Church; hotelkeeper.

Garloff, Annie - near Myerstown.

Gerhart, Zacharias - Green Lane, Mont. Co.

Gibble, Willis - Lititz; a Dunkard.

Grace Reformed Church - Northampton.

Groh, Calvin - Schaefferstown.

Gross ---, - Snyder County.

Gruver, Mrs. Orville - Cementon, Lehigh Co..

Hassler, A.E.

Hatzell, ---.

Heister, Adam - Strausstown.

Held, Rev. Cyrus E. - Sumneytown - served Friedens Union Church Sumneytown and Keelor's, from Nov. 1, 1933 to Nov. 1, 1960 when he resigned due to ill health and impaired eyesight. He died June 21, 1940. He was the pastor of the Lutheran congregations during Rev. Brendle's pastorate.

Helfrich, Rev. William -- Bath.

Hertz, Dr. - Lititz.

Hetrick, Dawson - Schaefferstown. Thomas R. Brendle's schoolmate.

Hiltebeitel, Jonas - Green Lane.

Hoffman, Charles - Egypt.

Hoffman, Thomas F., 1905-1985 - Egypt. Storekeeper. Deacon and elder in Rev. Brendle's church in Egypt.

Hommel, Mrs. Rudolf.

Hommel, Rudolf - 1887-1950. See Item Number 1741.

Hummel, Mrs.

Hunters of Sumneytown.

Issett, Mrs. Hannah - Sumneytown - sister of James Jacoby. Member of Rev. Brendle's church. Her husband was a doctor.

Jacoby, Jim - Sumneytown - 1855-1942 - The Brendle family spent Christmas with Jim and his wife every year.

Jacoby, Mrs. James. - 1836-1929 - A member of Rev. Brendle's church.

Johnson, Mrs. Charles - Egypt.

K-, Mrs. - a mid-wife at Laurys.

Keelor's Church, Frederick, Montgomery County - One of three churches of the Old Goshenhoppen Charge served by Rev. Brendle from 1913-1926.

Kegel, Prof. - Lehigh University.

Kern, Mrs. Joseph.

Kilmer, Jane - Mrs. T.R. Brendle's aunt, formerly of Myerstown. In her latter years she lived with the Brendle family in Egypt.

Kleckner, Allen A. "Steady," 1882-1960 - He had a newspaper agency located directly across the street from Rev. Brendle's parsonage in Egypt.

Kleckner, old Mrs. - Egypt.

Koch, Mrs. Mary, - Rev. Brendle's neighbor in Egypt; wife of William Koch.

Koch, William - Egypt.

Kohler, Dallas R., 1875-1963 - Egypt. Coal dealer. Church elder for many years.

Kohler, Mrs. Louis

Kuhns, Harold, 1886-1940 - Egypt. Church organist in Egypt. Teacher of languages in the Whitehall High School.

Landis, William - superintendent of schools in Egypt.

Laub, Clarence.

Laubach, Francis E., 1885-1964 - Ballietsville. Carpenter foreman.

Laurys Grange, Lehigh Co.

Leh, Dr. Henry D., 1861-1931 - Egypt.

Leh, Orsville P., 1859-1941 - Egypt. School teacher.

Leiby, Rev. Amandus - successor to the Rev. Thomas Leinbach, pastor at Bernville, Strausstown, etc. around 1900.

Leinbach, Rev. Tom - pastor at Bernville, Strausstown.

Leinbach, Rev. Samuel A. - pastor of the Egypt Reformed Church from 1868-1884.

Levengood, Ellen - Treichlers.

Lick, David E. - Fredericksburg. Co-author with Rev. Brendle of *Plant Names and Plant Lore Among the Pennsylvania Germans*, published by the Pennsylvania German Society in 1923.

Light, Mason - Allentown.

Lindenmuth, Mrs. Morris (Erma M.), 1895-1967 - Egypt. Housewife. She possessed a beautiful alto voice and sang in the choir of the Egypt Union Church for many years. Her husband operated a bakery.

Mantz, ---, Miller's Church, Laurys. See below.

Meissner, Mrs. Catherine S., 1888-1960 - Lehighton. Housewife.

Mickley, Edwin, 1882-1945 - Perkasie. Farmer.

Mickley, Oscar, 1892-1970 - Farmer. Lived in Egypt and Schnecksville.

Miller, Tom - Schaefferstown.

Miller's Church - St. John's United Church of Christ, Laurys - one of the three churches in the Egypt Charge which Rev. Brendle served from 1926 to 1961.

Milson, Charles - Popular Justice of the Peace in West Catasauqua.

Minner, Dr. J. Edwin S., d. 1970 at the age of 81 - Egypt. Physician and banker. He was born in Bechtelsville in Berks County. He began his practice in Egypt in 1911 and organized the Egypt bank in 1918.

Mitman, Mrs. Mantana - Northampton.

Mock, Peter - Schaefferstown. A friend of the Brendle family.

Moser, Dan - Anise, Mont. Co.

Moyer, Anna - Mrs. Elizabeth Moyer's daughter.

Musselman, Henry.

Musselman, Mrs. Clem - Egypt.

Nagel, Mrs. Minnie S., 1889-1974 - Northampton and Walnutport. Daughter of Mrs. Ed Wagner. Factory supervisor.

Newgard, George - He lived between Egypt and Ormrod.

Newhards - lived between Egypt and Ormrod.

Nothstein, Mrs. Pierce (Mabel E.), 1881-1960 - Ormrod.

Nothstein, Pierce F., 1878-1956 - Ormrod. Cement plant worker.

Old Goshenhoppen - U.C.C. congregation in Montgomery County. Rev. Brendle served this church from 1913-1926.

Peters, Alfred - Sexton of Miller's Church at Laurys.

Peters, Leslie - Laurys.

Peters, Richard.

Reed, Cal - Sumneytown.

Reinsmith, Mrs. Hobart - Bath.

Remaley, Mrs. Raymond (Mary) - Egypt.

Remaley, Norman A., 1877-1950. Egypt. Cement mill worker.

Renninger, Gus - Falkner Swamp.

Richard, ---, - Catasauqua, formerly of Monroe County; his mother was a Beidel.

Ritter, Astor E., 1874-1943. Prominent farmer at Wennersville, South Whitehall Township, Lehigh County.

Roth, John - Cementon, Lehigh Co.

Roth, Mrs. Harold - Cementon. Mrs. Roth's grandmother.

Roush, Rev. J.L. - Center County.

Rudoph, Mrs. - Cementon.

Schaeffer, Polly - Cementon.

Schaeffer, Robert - Northampton.

Scheidys Sunday School - rural Sunday School in the vicinity of Egypt.

Scheirer, Russell H., 1897-1959 - undertaker of Siegersville; a native of Allentown, who spent his boyhood there.

Scholl, Dr. Harvey - Green Lane.

Schumacher, Hattie - Treichlers.

Semmel, Carson A., 1879-1952 - Egypt. Member of Egypt Lutheran Church.

Shafer, Rev. F.R. - Schaefferstown.

Shoemaker - janitor at Old Goshenhoppen.

Shupp, John Henry, 1875-1945 - Mechanicsville. Fireman, Lehigh Portland Cement Company. Grandfather of Leonard E. Shupp.

Slifer, Rev. Franklin - church near Quakertown.

Smith, Isaac - Green Lane - 1855-1941, A farmer reknowned for his philanthropic activities. He donated a large tract of land to the Green Lane borough for a recreation area and park. It is now known as the Isaac R. Smith Park. (A neighbor of Rev. Brendle)

Smith, Preston - cashier of the Egypt Bank.

Smith, Rev. Sidney S., 1898-1956 - Northampton.

Snyder, Charles - Ballietsville. Carpenter. He died in December of 1936.

Snyder, Mrs. - Eagle Point.

Snyder, Mrs. Charles - mother of Mrs. Wotring.

Solt, Hattie F. (Mrs. William H.), 1889-1964 -Egypt. Housewife.

Sowers, Frank F. - 1877-1963 He had a long and sucessful career which embraced service as teacher, merchant and banker over more than fifty years. A prime mover in the reorganization of the First National Bank of Green Lane during the depression years. He headed the bank as president for twenty years until his retirement. He took an active interest in church and fraternal affairs. He taught school at Hartzell Academy in Sumneytown for thirteen years, after which he became a retail merchant as the owner and operator of the Green Lane General Merchandise Store.

Sowers, John - Sumneytown - 1875-1951. Operated a small grocery store known as Meadow View. Located between Green Lane and Sumneytown.

Sowers' Store - Green Lane, Mont. Co.

Stahl, Isaac S. - of Stahl's pottery, Powder Valley.

Steckel, Frank N., 1887-1971 - Cementon. Barber for 50 years. According to Rev. Brendle an outstanding story teller.

Sterner, Frank, 1890-1954 - Egypt. Plasterer and bricklayer.

Stetler, Mrs. Robert - nee Kennel.

"Sticks" Surface, Egypt = Howard E. Zerfess.

Stoudt, J.B. = **Rev. John Baer Stoudt, the father of John Joseph Stoudt.**

Strauss, Mrs. Lottie - Treichlers.

Strauss, William.

Summers, Helen.

Summers, Henry - Green Lane - 1850-1931, A painter and paper hanger. A member of Rev. Brendle's church.

Troxell, David E., 1869-1937. Allentown. Elevator operator.

Troxell, Henry S., 1875-1936 - Ruchsville. Farmer. Member of St. John's Church, Mickleys, Lehigh Co.

Troxell, Mrs. David (Alice M.), 1874-1948. Allentown. Housewife.

Troxell, William S. - "Pumpernickle Bill," 1893-1957 - Allentown, PA. A graduate of Kutztown State Normal School in 1913; he taught in rural schools for five years.

Upon the death in February of 1925 of Solomon DeLong, who had written the "Obediah Crouthammel" dialect column in the Allentown Morning Call for a period of twelve years, Troxell succeeded DeLong and called himself "Pumpernickle Bill." In May of 1926 Troxell became a full-time member of the Call staff. For the next 31 years the "Pumpernickle Bill" column appeared daily with the exception of Sunday.

Troxell, Willoughby H., 1870-1945 - Farmer and innkeeper of Goosebone Inn, located between Egypt and Laurys. He was known as the "Goosebone Man" due to his weather predictions every Thanksgiving.

Undertaker, an old - Sumneytown.

Unger, C.W. - co-author of *Folk Medicine of the Pennsylvania Germans.*

Wagner, Mrs. Ed (Magdalene E.), 1871-1948 - Northampton. Housewife.

Walck, Elmer - Long Run, near Weisport.

Wenger, Abraham, 1856-1941 - Egypt. Uncle of Willis Gibble of Lititz. Formerly of Lancaster County where he was at one time warden fo the county prison. Moved with his family to Egypt in 1919. Poultry farmer. Close friend of the Brendle family.

Werley, Robert O., 1893-1968 - Egypt hotel owner, ca. 1917-1923, and banker, after 1924.

Werner, David - Myerstown.

Whitman, Horace - Woxall.

Wilson, Charles - operator of a boarding house at Promised Land, Pike County.

Wolford, Rev. W.O.

Worman, Ray A. - Egypt - Inspector with the State Highway Department.

Wotring, Hilda.

Wotring, Mrs. Sydney (Ellen J. Snyder), 1884-1970. Ballietsville. Housewife.

Wotring, Sydney H., 1889-1969.

Wright, Mrs. Orlando (Annie E.), 1889-1959. Housewife. For many years she was a member of the Egypt Church Choir.

Wright, Orlando - Egypt.

Xander, Norman L., 1894-1966 - Lived between Ruchsville and Meyersville. Farmer.

Young, ---, - Swartzville, near Muddy Creek Church, Lancaster County.

Zepp, Jess - Sumneytown.

Zerfass, Howard E. "Sticks," 1902-1965 - Popular baseball player in his youth. Police officer in Egypt = Surface, "Sticks."

Ziegler, Harvey - Souderton.

Ziegler, Mrs. Harvey - Egypt.

Bibliography

Beam, C. Richard. "Eulenspiegel in Pennsylvania." *Eulenspiegel-Jahrbuch* 10. Neumünster: Wachholtz, 1970.

Botkin, B.A. *A Treasury of American Folklore.* New York: Crown, 1944.

Brendle, A.S. *A Brief History of Schaefferstown.* Schaefferstown: Historic Schaefferstown, 1979.

Brendle, Thomas R., ed. *The Little Herald* 1-5 (1919-1923). Published Bi-monthly by the Joint Consistory of the Old Goshenhoppen Charge. Green Lane, PA.

_____, ed. *The Perkiomen Region* 1-4(1921-1926). Published by the Historical and Natural Science Society of the Perkiomen Region. Pennsburg, PA.

_____. "Customs of the Year in the Dutch Country." *The Pennsylvania Dutchman* 3.12 (1951): 1+.

_____. "Moses Dissinger: Evangelist and Patriot." *William Rittenhouse and Moses Dissinger: Two Eminent Pennsylvania Germans.* Scottdale: Pennsylvania German Society, 1959. 93-192.

_____. "Farewell Sermon." *Historic Schaefferstown Record* 9 (1975): 50-56.

_____, and William S. Troxell. *Pennsylvania German Folk Tales, Legends, Once-Upon-a-Time Stories, Maxims and Sayings Spoken in the Dialect Popularly Known as Pennsylvania Dutch.* Proceedings of the Pennsylvania German Society 45. Norristown: The Pennsylvania German Society, 1944.

_____, and William S. Troxell. "Pennsylvania German Songs." *Pennsylvania Songs and Legends.* Ed. George Korson. Baltimore: Johns Hopkins UP, 1949. 62-128.

_____, and Claude W. Unger. *Folk Medicine of the Pennsylvania Germans: The Non-Occult Cures.* Proceedings of the Pennsylvania German Society 45. Norristown: The Pennsylvania German Society, 1935.

Buffington, Albert F., ed. *The Reichard Collection of Early Pennsylvania German Dialogues and Plays.* Pennsylvania German Society 61. Lancaster: Pennsylvania German Society, 1962.

Dorson, Richard M. "German Pennsylvania." *American Folklore.* Chicago: U of Chicago Press, 1959. 76-90.

_____. "Pennsylvania Dutchmen." *Regional Folklore in the United States: Buying the Wind.* Chicago: U of Chicago Press, 1964. 107-61.

"Funeral Rites Conducted for William S. Troxell." *Morning Call* (Allentown, PA), 15 Aug. 1957.

The History of St. Paul's United Church of Christ (Formerly St. Paul's Reformed, Schaefferstown, PA.) Published by Request of the Church Council in 1965.

Huber, Charles H., ed. *Schaefferstown, Pennsylvania*, 1763-1963. Schaefferstown: Schaefferstown Bicentennial Committee, 1963.

Klees, Fredric. *The Pennsylvania Dutch*. New York: Macmillan, 1950.

Korson, George. *Black Rock: A Mining Folklore of the Pennsylvania Dutch*. Baltimore: Johns Hopkins UP, 1960.

Lambert, Marcus Bachman. *A Dictionary of the Non-English Words of the Pennsylvania German Dialect*. Lancaster: The Pennsylvania German Society, 1924.

Lick, David E., and Thomas R. Brendle. *Plant Names and Plant Lore Among the Pennsylvania Germans*. Proceedings of the Pennsylvania German Society 33. Norristown: The Pennsylvania German Society, 1923.

Milbury, Helen Brendle. "My Father, Thomas Royce Brendle." *Historic Schaefferstown Record* 12 (1978): 52-55.

Stoudt, John Baer. *The Folklore of the Pennsylvania Germans*. Philadelphia: Campbell, 1916.

"The Tragedy of Old Schaefferstown." *The Pennsylvania Dutchman* 2.6(1950): 2.

Yoder, Don. *Pennsylvania Spirituals*. Lancaster: Pennsylvania Folklife Society, 1961.

_____. "Pennsylvania German Folklore Research: A Historical Analysis." *The German Language in America: A Symposium*. Ed. Glenn C. Gilbert. Austin: U of Texas P, 1971. 70-105.

_____. "The Saint's Legend in the Pennsylvania German Folk-Culture." *American Folk Legend: A Symposium*. Ed. Wayland D. Hand. Berkeley: U of California **Press,** 1971. 157-183.

_____. "Hohman and Romanus: Origins and Diffusion of the Pennsylvania German Powwow Manual." *American Folk Medicine: A Symposium*. Ed. Wayland D. Hand. Berkeley: U of California **Press,** 1976. 235-48.